COMPUTER OUTSOURCING
MANAGING THE TRANSFER OF INFORMATION SYSTEMS

Thomas R. Mylott III

PRENTICE HALL
Englewood Cliffs, New Jersey 07632

Prentice-Hall International (UK) Limited, *London*
Prentice-Hall of Australia Pty. Limited, *Sydney*
Prentice-Hall Canada, Inc., *Toronto*
Prentice-Hall Hispanoamericana, S.A., *Mexico*
Prentice-Hall of India Private Limited, *New Delhi*
Prentice-Hall of Japan, Inc., *Tokyo*
Simon & Schuster Asia Pte. Ltd., *Singapore*
Editora Prentice-Hall do Brasil, Ltda., *Rio de Janerio*

This publication is designed to provide accurate and authoritative information in regard to the subject matter covered. It is sold with the understanding that the publisher is not engaged in rendering legal, accounting, or other
professional service. If legal advice or other expert assistance is required, the
services of a competent professional person should be sought.

*. . . From the Declaration of Principles jointly adopted by a Committee of the
American Bar Association and a Committee of Publishers and Associations.*

10 9 8 7 6 5 4 3 2 1

Library of Congress Cataloging-in-Publication Data

Mylott, Thomas R.
  Computer outsourcing : managing the transition of information sys-
tems / Thomas R. Mylott III.
    p. cm.
  Includes index.
  ISBN 0-13-127614-X
  1. Electronic data processing departments—Contracting out. 2.
Information resources management. I. Title.
  HF5548.2.M94   1995
  658′.05—dc20   94-42556
                                                            CIP

ISBN 0-13-127614-X

PRENTICE HALL
Career & Personal Development
Englewood Cliffs, NJ 07632

Simon & Schuster, A Paramount Communications Company

Printed in the United States of America

In the same way that only Nixon could go to China, only I could write this book in this way. However, I'm not to blame for any parts you dislike. That is the fault of others who, although they helped me substantially in putting this book together, failed to rap my fingers when I was composing that section.

The person who had the best opportunity to stop me is Bonnie A. Savage, Esq. Her insights, assistance, and encouragement made a three point attempt from half-court seem like a slam-dunk. Peter S. Vogel, Esq. also could have stopped me, but instead offered useful comments and suggestions.

I also make a special acknowledgment to Win (pronounced "Waaaah"), who did occasionally stop me by eating unsuitable (and, I was to learn, indigestable) parts of several chapters.

PREFACE IX

1. The Ten Commandants of Outsourcing 1
    • Ten phrases to help you remember this book's cate-
    chism.

PART I: OUTSOURCING 101 7

2. There Is No Such Word As Outsourcing 9
    • An introduction to outsourcing and why you need to
    add it to your vocabulary.

3. How Outsourcing Can Solve All Your Problems and Let
    You Retire Rich and Young 21
    • Outsourcing offers myriad advantages; this chapter
    reveals them; so pack your bags for St. Tropez.

4. Why Outsourcing Users Become Guests on TV Talk
    Shows 35
    • Your choice: either continuously monitor Geraldo or
    learn outsourcing's disadvantages in this chapter.

5. Help, I Need Somebody—Not Just Anybody! 53
    • Even if you make your own clothes and re-build your
    car's engine annually, it takes more than two hands to
    handle an outsourcing transaction.

6. There is a Cavalry for Your Calvary 69
    • How to bugle for consultants, without getting F Troop,
    General Custer, or the Boogie Woogie Bugle Boy from
    Company B.

7. Have I Got a Deal for You 87
    • Don't let that big promotion or the toaster you'll get
    for outsourcing influence you. You must approach the

subject with an open mind and a clear head. This chapter
will help you decide which way to go.

8.   Beware of Bargains in Parachutes and Outsourcing
     Agreements. 107
     • Would you believe a vendor who said, "We'll respect
     you at quarter end?" Or, how about, "The report's in the
     mail?" You need an overview of common outsourcing
     vendor strategies. They're here.

**PART II: OUTSOURCING UNDERGOES MANAGEMENT
TRAINING 115**

9.   The Value of Maps in Mine Fields: Managing the Transi-
     tion to Outsourcing 117
     • Tip toe through the turnover problems of who, what,
     when, and how to organize that transition.

10. No Bad Dogs: Managing the Relationship After the Tran-
     sition 143
     • Canine Obedience Academy: It's not just for outsourcers
     anymore.

11. "Fifty" Ways To Leave Your Vendor 165
     • Have a way to turnback, Jack. Make a self-defense plan,
     Stan. Tell the vendor, "I'll see ya," Leah, and get yourself
     free.

PART III: OUTSOURCING GOES TO LAW SCHOOL 187
     • The following chapters illustrate, discuss, and offer
     checklists for contract provisions relevant to an outsourc-
     ing agreement. Don't worry; your perusal thereof won't
     turn you into an attorney. But after reviewing them,
     you'll know more about outsourcing contracts than do
     most lawyers.

12. Description of Services 189
13. Additional Services 201
14. Fees 205
15. Turnover 211
16. Schedules 215
17. Liaisons 219
18. Existing Employees 227
19. Existing Software License's 237
20. Existing Hardware-Related Agreements 249
21. Performance Standards 255
22. Backup and Disaster Recovery 269
23. Self-Defense 277
24. Dispute Resolution 287
25. Warranties and Limitations of Liability 295
26. Termination and Expiration 303
27. Turnback 311
28. Change of Character and Substitution 327
29. Asset Transfers and Equity Infusions 331
30. Definitions 335
31. Assignment 337
32. Miscellaneous Provisions 339

PART IV: APPENDICES 349

33. Sample Outsourcing Contract 351
34. Glossary 371
35. Index 379

LIST OF CHECKLISTS

I.   Evaluating Your Need For Help 63

II.   Cost and Performance Measures for Assessing Your Current IS Department 103

III.   Possible Dispositions for Hardware and Tangible Property 139

IV.   Preparing to Leave Your Vendor 182

V.   Description of Services 196

VI.   Additional Services 202

VII.   Fees 209

VIII.   Turnover 212

IX.   Schedules 216

X.   Liaisons 221

XI.   Existing Employees 233

XII.   Existing Software Licenses 245

XIII.   Existing Hardware-Related Agreements 251

XIV.   Performance Standards 264

XV.   Backup and Disaster Recovery 272

XVI.   Self-Defense 283

XVII.   Dispute Resolution 292

XVIII.   Warranties and Limitations of Liability 298

XIX.   Termination and Expiration 307

XX.   Turnback 315

XXI.   Change of Character and Substitution 329

XXII.   Asset Transfers and Equity Infusions 332

WHY A BOOK ON OUTSOURCING?

More and more companies are betting on computer outsourcing—eliminating their own data processing operations and buying such services from an outside source. Every week the computer industry press announces another outsourcing deal. The stakes are enormous and increasing. *Fortune* magazine reported that the $7.2 billion spent on computer outsourcing in 1990 would more than double in five years. Experts continue to project a twenty percent annual growth rate. "Outsourcing appears to have the momentum of a tidal wave," according to First Boston Corporation.

The faithful believe that outsourcing can deliver significant cost reductions. One major bank estimates that it saves nearly 20% in certain accounting costs through outsourcing. AMTRAK believes it will save $100 million during its ten year outsourcing agreement. Yet not everyone agrees. U.S. Representative Dingell described an outsourcing contract for the EPA as "shameful, embarrassing, and the worst example of government contracting I have ever seen." Both views may be correct: outsourcing can be either a cost savior or a calamity.

Every company with a computer larger than a desk-top is a candidate for outsourcing. But businesses that want to outsource are at an extreme disadvantage in considering, negotiating, and supervising an outsourcing relationship. Here's why: the outsourcing vendor has all the expertise and the potential customer has none. Worse yet, there is no neutral source of any relevant information. Executives, managers, and other professionals who want to know more need information from somewhere other than vendors. *Computer Outsourcing* is intended to provide a source for this essential information.

Successful management of outsourcing requires knowledge in three distinct areas: business, computers, and computer law. This book offers you a tool with which to weave these disparate strands.

WHO SHOULD READ THIS BOOK?

Potential outsourcing customers, or users, are in the cross-hairs of this book. Moreover, you will find the chapters that follow are unconcerned about the tender feelings of some outsourcing vendors. This is not to say that outsourcing vendors are evil miscreants formed out of primeval slime — some of my best friends are outsourcers — but rather that these vendors don't need any help; they are already outsourcing experts. It's users who need the help. So the focus here is on outsourcing customers and their problems. It is precisely because a move to outsourcing can be one of a company's best moves that users require assistance to make sure they get everything they intend.

Computer Outsourcing will benefit anyone whose company is considering outsourcing; anyone who wants more information on outsourcing; anyone who needs detailed information on outsourcing contracts; and anyone who works for a company that has already made the decision to outsource.

WHY SHOULD YOU READ IT?

There is no other source for all the information packed into these pages. Here you can learn about:

- What outsourcing is.
- The advantages and disadvantages of outsourcing.
- Why you will need help in coping with an outsourcing transaction.
- What kind of help you will require.
- Where you can get that help.
- How to decide about outsourcing.
- Outsourcing vendors' strategies.
- How to manage the transition to outsourcing.
- How to keep your vendor on its toes and off yours.
- How to leave an outsourcing relationship.

- What provisions to include in an outsourcing agreement and why.

For those who want a full explanation, there are in-depth discussions of all the issues. For those who want a quick overview, there are numerous checklists. If you don't have any idea what the terms of an outsourcing contract should look like, you will find sample contract provisions.

The kind of help these pages offer would cost you plenty in the open market. That's why, if you can use even just one atom of an idea in this book, your return on investment will be a thousand-fold.

Even if you are not interested in outsourcing, you should learn why your competitors are.

WHY IS THIS AUTHOR WORTH READING?

Your time is valuable; you don't want to waste it. You don't want to read a book about the Himalayas written by someone who has only studied the topographical maps. You want someone who has climbed Everest and hired Sherpas. Your author has been involved with computers since 1967, has worked for outsourcing companies as a programmer and consultant, and is an attorney whose practice has involved computer matters exclusively. Moreover, he has negotiated a number of outsourcing transactions and drafted outsourcing agreements.

PARLEZ-VOUS COBOL, SQL, OR C++?

You are alone right now, aren't you? Or, if you have company, they can't see what you're reading, can they? Truth be told, all over America, in some of the best families, among people who otherwise have all the trappings of success, there are some confused souls who do not speak COBOL, or SQL, or C++. These people are missing out on a vast and rich vocabulary of computer terms. Some of these technical words have so many different meanings that even the speaker doesn't know what he or she is talking about. While jargon free, or at least jargon-lite, this book nevertheless assumes that you have a working knowledge of a computer-oriented vocabulary. There may be some of you who are not as computer literate as others. Therefore, in the appendices, you will find a glossary of computer and legal terms. They deserve each other.

While on the subject of vocabulary, this book has taken a few liberties of its own. You will find that *Computer Outsourcing*, like the computer trade press, uses "information systems," "IS," "data processing," and "DP" interchangeably as synonyms. Purists may debate the propriety of this approach and academics will surely condemn it, but so what? To compound its felony, this book uses the following variants of the non-word "outsourcing:"

1. "Outsource" as in "to outsource" meaning to obtain outsourcing services; and

2. "Outsourcer" as in "an outsourcer" or "vendor" meaning the vendor of outsourcing services.

A MATTER OF STYLE

You will convince no one that you want to read a book about outsourcing for pleasure or to discover how it all turns out in the end. With that in mind, your author has approached the subject in a manner you may find more facetious and irreverent than is the norm. Search as you may, you will uncover no intent to offend or injure anyone. Yet in these days when PC can mean more than personal computer, it is inevitable that something in here will offend someone. The offense is unintentional.

THE STRUCTURE

Computer Outsourcing has three parts. Part I is an introduction to outsourcing. It explains outsourcing, its advantages and disadvantages, and how to make the decision to outsource.

Part II discusses the management of outsourcing. It will take you through the transfer of your existing operations to the outsourcer, how to keep the vendor in line, and how to terminate your outsourcing relationship.

Part III plunges into the details of an outsourcing contract once you've decided to outsource. It provides sample contract provisions and discusses those provisions.

Specifically, here's how this book organizes the topics:

Chapter 1:   Ten guidelines for outsourcing transactions.

Part I

Chapter 2:   Description of outsourcing.

Chapter 3:   Advantages of outsourcing.

Chapter 4:   Disadvantages of outsourcing.

Chapter 5:   Why you will need help.

Chapter 6:   Where you can get that help.

Chapter 7:   How to make the decision.

Chapter 8:   Vendor strategies during negotiation.

Part II

Chapter 9:   How to manage the transition.

Chapter 10: How to manage the vendor.

Chapter 11: How to terminate the relationship.

Part III

Chapters 12 through 32 provide sample contract provisions, discussion of those provisions, and related checklists.

Part IV

Appendices

COVER TO COVER

There are many people who like to start at the first page and work their way to the end of a book. Remember that teacher who told you always to read the table of contents before you read the book? Not bad advice, but since life does not move in a linear progression, why should reading? You can read *Computer Outsourcing* from cover to cover, but you don't have to. This book can serve as a reference for outsourcing issues. For instance, if you are familiar with outsourcing and need advice only on the contract, read Part III first. If you have an existing outsourcing agreement and you want to terminate it, see Chapter 11 first.

Of course, you can read the topics in the order of your interest. You can also use the sample contract provisions as a way to organize your reading. When useful, there is a cross reference from the chapter containing a sample provision to another chapter for additional information.

Using the checklists is another way of organizing your research. The listing following the Table of Contents will help you locate each checklist quickly and easily.

CHAPTER 1

THE TEN COMMANDMENTS OF OUTSOURCING

Say the following phrases to yourself and at least one of them will evoke memories: "Heroes in a half-shell," "It's the economy, stupid," "To be or not to be," "Do be do be do," "I like Ike," "Play it again, Sam," "Hotel, motel, Holiday Inn," and "Gallia est omnis divisa in partes tres."

Not only will at least one of these be familiar, but you will also be able to identify its source, perhaps sing the song, recite the campaign platform, or translate the phrase into ancient Greek. Whatever you remember, the phrase was your conduit to the memory.

This chapter has ten phrases to help you remember key messages in this book. Keep them in mind when evaluating and negotiating an outsourcing transaction.

And now, the Ten Commandments of Outsourcing.

I. LOOK BOTH WAYS.

II. REMEMBER THE BERLIN WALL.

III. BEAT ME, WHIP ME, MAKE ME WRITE BAD CHECKS.

IV. DON'T GO STEADY UNLESS YOU GET A RING.

V. TRUST, BUT VERIFY.

VI. WRITE THE DIVORCE DECREE BEFORE YOU GET MARRIED.

VII. KEEP A CHECKING ACCOUNT IN YOUR NAME ONLY.

VIII.   COUNT YOUR OWN CHICKENS.

  IX.   FORGET ABOUT THE IMPOSSIBLE DREAM.

   X.   TOUGH LOVE MAY BE TOUGH ENOUGH.

Let's take a closer look at each of these commandments to see how they apply to outsourcing.

I. LOOK BOTH WAYS

Weigh the advantages and disadvantages of outsourcing carefully before you plunge into an outsourcing relationship.

Advantages:

1) Fix costs.
2) Control costs.
3) Pay as you go.
4) Extend useful life of obsolete technology.
5) Obtain expertise.
6) Focus on your core business.
7) Minimize negotiation cycles.
8) Attain technological independence.
9) Minimize IS management responsibilities.
10) Reduce attention to computer technology changes.
11) Gain quick access to advanced technology.

Disadvantages:

1) Total dependence on the outsourcing vendor.
2) Risk to third party confidentiality.
3) Increased security risk.
4) Loss of control in fulfilling your IS needs.
5) Change in accountability.
6) Loss of expertise.
7) Risk of technical paralysis.

8) Constituent issues, such as employee issues.

II. REMEMBER THE BERLIN WALL

The wall that separated East Berlin from West Berlin was surely one of the 20th Century's most obscene edifices. But you cannot dispute its effectiveness while it stood. To leave East Berlin, one first had to climb across a tangle of barbed wire. Successful climbers then navigated a mine field. After that, those still in one piece had to scale the wall itself. All through the process the guards were shooting to kill. The wall was sufficiently effective that few escaped over it.

When describing the services that an outsourcer is to provide, you want to build a structure like the Berlin Wall. You need a design such that none of the services you want will slip through the cracks. First, have a specific list of services, and, second, have a catch-all for those services that you forgot to list in the first part. What you leave out of the services definition will become additional service for which you must pay extra.

III. BEAT ME, WHIP ME, MAKE ME WRITE BAD CHECKS

If you plan to use outsourcing to control costs, you must put effective cost control mechanisms in place. You need to think creatively and realistically when designing the structure. For instance, one of outsourcing's attractions is your ability to pay fees based on your usage of the outsourcer's services. Those services consist mostly of IS services. When in the history of your company has its usage of IS services from one month to the next, or from one year to the next, actually decreased? Your long term IS services usage graph will always be upwardly sloping, even if during a month or a quarter your use declines. Your tendency will be to increase use and, therefore, increase your cost.

Think creatively about other pricing structures such as sharing savings or dividing profits. Keep in mind that the vendor's profits are often back-end loaded. The vendor makes most of its profits in the later years of the relationship. Be very careful about "additional services" provisions.

IV. DON'T GO STEADY UNLESS YOU GET A RING

Do not agree to obtain all your IS services exclusively from the vendor without a very, very good reason.

Exclusivity means that you agree that you will use the outsourcer for all of your IS needs. The first problem is one of definition: what are those needs? The second problem is that agreeing to exclusivity can lock you into old and aging technology. Third, exclusivity removes an effective tool for keeping the vendor honest.

What's a good reason to agree to exclusivity? Perhaps the vendor offers you an extremely sweet deal. If you are inclined to drift toward exclusivity, try to define the range of services that are exclusive, such as your existing applications. Moreover, try to insert a provision that lets you move to a new technology, such as LAN technology, without necessarily using your current outsourcing vendor.

V. TRUST, BUT VERIFY

Do not assume that the outsourcer will back up your part of its operations, or that it has a disaster recovery plan, or that its disaster recovery plan will work when push comes to shove.

Determine what the vendor's backup and disaster recovery plans for you are. If those plans are satisfactory, incorporate them into your agreement. If they are unsatisfactory, fix the plans before you sign on the dotted line.

VI. WRITE THE DIVORCE DECREE BEFORE YOU GET MARRIED

An outsourcing relationship resembles a marriage. In a business sense, the relationship will be extremely intimate, and the outsourcing customer must place a great deal of trust in the vendor. Likewise, getting out of the relationship can lead to a very, very messy divorce.

Unlike all marriages, all outsourcing relationships end. Plan for the end before you begin. Your contract should include provisions for the transfer of your data and software on magnetic media, and of your IS operations back to you or to another outsourcer at the end of the relationship.

VII. KEEP A CHECKING ACCOUNT IN YOUR NAME ONLY

You need to have a way to commence your own IS operations again on very short notice. To do so:

A. *Take good pictures:* Make and keep regular copies of your software, data, and production documentation.

B. *Go to jump school:* If possible be able to bail out of your outsourcing agreement and hit the ground ready to fight through to an alternative means of obtaining IS services.

C. *What's mine is mine:* Maintain an express right to your data and the media on which it is recorded, but temper this with fiscal and technical sense.

VIII. COUNT YOUR OWN CHICKENS

Inventory your existing software and make certain that your outsourcing vendor is properly authorized to use that software on your behalf. Software from third parties is a problem in outsourcing relationships. In almost every instance, outsourcing is a breach of your existing software agreement. Some software licenses expressly prohibit outsourcing. Nearly every software license agreement has a nondisclosure provision which you will breach by giving your software to the vendor.

Bottom line, you need the software licensor's written authority to let your outsourcer use your software for your benefit. Currently this is a big issue in software licensing and outsourcing that has spawned more than one lawsuit between software vendors and outsourcers. Be aware that some outsourcing companies tend to understate the seriousness of this issue.

Also, don't forget to protect your in-house software that you let the vendor run for you. In other words, grant the vendor a license that preserves your rights. Don't try this at home; dealing with software licenses is a job for your attorney.

IX. FORGET ABOUT THE IMPOSSIBLE DREAM

You need to establish concrete, objective performance standards for the outsourcer. A vendor's vague promises of how well it will treat you are unattainable dreams that can only become your nightmares.

X. TOUGH LOVE MAY BE TOUGH ENOUGH

Have a way to punish your vendor's performance failures without killing the vendor or committing suicide. You need to be able to motivate your vendor without having to litigate.

PART ONE

OUTSOURCING 101

"Try it; you'll like it" is bad advice when applied to outsourcing. You need to understand the good, the bad, and the ugly before plunging in. This part will introduce you to outsourcing and tell you the basics you need to know.

CHAPTER 2

THERE IS NO SUCH WORD AS OUTSOURCING

Go ahead, make my vocabulary. There is no such word as "outsourcing." Look it up. It's not in the dictionary. This book discusses a subject based on a word that does not exist—at least officially. So what. "H-bomb" wasn't in *Webster's* until it turned Bikini Atoll into glass. Eventually "outsourcing" will have its day in lexicography, but in the meantime the billion dollar outsourcing industry will have mushroomed into tens of billions.

Outsourcing is a technical buzz word, which is to say a word developed so that those who know what it means can believe themselves superior to those who do not know. Don't worry, though, if you don't know a bit from a byte or if you can't do long division in hexadecimal. Before you read another three paragraphs you will know at least one definition for the word outsourcing.

First, though, there is outsourcing and there is outsourcing. When this book refers to outsourcing it means computer outsourcing—the real outsourcing. Some non-computer industries have tried to usurp the word as their own. When GM has another company make a part that UAW workers used to make, both sides have the effrontery to call it outsourcing. This corruption of a non-existent word is oozing throughout industry like lawyers' commercials on television and should not be tolerated.

What is particularly strange about the word outsourcing is that another buzz word would have been more obvious and more memorable to describe the transactions involved. Your existing computer operations are referred to as in-house systems. So why, you might ask, when a company seeks information technology services from the outside, the appropriate term isn't "out-housing?" That answer is, however, beyond the scope of this book.

OUTSOURCING'S 57 VARIETIES

Computer outsourcing means engaging someone outside of your company to perform information systems services for you. There are three major categories of outsourcing that describe the arrangement with the outsourcing vendor: service bureau, time-sharing, and facilities management.

A service bureau is an IS "black box." You send your data to the outsourcer and the outsourcer returns your output. A service bureau customer may have no idea of what transpires at the outsourcer's facilities; the outsourcer might as well be an out-sorcerer.

In time-sharing you have a connection to the outsourcer's facilities and via this connection can use the vendor's computer resources. The outsourcer provides the computer resources at a remote location, but generally does not know how you are using those resources.

In facilities management, you provide the computer resources on your premises, and the outsourcer provides the managerial expertise to deliver your agreed upon results.

There are three categories of outsourcing that describe the breadth of outsourcing services you can receive: full outsourcing, selective outsourcing, and everything-in-between outsourcing. In full outsourcing, the vendor is in charge of all your IS applications. In selective outsourcing, the vendor provides services for one or a few applications such as payroll. Everything-in-between outsourcing is exactly that.

For the gourmet reader, a cooking analogy might help. If you hire someone to prepare your meals, you have outsourced your food preparation services, which is to say you've hired a chef. (People who outsource food preparation don't hire mere cooks.) If the chef cooks off premises and delivers, then you have the service bureau form of outsourcing for your food. If the chef lets you use a shelf in his or her oven, you're time-sharing that oven. If the chef takes over your kitchen and completely runs it, you have the facilities management form of outsourcing. If you sell your kitchen, appliances and all, to your chef, then you have the most extensive form of outsourcing, full outsourcing. If instead you hire a chef just to prepare your pastries, you have selective outsourcing of the dessert function.

Reasonable people may disagree whether service bureau, time-sharing, and facilities management services should all be included in the definition of outsourcing. While there can be significant differences between service bureau, time-sharing, and facilities management relationships, there are more similarities than there are differences. For our purposes, outsourcing means any permutation or combination of service bureau, time-sharing, or facilities management services, whether full, selective, or in-between, and any other relationship where an outsider performs a substantial portion of your IS services. This definition could also include some of the common disaster recovery arrangements.

The difference between outsourcing and any other IS service relationship is more one of degree rather than content. For example, when your company hired a consultant programmer to write software for that nifty little sales report you liked so much, in a way the company outsourced those programming services. But the limited duration and restricted scope of the project would lead few people to call it outsourcing. On the other hand, if you engaged a consulting firm to do all of your software development for the next ten years, you would be outsourcing your software development. If you are inclined toward cross-examination, you might want to ascertain how long a programming engagement must last before it becomes outsourcing. The short answer is that anyone who claims to know, doesn't. Moreover, the answer doesn't matter. The ideas and strategies discussed in the succeeding parts are applicable to and useful in service agreements that are less than full outsourcing, as well as in extensive outsourcing transactions.

More important than trying to affix a precise name to your transaction is to determine if any of the following elements are present. If so, then you have outsourcing attributes in your transaction and this book can help you manage the transaction.

1) Is someone (a "vendor") to provide computer-related services for you?

2) Is operating a computer system part of those computer services?

3) Will any of your company's daily work depend upon the vendor's performance?

4) Will any of your company's recurring work depend upon the vendor's performance?

5) Is your company's involvement to be confined to data entry and the receipt of reports?

6) Will your agreement with the vendor last for two years or more?

7) Will the vendor replace more than ten percent of your existing IS function, that is, of services currently performed by your IS department?

8) Will the vendor supply all the IS services necessary for a particular business application, e.g., is the vendor to perform all your payroll services or health claims processing?

9) Are you selling any hardware or other assets to the vendor?

10) Is the vendor to perform services that your IS department previously performed?

The more "yes" answers you give to the above questions, the closer your transaction is to a full outsourcing transaction.

Don't Know Much About History

A brief history of outsourcing is worth reviewing. Most people credit Ross Perot with starting outsourcing. Whether he deserves the credit or not is beside the point. He's the first person to have become a billionaire because of it, and the first company he founded, Electronic Data Systems (EDS), remains the largest player in the industry. He is also the first computer professional to run for president. Thus, the political impact of outsourcing is easy to establish. Perhaps Bill Gates will be the first presidential candidate who got his start in operating system software.

THE DAWN OF OUTSOURCING

Outsourcing was around at the dawn of the computer age, when computers had vacuum tubes and you could still see a transistor with the naked eye. Outsourcing in the form of service bureaus got its start at a time when a computer as powerful as your PC would not fit within the city limits of Denver. Service bureaus have for years made an impact in several industries, particularly in banking, insurance claims, payroll, and tax processing.

Back when baby boomers were crawling, if you needed the speed and efficiency of a computer, but didn't want the trouble and expense of buying one, you could turn to a service bureau. Consider, for example, a manufacturer with numerous customer accounts. Until computer technology, each account required a hand or an adding machine calculation of purchases, credits, returns, payments, late payment fees, interest, etc. This was a slow process at best and one prone to frequent error.

Yet, even after the availability of commercial computers, only the largest companies acquired them. Early computers were expensive, massive, required special operating environments, and required specially trained people to program and operate them.

A service bureau made money because it had enough customers to make owning a computer cost-effective and it could specialize in one application such as payroll. Service bureaus were able to accelerate paycheck processing and improve accuracy. Sending time cards to a service bureau for processing saved you the expense of all the people in the payroll department calculating pay and writing checks. When all costs were added up, the service bureau had economies of scale in processing that many employers were unable to match.

This same principle has worked well in a number of business applications. Outsourcing has been particularly successful in regulated industries where the IS needs from one company to the next are closely parallel, if not identical. Banking has been a good example. Until the S&L debacle, government kept a tight rein on depository institutions. So, for many years, one bank's data processing closely resembled another. Bank processing has been a good business for outsourcers. Areas such as credit card processing and check processing fit well into the outsourcing purview. An outsourcer could often use the same hardware and software to process multiple banks' work.

Another area subject to much outsourcing has been insurance claims processing. Large health insurers such as BlueCross/BlueShield have relied on outsourcing for many years. Outsourcing has also been widespread in Medicare and Medicaid claims processing.

KEEPING UP WITH THE JONESES' COMPUTERS

As increasing numbers of computers landed in corporate America, some companies found the management of data processing expensive and difficult. Software seemed to generate an endless stream of problems, computer programmers (even the men) rarely fit the "organization man" model, and what was supposed to be saving money was costing increasing amounts of money. Enter the concept of facilities management, also known as "FM." For a stable, often fixed, price a facilities management company assumed the responsibility for a customer's data processing operations. Key to the success of FM relationships was the delineation of services to be provided by the facilities management company. The FM vendor promised a specific set of services at an agreed fee. If the customer wanted services not specified, the customer paid for each such additional service. Vendors have made considerable profits on additional services.

THE ROCHESTER QUAKE

For many years outsourcing had been a profitable and growing business. Yet, many large corporations were reluctant to outsource until a transaction in 1989 shook the outsourcing industry and the corporate world. In that year Eastman Kodak Company of Rochester, New York outsourced to an IBM subsidiary, Integrated Systems Solutions Corporation (ISSC). Rumor has it that IBM created ISSC just to entice Kodak. ISSC agreed to build and operate a computer center for Kodak and thereby replace the work done by four existing Kodak facilities. Three hundred Kodak employees became IBM employees. Kodak estimated its savings at fifty percent of its data processing cost. Since 1989 ISSC has signed up other large corporations as well.

Once a corporation the size and prominence of Kodak went to outsourcing, other companies took notice. No longer would an enterprise get strange looks for having an outsider perform its IS function. All of a sudden outsourcing became fashionable for the Fortune 500.

Since the Kodak deal, the outsourcing business has exploded. Hardly a week goes by without an announcement of a deal larger than one made the week before. The total value of some transactions are now in excess of a billion dollars. Deals of 100 million or more are so commonplace that they hardly create a ripple. Estimates of the outsourcing industry's growth put the increase at around twenty percent a year.

THE AFTER-SHOCK

While Kodak, before outsourcing, was in fact a progressive user of IS technology, it did not have a substantial reputation as such. Many of outsourcing's critics have opined that a technologically advanced enterprise would never do a deal. Xerox Corporation, on the other hand, did have a reputation of soaring on technology's leading edge. And in 1994, Xerox entered into a 3.2 billion dollar outsourcing transaction. News reports of the critics' consuming quantities of large black birds are undoubtedly exaggerated. Most likely, historians will view the Xerox deal as having vaporized the last barriers of outsourcing reticence in U.S. businesses.

FROM FANS TO FANATICS

While thousands of small and medium sized companies have outsourced, the press has focused on the corporate nobility. And that list reads like a who's who of corporate America.

Here are some outsourcing transactions completed since Kodak:

Company	_Reported Deal_
General Dynamics	$3 billion
National Car Rental	$500 million
Inland Revenue (U.K.)	$1.5 billion
First City Bank Corp.	$600 million
Continental Bank	$700 million
Enron Corp.	$750 million
Xerox	$3.2 billion

First Boston Corporation is correct; outsourcing does have the momentum of a tidal wave. It has become tsunami. The impetus to outsource is so great that on many occasions it has washed common and business sense over the side.

This is often the case when economic realities force business to change. The frenzy over outsourcing is part of the rapid, traumatic, and absolutely necessary re-structuring of corporate-America. With sledge-hammer like force, companies have realized that they must change to compete in the global marketplace. From Main Street to Wall Street, American businesses have acknowledged that survival requires evolving from hierarchial, inflexible dinosaurs—bloated with personnel and inventory—to trim, flexible, and nimble enterprises. This awakening has generated such concepts and associated buzzwords as downsizing, re-structuring, re-engineering, and just-in-time manufacturing.

Hundreds of thousands of people have lost their jobs, but at the same time, new businesses have sprouted throughout the country. Perhaps more impressive has been the near miraculous transformation of many sectors of U.S. industry. Except for people on hallucinogens, who would have ever believed that U.S. auto manufacturers could change and then rival, let alone surpass, the Japanese in quality, performance, and price? You have the right to remain silent, but you had your doubts, didn't you?

While the major political parties want to claim credit for this amazing transformation, the real credit goes to U.S. business. Those companies that are not evaluating and implementing new ways to compete, slash costs, innovate, and satisfy customers will vanish before the second millennium starts.

This does not mean that every company must downsize, re-structure, or outsource, but rather that every company should evaluate these and other strategies. The concepts merit more than one look. Because the business environment is in so much flux, surviving companies will re-evaluate frequently.

Outsourcing is clearly part of this phenomenon. Outsourcing IS functions can help keep the corporate body lean and flexible. With a successful outsourcing transaction, you don't need the bricks, mortar, computers, or people on your books. They belong to the outsourcer or are at least the outsourcer's problem. You can transform your fixed costs into variable costs or vice versa. Chapter 3 explores the advantages of outsourcing in much greater detail.

THE TAO OF OUTSOURCING

A fundamental belief of Taoism is that good and evil exist in balance. For every advantage there is a disadvantage.

Likewise there is a dark side to outsourcing. Many outsourcing transactions have happened for the wrong reasons or at least without sufficient consideration of the long term consequences. These transactions in the banking industry became so common that in 1992 the U.S. General Accounting Office investigated outsourcing in this industry and reported their conclusions to Congress with recommendations for government action. Here's a sample of what they had to say:

> Federal regulatory agencies for banks and savings associations
> found unusual contracting arrangements between depository
> institutions and data processing servicers through their reviews of

depository institutions. These arrangements included awarding data processing contracts to companies after the company agreed to purchase bank assets, such as computer equipment, at substantially higher prices than the market value and agreeing to provide capital to the institution by purchasing stock from the bank.

Arrangements such as these allow banks to maintain capital, defer losses on the disposition of assets, and show an increase in financial value on the balance sheet. But since these arrangements involve banks paying higher fees over the life of the contract, the banks' books were "artificially inflated" and did not reflect the true financial picture of the institution. The regulatory agencies were concerned that these types of arrangements could have an adverse effect on the financial soundness of the institution. As a result, the agencies issued a number of guidelines to depository institutions and their examiners concerning these arrangements. Recently, FDIC proposed a rule that would require banks to prove that contracts they sign with vendors will not jeopardize bank safety and soundness. (*Depository Institutions Contracting Practices With Data Processing Servicers.* United States General Accounting Office, February 1992)

Why does the government rage? One of the fundamental truths of human existence is that bureaucrats constantly must justify their existence. Whether you worry about the same things as the GAO and the FDIC, bank outsourcing has clearly become a government hot button. There are other problems with outsourcing as well. Chapter 4 explores the disadvantages of outsourcing in more detail.

THE CRYSTAL BALL

Computer technology has changed so much in the past decades, that anyone making long-term predictions should speculate at the end of a 1-900 telephone number giving psychic, not written, advice. In the year 2525, all data processing services may come out of a wall outlet or through a pocket cellular mainframe, but in the next few years, developments should be more modest. Here's a list of outsourcing trends you can take to the bank.

1. Outsourcing will continue to expand at a rapid pace.

2. Outsourcing will become one-stop shopping for IS services and resources. More outsourcing transactions will have the outsourcer acquiring hardware and software, and building applications and data centers for specific customers. Outsourcers will act as systems integrators, with the goal of transferring turnkey operations to customers at the transaction's end.

3. There will be increased interest in outsourcing voice and data networks.

4. Outsourcers will provide increased client-server technology.

5. The choices for specialized technology available through outsourcing will increase dramatically—especially in the following areas:

　　—Health claims processing and administration

　　—Workers compensation claims processing and administration

　　—Business reply mail processing

　　—Property tax collection

　　—Parking ticket management and collection

　　—Interoffice and office-to-home video transmission services

　　—Optical scanning (imaging) of data entry and mail

Now, for that 1-900 number . . . .

CHAPTER 3

HOW OUTSOURCING CAN SOLVE ALL YOUR PROBLEMS AND LET YOU RETIRE RICH AND YOUNG

(THE ADVANTAGES OF OUTSOURCING)

Outsourcing has many advantages. To determine if you or your company can benefit, take this cyber-sanity test. Would or should your company do any of the following:

1. Render lard to make soap for the washrooms?

2. Build a dam to provide electricity for your offices?

3. String telephone cables for long distance service?

4. Sculpt a reservoir for drinking water?

5. Encourage employees to count in hexadecimal (base 16)?

6. Enjoy frequent meetings with computer salespeople?

The correct answer to all six is no. If you aced the test, read on. There is still hope for you.

If you answered yes to any of these questions, your company is a dubious candidate for outsourcing, and you need therapy.

COMPUTERS TO RESCUE YOU FROM COMPUTERS

The computer revolution has spawned its own challenges. For some people, the travails of managing computers and computer personnel significantly undermine many of the technology's benefits. It seems the harder you struggle to stay current, the faster the technology changes. And the technology is the easy part. Computer professionals rank up there with opera stars and professional athletes in the difficulty of managing them.

Countless users have asked themselves why can't they receive the benefits of computer technology without all the hassles. Outsourcing is one answer.

Outsourcing can save you money, create money, catapult you into new technologies, cut your tranquilizer costs, and enhance your social life. Of course, you won't present outsourcing options to your CEO using all of these reasons. Instead, your formal presentation will reveal that there are strategic, financial, and technical reasons why a company might choose to outsource its IS processing. To assist you in that sales pitch, the rest of this chapter focuses on outsourcing's advantages—which, incidentally, are similar to the reasons why you should not make your own soap.

HAVE SOMEONE ELSE DO YOUR LAUNDRY

In some ways, the reasons for obtaining outsourcing services are similar to the reasons for obtaining any other service. To outsource or not is a version of the classic "make or buy" and "own or lease" analyses. In choosing outsourcing services, a business chooses to buy data processing services rather than to supply its own. So the first advantage of outsourcing is that the outsourcing customer can acquire computer services rather than acquiring an IS department. In buying computer services, the buyer avoids having to obtain computers, computer software, computer professionals, computer operators, and other related goods, services, and personnel. And if a company already has an information systems department, outsourcing can eliminate it or shrink it.

Most companies that acquire outsourcing services do so to obtain those services. While this may seem an insultingly obvious reason, there are many other good reasons for entering into outsourcing agreements, such as the following reasons.

PRINT MONEY TO IMPROVE THE BALANCE SHEET

One of the other reasons for outsourcing is the desire to improve the company's balance sheet. In a Government Accounting Office (GAO) study, forty percent of the outsourcing vendors surveyed said that the purchase of their customers' equity or assets was a condition of obtaining the outsourcing contract award. The sale of additional equity changes the balance sheet by definition. Thus, outsourcing can give you a needed cash infusion.

GET OFF YOUR ASSETS TO IMPROVE THE BALANCE SHEET

Another way to improve a balance sheet is to unload non-performing assets. Removing data processing assets from the books by selling them to the outsourcing vendor will free up some capital (or even cash). Sometimes a business can actually make money on the computer assets it sells. In that GAO report, quoted in Chapter 1, the government was quite upset that many outsourcers were paying much more than "fair market value" for their customers' computer assets—a fact unlikely to cause other companies to reject outsourcing out of hand. Maybe you too can transform non-revenue yielding assets into cash. This abracadabra with computer assets is similar to deals in the 1980s where businesses sitting on valuable land or pondering the view from their skyscrapers realized they could turn their lead-weight real-estate assets into gold through the alchemy of sales and lease-backs. "Free the non-performing assets" does have a nice financial and political ring to it.

THE DP DIET TO CUT COMPUTER COSTS

For many comptrollers, the IS budget has grown like the eggplant that ate Chicago, leaving their companies with bad cases of cost indigestion. One of the undisputed facts of changes in computer technology has been the plunging costs of computer power. Undoubtedly you have heard something like this: If a Mercedes-Benz had gone down in price by the same percentage as have computers, it would cost only $1.00. (And of course this was true in 1812—when you had that gold dollar in mint condition and no one knew how to spell inflation.) Reasoning right along, the uninitiated believe that computer costs should swirl away into insignificant sums like grease treated with Drano.

The reality has been different. Yes, the costs of computer power have dropped off a cliff, but everyone from kindergarten to the board room and the Pentagon has found uses for this power and demanded more. So while each unit of computer power and each unit of computer storage has decreased in price, the demand for computer power and storage has blasted through the roof.

Worse yet, in evaluating these increasing data processing costs, only a soothsayer can tell if there is a light at the end of the tunnel or an approaching train. Enter the marketing opportunity for outsourcing vendors. Many outsourcers will guarantee in writing to slash IS costs.

PUT A LID ON COMPUTER COSTS

For many companies, IS processing costs are like secret projects in the national defense budget. Chief financial officers can show the bottom line cost, but often have difficulty explaining the how and why of those expenses. Not only do computer budgets expand, but they tend to increase at an unpredictable rate. Many enterprises have trouble determining from one year to the next what their information systems outlays should be. Having a fixed cost for data processing, or at least controlling the cost, is attractive to the financial people in a company.

Fixing or controlling costs through outsourcing is like exchanging a variable rate mortgage for a fixed rate one. The outsourcer, like a mortgage company, absorbs the risk of IS cost increases. If you have ever been on the rollercoaster of variable rates, you know that your stomach, if not your cash flow, will appreciate the element of certainty that outsourcing can provide. Computer cost control gets the attention of even the most spendthrift CFOs.

Pay as you go

Another of the rock-in-the-shoe problems of having IS facilities is that rather than your paying for just what you use, your processing involves a great deal of overhead costs. You must make large outlays for data centers, hardware, software, and personnel. You spend a lot of money before getting anything in return. Then you have to pay the rent, service the hardware, and pay the employees regardless of whether that corporate IS function (i.e., plant, equipment, and people) is at that moment performing any useful function or if it is even operable. For IS expenditures in general, you must open your wallet in advance and without knowing that you will use what you have bought.

Typical outsourcing transactions, on the other hand, have fee structures based on a usage algorithm. In other words, you pay as you use, and you don't pay for bricks, mortar, hardware, software, and people that you don't use. You transfer fixed costs to lower variable costs, and you let the outsourcer worry about its investment in computer resources.

Take a smart pill by hiring IS expertise

For all the money that your company may be willing to spend on computer personnel, finding people with the necessary management and professional skills is difficult. Complicating matters even more is the fact that computer expertise is volatile. The most effective and useful management and staff professionals must divert significant time and energy to remain current with computer technology developments.

Companies with outdated computer skills risk several things. The first is the risk of increased costs. Old software often costs more to maintain than does new software and also may be more difficult to maintain than new software. The second risk is that the use of old technology and skills incurs an opportunity cost for the enterprise. Improvements in computer technology can cut costs, such as the way automated teller machines reduced the cost of providing bank teller services. Potential lost savings are a risk of antiquated data processing expertise as well.

Defections from the information systems department are a third problem that frequently occurs when a business allows its computer expertise to decline. IS professionals, both management and staff, fear their own technical obsolescence. These professionals are quick to jump ship when their employers fail to invest in state-of-the-art computer systems and the related training. The employees that remain tend to be the least skillful.

Outsourcing is an opportunity to acquire expertise in computer technology. Often an outsourcer's expertise will exceed yours. Some vendors are experts in telecommunications, while others are proficient in keeping large systems operating at maximum efficiency. So you might outsource all or part of your data processing operations as the cheapest way to obtain, manage, and retain the necessary expertise.

Reach for the Grey Poupon to improve quality

Employing a higher level of expertise may improve the quality of the resulting product or service. Many outsourcing vendors are able to deliver significant improvements in computer services over a user's in-house processing. These improvements arise out of a number of skills that the vendor brings to the table: IS expertise; economies of scale; and concentration on providing IS services to its customers. Outsourcing enables some companies to pour their American mustard down the drain and use French mustard from an adjacent Rolls Royce.

Stick to knitting and focus on your business

Another reason to delegate data processing to an outsider is to focus on your core business. With outsourcing, your management can concentrate on your company's products and services while someone else worries about the computers. This concept is very attractive to many businesses. All the time, money, and uncertainty involved in corporate IS processing diverts time, money, and attention from the central business of the enterprise. Outsourcing can present a useful way to focus on line operations and to reduce wasted energy on what is essentially a staff function.

Stick to Knitting a Sweater and Focus on Software Development

While focusing on a company's core business is an important advantage of outsourcing, you should not underrate an analogue within the IS department. If you outsource your existing applications and the associated maintenance obligations, you free your retained programming staff to concentrate on new development. Not only will this change increase the chances that your staff actually develops new applications, but their morale will skyrocket.

Eschew the Fat and Let Your Outsourcer Do the Negotiating

For a business to manage and use its computer system well, it must take advantage of the significant and constant changes in the computer industry. More often than not, the changes in technology mandate constant acquisitions of software and hardware. These frequent acquisitions require a cycle of negotiation with hardware and software vendors. In many instances these vendors do not work together and have differing business practices that are at odds with one another. And because of the rapidly changing technology, new vendors are popping up all the time—which adds another potential vendor to investigate and with which to negotiate. Adding confusion to the product mix, are the economic ups and downs of nearly every computer hardware and software vendor. Almost all major computer vendors have experienced acute financial and technological problems in the recent past. The reports that XYZ Computer Corp. is abandoning a product line, losing money in every quarter, laying off thousands, or "re-structuring" have become monotonous. If you run your IS in-house, you must adapt to these computer vendors, accommodate their variable business fortunes, and negotiate new software and hardware agreements in that context. Outsourcing provides a way to avoid all of these chores.

Outsourcing vendors are well-equipped to accommodate the repetitive cycle of negotiation with hardware and software vendors. Many outsourcers have volume purchasing agreements that users cannot hope to equal. This is one way outsourcing can serve as one-stop shopping for computer services. The outsourcer becomes responsible for all negotiations and arranges for all hardware and software. You worry only about the outsourcer's monthly bills.

LEAVE UNIX TO 1000 AND 1 ARABIAN NIGHTS WHILE THE VENDOR TRACKS TECHNOLOGY

It is almost impossible today to manage computer systems and remain unaware of changes in computer technology. The changes occur constantly. The economics of the technology change constantly, too. And, the ability to keep existing systems in good repair diminishes rapidly over a short period of time. Committing to one manufacturer's computer system is often necessary, but can severely restrict future choices. Likewise, choosing a system of a certain size will influence the selection of possible growth paths.

By outsourcing, a company may choose to avoid all of those problems—let the outsourcer worry about where the technology is going, let the outsourcer worry about keeping everything in good repair, let the outsourcer worry about maintaining the myriad components' compatibility. A business can fire its sooth-sayer and let someone else predict the future of computer technology.

In essence, outsourcing is a route to technological independence. Users can reduce their dependency on particular computer vendors and specific hardware and software configurations. Moreover, a business can gain substantial flexibility in matching available computer resources to its fluctuating requirements. Management can forget about what model CPU or what operating system version it's using and let the outsourcing vendor get ulcers. As long as the application software is compatible with the vendor's computer systems, certain specific characteristics of the technology become irrelevant.

Cancel your Valium prescription because the vendor manages IS

You may have dreamed of reducing your company's labor requirements. Staff employees such as those in the computer department contribute little, if anything, directly to the bottom line. In particular, data processing staffs often appear overpaid and troublesome.

If you want to minimize your IS management responsibilities, outsourcing creates an opportunity to rid a company of not only its computer staff, but also its entire information systems department.

It slices; it dices; over 1000 uses: obtain advanced technology

Often an outsourcing vendor represents a source of technology otherwise unobtainable for a business. Certain advanced technology might be beyond your company's financial resources or technical abilities. For instance, sprawling network tentacles are rapidly outstripping the technical and administrative capabilities of all but the most sophisticated users. There are topologies, protocols, switches, bridges, modems, cables, backbones, circuits, relays, routers, servers, peripherals, and multiple software layers which must all sing in harmony lest the network fall flat. Yet there are outsourcing vendors that can deliver a full symphony of network facilities.

Many outsourcers can offer technology far above what many companies could ever hope to achieve on their own. These outsourcing vendors represent an opportunity for your business to access advanced technology without having to invest in it—or even understand it.

If it ain't broke, don't fix it, and retain proven technology

Outsourcing can allow you to use "obsolete" technology beyond its so-called life-span.

The whirlwind of change in computer technology often forces upgrades to new technology even when the prior technology was sufficient. Over time, software and hardware become more expensive to maintain. Perhaps you have several perfectly useful applications written in Autocoder (a 1960's programming language). The only trouble is that ten years ago your last Autocoder programmer retired, forwarding address unknown. Or maybe you cannot justify acquiring a replacement for your now barely maintainable 1970's era system, but you've been running well-settled applications on it for years. As the third party maintenance company keeps raising prices and warning that certain parts may become unavailable, you may conclude the maintenance costs to be unbearable or the risk of having no maintenance unacceptable.

Some outsourcing vendors can provide an alternative. They may have several customers that need Autocoder maintenance and so can justify keeping an Autocoder programmer alive as well as employed. Or they may be able to run your old software in emulation mode on their new machines—keeping those time worn and treasured routines around for another production cycle. They may even keep an "obsolete" system around because they have enough business running on it to justify the high cost of maintenance. More likely, they even do their own maintenance. By outsourcing to an "old" system, you might avoid having a problem conversion to a new system.

HIRE AN EXPERT, NOT A HACKER, BY CHOOSING A SPECIALIST

Through outsourcing you can gain access to advanced software applications. Some vendors specialize in certain applications, such as insurance and payroll. Those vendors not only offer overall data processing expertise, but also provide a particular application expertise. They may be your least expensive route to the software technology and the expert assistance to exploit that technology.

In the software market, there really are some better mousetraps. Even when an outsourcer's mousetraps are no better than your own, their rat-catchers may be experts. Some vendors can offer superior operations and application administration in addition to their advanced software.

In health care and insurance applications, in particular, a user can obtain access to specialized software and personnel through outsourcing. Many users lack the requisite expertise in these areas and cannot afford to acquire and maintain that expertise. Once upon a time, for example, automobile insurance for vehicles registered in the Commonwealth of Massachusetts fell into this category. The rules and regulations for rating and writing automobile policies were so complicated, and so unlike other states, that many insurers who processed their automobile policies for every other state outsourced their Massachusetts' processing to specialists.

Selectively outsourcing an application that is new to your company is an excellent way of evaluating the application's performance. You get a "test drive" without the hassle of bringing it up to speed in-house. You can get the processing benefits with minimal training and no conversion effort.

BEND IT, SHAPE IT, ANY WAY YOU WANT IT: OUTSOURCING CAN ADD FLEXIBILITY

At its best, outsourcing adds valuable flexibility to your information services. In a perfect world, a company never has too many data centers and never acquires or divests a business without having all its data processing lined up. Yet, by counting the number of law school graduates, it's easy to conclude that a perfect world remains a dream.

Hiring an outsourcer is one way to consolidate those data centers which seem to have sprouted up all over the land, and which you have been unable politically to merge into your super cheap facility in North Dakota where you're the only employer for 500 miles that pays in cash.

On the other hand, maybe your employer is an acquisitive company and likes to buy and sell other businesses. Usually, the worst fit between formerly independent companies lies in the IS functions. Outsourcing is a quick way to bring a new subsidiary or a merged entity into the fold while shedding the fixed cost of the prior operation.

Not every operation needs the same quantity of IS services from one month to the next. Many businesses have peak operating requirements. Seasonal businesses, cyclical businesses, and many retailing businesses have a time of year, like the Christmas season, or a point in the business cycle, like periods of mushrooming home sales, where they need every nanosecond of computer power on tap. Too often, these companies must maintain the IS capacity to accommodate the peaks, even if their average needs are closer to the valleys. By selective outsourcing, you may be able to keep enough IS resources in-house to meet your average needs, while filling the gaps in the peak periods.

Outsourcing is oil that you can pour on the rough seas of variable usage requirements. You can smooth out crests and troughs of usage as well as costs. At the same time outsourcing adds an element of navigation to an uncertain course.

THE OUTSOURCING MENU: PRIX FIXE OR À LA CARTE

Numerous types of outsourcing transactions are available. These are a few examples of activities that have been outsourced:

- All IS functions and facilities.
- Medical claims processing for the company's self-insured medical benefits plan.
- Payroll.
- Insurance policy rating and writing.
- All network services.
- Accounts receivable billing and collection.
- Delinquent property tax collection.
- Medicare/Medicaid claims review and payment.

You could be the next winner

Outsourcing has been a boon to many enterprises—including outsourcing vendors. The billions in revenue banked by the outsourcing industry indicate a mushrooming flock of blissful converts. Yet, while outsourcing may be a path to IS nirvana, this stairway to heaven is an unmapped mine field. The next chapter will give you a metal detector.

CHAPTER 4

WHY OUTSOURCING USERS BECOME GUESTS ON TV TALK SHOWS

(DISADVANTAGES OF OUTSOURCING)

You must have missed that episode on Sally Jessy where the studio was full of top executives from major corporations. The TV cameras blurred their faces with multi-colored checkerboards. The caption under each guest said either "Received big promotion after outsourcing, but still can't sleep without chemicals," or "On the outs with outsourcing." If you missed that show, don't worry. It will be repeated.

There is no disputing that outsourcing could be your company's island paradise. However, getting there involves a swim through shark-infested waters. To avoid substantial injury to the corporate body, you must know the enemy and choose the best shark repellant. To do so, you need a thorough understanding of the potential disadvantages of outsourcing.

BUYING SWAMPLAND

Everyone has heard stories of marvelous Florida "waterfront" property that actually writhed with alligators and poisonous snakes and stories of the poor souls who scrambled to buy a place to work on their tans. These buyers purchased water and beach front, but with aquatic characteristics totally unlike what they intended. They bought swampland when they wanted sand and waves.

The Florida stories often contained an element of fraud that does not exist in the outsourcing industry. However, if

35

you are not careful, even an outsourcer with the best intentions can sell you swampland. If you and your outsourcing contract fail to describe clearly what you want and how the relationship will work, the vendor may fail to provide the benefits you seek from outsourcing. So the first disadvantage of outsourcing is, quite simply, that you may fail to receive the many advantages of those services.

THE HEART-LUNG MACHINE MEANS TOTAL DEPENDENCE

In the full-blown outsourcing relationship, the end user is totally dependent upon the vendor to provide all information systems' services. Indeed, this dependency may have been a significant motivation for entering that relationship in the first place.

The disadvantages, though, of this total dependence are many and significant. No work will be performed without the outsourcing vendor's cooperation. No software will be changed without the outsourcing vendor's acquiescence. Without the vendor's participation, no data will enter the computer system nor will any reports come out. You become the patient and the outsourcer is your hospital, physician, life-support machine, and blood donor all wrapped up in a data center. You need the vendor, like you need air, water, and hemoglobin. If the vendor makes a bad decision, you get sick; if it trips over your oxygen hoses, you choke; and if it turns off the life-support . . . .

SHOTGUN WEDDINGS MEAN AN UNUSUAL BUSINESS RELATIONSHIP

Most outsourcing relationships are like marriages. In neither instance is it possible to be a little married. While people presume intimacy in marriages, in most business relationships things are supposed to happen at arm's length. But in outsourcing, the vendor and the user are on intimate terms. They are like newlyweds in a very small one-room apartment. Both parties have great hopes for the future, yet each can easily rattle the other's nerves. There is little chance of privacy and there are few secrets.

But newlyweds are actually much better off than are outsourcing customers. At least in theory, the partners to wedded bliss are in equal positions. Each shares the same risk of intrusion from the other. This is not so in outsourcing where only the user is so dependent and risks exposure. So even the outsourcing analogy to marriage breaks down, unless your idea of marriage is the feudal concept of male dominant nuclear families, where the men get the bomb and the women and children get the fallout.

There is a persuasive argument that the relationships of outsourcers to their customers more closely resemble those of physicians, accountants, or attorneys to their patients and their clients. The law labels these professional relationships as "fiduciary relationships," and mandates special obligations on the part of the professionals. The law does not, however, recognize outsourcing transactions as fiduciary. Most outsourcers will claim that if the law considered their customer relationships as fiduciary, they would become intimate only with the bankruptcy statutes. There may be some truth in their view.

DON'T BLAME ME

Even worse for your company is that the potential liability problems of outsourcers mean they will do everything possible to shift the risk of the outsourcing relationship back to you.

In fact, the typical contract for outsourcing substantially reduces the risk for the vendor because it establishes only a minimum responsibility to the user. This is particularly true when a user signs its vendor's standard agreement.

The real world for the typical outsourcing customer is that the customer receives the vendor's services "as is." Could you imagine getting medical care on a heart-lung machine "as is?"

Worse yet, your total dependence during the outsourcing relationship can create problems at the end of the relationship. You risk becoming hostage to the vendor when you are ready to leave.

DON'T PEEK, BUT THERE IS A RISK TO CONFIDENTIALITY

Closely related, and an inevitable result of your total dependence on the outsourcing vendor, is a commensurate loss of confidentiality. Companies create information in many ways and from many sources. For instance, almost all businesses use computers to process their financial accounting information such as accounts payable, accounts receivable, and general ledger. In full outsourcing, all of these financial applications will be under the control and purview of the vendor. All of the automated information flowing through your company will pass under the vendor's eyes. The outsourcer may see commercially relevant information as well as confidential information.

The creation and demand for information within companies is only going to increase. Look at the rapid change in inter-office communications. What people once communicated by telephone calls and typewritten paper memoranda, they now increasingly do through electronic mail. But as many of the principal players in the Iran Contra debacle discovered, electronic mail messages sent to one another were not really erased when they pushed a button that said "erase." Those messages were later uncovered by Congressional committees searching the computers that performed the electronic mail function.

Likewise, the electronic mail in any corporation is subject to discovery by anyone who controls the computers that perform the mail functions. If your electronic mail functions are part of the data processing functions that are outsourced, the outsourcing vendor has access to all of the electronic mail within your business. You could lose the confidentiality of any data that you expose to the outsourced IS department, including intra- and inter-office communications.

Strategic software is any software that gives you a competitive advantage in your industry because your rivals don't have it. The confidential nature of any strategic software you possess can also be weakened through an outsourcing transaction. You may have software that can analyze sales in some special manner or control your inventory in a way that your competition would drool over. Airline reservation systems, for example, are strategic systems within the airline industry. Unfortunately, a European national railroad discovered that such reservation systems are industry dependent when it looked to an airline to convert airline software to railroad software. Some peculiar problems arose because railroads, unlike airlines, do not operate on a hub and spoke system. Imagine having to ride a train to New York from Nashville to get to Los Angeles.

Your strategic software may or may not fit the legal definition of a trade secret. Trade secrets are intellectual property of a special nature that most courts protect enthusiastically. In somewhat of an oversimplification, you can think of trade secrets as almost anything—software, ideas, processes, formulae—that is generally unknown in your industry and that gives you an advantage over your competitors who remain ignorant of your trade secret. The biggest threat to a trade secret's legal viability is disclosure. When the world knows about the trade secret, it's no longer secret and, thus, probably not protectable in court.

Outsourcing can compromise a user's trade secrets. First of all, disclosure to the vendor without the appropriate contractual safeguards may negate the requisite element of secrecy. Secondly, the vendor or its employees may make unauthorized disclosures. Finally, other customers of the outsourcer may gain unauthorized access to your trade secrets. The problem is two-fold: you can lose the legal advantages of claiming trade secrecy and you expose the secret to another's wandering eyes.

Even if you do not lose the confidential nature of your information or your legal claims to trade secrets, the outsourcing vendor will have access to your financial data and the financial results. This information can be very valuable to a vendor when it wants to negotiate with a user. The vendor can know the user's cost structure and thereby be well positioned to offer pricing in a manner that maximizes its negotiating leverage.

When you have outsourced, you can never be certain that the vendor hasn't peeked behind the curtain. This is not a big problem for a publicly-traded company since much of its financial information is subject to public disclosure. Undoubtedly, though, most companies would like to control the disclosure of such information as much as is both legal and possible. The bottom line is that since the vendor will have access to all the data pulsing though your outsourced computer applications, the outsourcer could compromise any information that you wanted to keep under wraps.

CAN YOU KEEP A SECRET?

When someone entrusts data or software to your company in confidence, you have a business and possibly a legal obligation to prevent disclosure. Remember what you learned in elementary school: few people will tell you a secret if you can't keep one. If you violate a written agreement where you promised to keep a secret, some people will haul you into court.

An outsourcing relationship may increase the difficulty of keeping other people's secrets. Most of the software that you have acquired from someone else, like a software licensor, is someone else's secret and, most likely, a trade secret. Yes, software licensors don't like your showing their software to anyone else. If you don't believe it, read the software license agreements that your company signed. Of course, when you bought the software, you focused only on the price, so reading the license now will be most enlightening. Odds are that somewhere amongst the dotted "i's" and crossed "t's" lurks a sentence that looks like the following: "End user agrees not to disclose the software to anyone other than the end user's employees and only after advising such employees of the confidential and proprietary nature of the software."

If there is such a sentence or words to that effect, then disclosing that software to your outsourcing vendor is a breach of that software license agreement. If the software licensor finds out, and odds are it will when maintenance time comes round, it could make your life very difficult. You may receive a polite letter for another license fee. Or, you could find yourself in court while the software vendor seeks an injunction to prohibit further use of its product. Don't get too worried about this now, though. Chapter 19 suggests ways to manage this problem. And while solving the problem may instill a desire to spill your guts to Geraldo, it's unlikely that the problem itself will force you to vacation at a correctional facility. Nevertheless, but for the outsourcing relationship, this problem would not exist.

You should also keep your customers' secrets. Whether you are formally obliged to maintain the confidentiality of your customers' information, business reasons usually compel you to refrain from such disclosures. How comfortable are you knowing that the outsourcing vendor, because of its access to all of your automated information, will have access to your customers' data as well?

Even secrets about you personally are at risk. After all, isn't it true that your company's automated personnel files contain your salary, address, home telephone, and dependents' names? An outsourcing vendor can snoop around in these files, too. Moreover, as health insurance claims become automated, the vendor may have access to health claims records and other information concerning the health of a user's employees.

All of these risks to confidentiality are primarily risks that the outsourcer will learn information that you might want or need to keep confidential. However, there is an additional risk over which the vendor has incomplete control: the risk of disclosure to the vendor's other customers.

One of the ways in which outsourcing vendors make money is to consolidate many data processing operations and use the same computer hardware and software for several customers at once, thereby achieving economies of scale. There are electronic and software techniques to inhibit unauthorized access to software and data. But an outsourcing customer must first evaluate how well its vendor will employ these available measures to protect the customers' data and software. Such an evaluation will be very difficult. Moreover, even the best measures used by outsourcing vendors are subject to a simple fact: the technology of breaking through protection schemes is more advanced than is the technology of protection.

Outsourcing complicates secrecy. Burglarizing a neighbor in your building will always be tactically easier than burglarizing someone down the street. Even a diligent outsourcing vendor cannot guarantee absolute protection from its other customers. Of course, those other customers have confidential data of their own at risk. But that is paltry assurance, indeed, that another customer will refrain from using whatever means are available to penetrate the security system and gain access to your confidential information. An outsourcing user must be particularly cautious and concerned with an outsourcing vendor who also provides services for a competitor.

THE KEY UNDER THE MAT ADDS A SECURITY RISK

Closely related to the risk to confidentiality is a risk to security. In some ways the risk to security might be better described as a loss of control over security. The security problems occur in two ways: physical security and electronic security. If the vendor moves your IS operations to a new site, usually the site of the vendor's consolidated operations, you will become subject to whatever level of security the vendor uses at that site. In many instances, that level of security will be better than the user's security it replaced. At the same time, the vendor's level of security could be lower than yours.

Worse yet, most users will be ignorant of the actual, as opposed to the theoretical, on-site physical security on a day-to-day basis. How is the vendor monitoring those people who have physical access to the site? How does the vendor monitor those who, although they have access to the site, may or may not have access to certain areas of the site? For instance, are the vendor's clerical employees allowed to go into the vendor's tape library and remove reels of tape? Can a programmer go into the machine room and sit in place of a machine operator and run the computers? What procedures exist for notifying the user when there has been a breach of security? What influence does the user have over resolving actual breaches of security or potential breaches of security? Irrespective of the answers, the vendor usually makes the final decision. And if the user disagrees with the vendor, the typical outsourcing relationship would provide no relief for the user.

Electronic security is the other kind of security for which the user is at risk. The more users there are on the same system, the greater the opportunity for a breach of electronic security.

These security breaches include a number of different ways in which an unauthorized individual may penetrate the outsourcer's computer system. Usually, such unauthorized access occurs by dialing into a computer system via a telephone, zigzagging through the password protection, and proceeding to examine and copy user files and software. In addition to snooping and copying, some intruders drag-race system resources and charge them to a user's account. A user and a vendor may remain unaware that a breach of electronic security has even occurred. The footprints left behind by the unauthorized user may appear simply as additional charges to one of the systems' users. The intruder could be another customer of the outsourcing vendor. That customer already has a legitimate means of access to the computer system and may be clever enough to bypass any security intended to protect one user from another.

IS INCONTINENCE IN ADDRESSING NEEDS

Businesses have needs that IS systems fulfill, and businesses must control their computer systems to meet those needs. Usually a company begins using a computer to fulfill specific business needs. Indeed, in a number of industries use of computer technology is essential. Imagine the credit card business without computers. Admit it, you can't.

A business in the U.S. economy encounters not only intense competition at home, but stunningly efficient competitors abroad. Every day, the "invisible hand" of Adam Smith, author of *The Wealth of Nations*, squeezes your company's throat. If your business is to breathe, let alone survive, it must adapt and surmount the competition. Information systems are one area where U.S. companies have a competitive advantage. But they did not secure that advantage, nor will they maintain it, if they fail to synchronize their needs with advancing technology. Replacing pens with punch cards instead of with keyboards and scanners is unlikely to keep you in front of the pack.

To function and maintain competitiveness, your business must tailor computer technology to fulfill your needs, both current and changing. Probably you are already among the converted and you did not need that sermon. But, consider how outsourcing shuffles the deck.

When you have your own IS department, you can identify needs and address them more readily than when you have outsourced. Your current IS staff should be in the best position to understand and implement the needs of your company's departments. Internal modification of your IS functions should compress the time interval between the articulation of business needs and their fulfillment.

When your data processing operations are in-house, you can tailor and tweak operations and needs as time and budget allow. Since many outsourcing relationships are for fixed services at fixed rates, any change in the services, other than volume, require additional negotiation with the vendor. Changes in volume generally do not require renegotiation; the outsourcing user will consume more of the same services, and usage charges will increase accordingly. However, when the user needs a change not in the volume or quantity of the services, but in the nature of those services, outsourcing relationships often adjust poorly. When data processing operations are in-house, management can adjust to changes in the nature of services. Even though many IS departments appear to be small independent kingdoms, any current problems with in-house data processing operations will only increase when the managers of those operations cease to be in the chain of command running downhill from your executive suites.

These control problems exist even when you want to install additional applications. Sometimes you can power up a new application readily, and you compensate the outsourcer merely by paying increased utilization charges. Other times, installing the application requires the outsourcing vendor to change its software and hardware configuration or revamp its telecommunications network. Few vendors will do this for free. Instead you must negotiate for these changes. In these circumstances, your negotiating leverage depends on just how much you want that new application.

In sum, in an outsourcing relationship, any modifications to your IS functions will be external to your business, and implemented by people who may be ignorant of your business and its special requirements. On the other hand, perhaps your IS department has been lacking in the needs fulfillment category. If so, outsourcing is a way to get rid of them. First, though, you might try a few selective personnel changes rather than firing the department.

Loss of control over the fulfillment of data processing needs does not always occur with outsourcing. On occasion, a sufficiently small or technologically backward enterprise may not have real control to lose. The outsourcing vendor may be in a far better position to negotiate, acquire, and finance the acquisition of additional data processing resources to service the end user. This can benefit certain end users who compensate the outsourcing vendor through a fee structure based on usage: the vendor in essence "finances" the user's acquisition of the additional resources.

It's not my job because you're not my boss anymore

An outsourcing relationship creates a different, and usually less effective, chain of authority and accountability than exists when your IS operations are in-house. To understand this, consider the different ways of handling a problem with an in-house operation versus an outsourced one.

When there is an in-house IS problem, management can pursue a number of remedies and procedures to effect a resolution. You can add resources to assist existing operations or to improve the existing functions. The in-house user often can adjust its operations to mitigate or avoid problems. You can "tune" your computer system by adjusting its hardware and software configuration. Depending upon its management style, a company can replace the managers responsible. Senior management can discipline or terminate middle management. The company can fire the data processing manager. In any case, your company itself chooses the solution.

In an outsourcing relationship, however, your contract with the vendor will govern your response to a problem.

Problems that were management or technical problems with in-house operations may explode into legal problems in an outsourcing relationship. You can always talk things over with the vendor; you can even sue. But most often a user will surrender its position to avoid litigation. Even if you want to support your local lawyers, unless your outsourcing agreement provides for accountability, you may not have a leg on which to stand.

Some things will never change: vendors are less likely to be responsive to your particular problems than are your own employees whose jobs are at stake. Rather than the priorities and style of your management, the law of services and the outsourcing contract govern accountability in an outsourcing relationship.

THE SMART RATS ARE FIRST TO LEAVE A SINKING SHIP

Get out of the way: your top IS talent may knock you over in its rush to leave when word of your impending outsourcing deal spreads. Don't blame your employees. Part of your motivation to outsource probably was to reduce their numbers. Along with your payroll reduction, though, you will lose individuals who know your company's computer applications and how those applications relate to the business objectives and needs of the company.

Many outsourcing deals provide that the outsourcing vendor will employ the user's computer personnel. In those circumstances, a user can tap the technical expertise it previously employed. Too often, however, your IS personnel will feel betrayed or unappreciated and resent a transfer to a new employer, especially a transfer achieved without the employees' knowledge or consent. Don't be surprised if those knowledgeable employees you so graciously transferred to the vendor leave their new employer in a short period of time. When the people go, their expertise follows. So the expertise those employees possessed will cease to be available, even for a fee through the vendor. Furthermore, you will notice that working on projects other than your company's will dilute the expertise of even those top performers who stay with the outsourcer.

Among the people employed in data processing endeavors are a greater than typical percentage of unusual and eccentric personalities. Often these employees are *prima donnas* who believe that they are underpaid and that they merit greater consideration than their employers give them. When, as part of its outsourcing agreement, a company transfers these employees to an outsourcing vendor, whatever feelings of unhappiness the employees felt in the past will increase. They may feel that they are simply servants or worse, to be transferred from one master to another. In such circumstances, the risk of deliberate sabotage clearly increases. More likely, though, outsourcing severs whatever bonds of loyalty may have motivated such employees. The company's transfer of these employees is certain to undermine their desire to remain and their motivation to perform at a high level.

You will want to retain some of your best and brightest IS people to oversee the transition to outsourcing, or to work in those areas or applications not outsourced. Unfortunately for you, the centrifugal force that outsourcing creates will probably cause attrition even in these ranks. When you enter into a large outsourcing relationship, you are no longer a major DP shop and the career path to top management becomes poorly marked, if any path even remains. Many of your new hires will be IS personnel who care little about their career paths and state of the art technology—or who expect you to train them so they can get a "real" IS job.

With phasers set on stun, you risk technical paralysis

Once locked into an outsourcing agreement, the user may not be able to keep pace with technological change. You may suffer technical paralysis and lose your ability to use improvements in computer technology.

The typical outsourcing vendor emphasizes and sells the concept that data processing services are software and hardware independent. Further, as part of persuading a particular customer to engage a vendor, the vendor will emphasize that the customer no longer need worry about staying current with changes in the technology.

Many users benefit from such a situation. As long as the data processing work gets done, and the cost of doing that work does not increase or increases at a fixed rate, many users will be satisfied. They will not need to determine if the most recent release of the operating system is compatible with the most recent release of something else. As a customer, the user can disregard a cost/benefit analysis for some new item of hardware. In fact, many users choose to outsource to avoid dealing with technological change.

On the other hand, much of what changes in computer technology are improvements—either increasing the amount of work performed without increasing costs, or decreasing costs for a given unit of work. While avoiding concerns with technological change, you may miss the benefits it can bring. At minimum you will be at the mercy of the vendor as to whether and how changing computer technology will affect you.

You will have great difficulty convincing your vendor to implement radical improvements in technology. For instance, when personal computers became well established in offices, some outsourcing vendors were reluctant to extend the advantages of personal computers to their customers. Since the outsourcing vendors depended mainly on the revenues derived from Central Processing Units, they had little incentive to distribute data processing operations to work stations. Vendors have also been uncomfortable with methods of charging for use of the particular work stations. As a result some users had to delay receiving the benefits of personal computers or maintain their own staffs to implement them outside of their outsourcing relationships. Consequently, data and control problems ensued from having multiple systems lacking central coordination.

These problems in technological flexibility will occur even if the change in technology is not major, but is only incremental or affects few companies. Outsourcers usually make more money by superior management of aging technology than they do by riding on the leading edge.

Generally, an outsourcing relationship significantly diminishes a user's ability to respond to changes in computer technology. Entering into an outsourcing agreement will substantially reduce choices and therefore flexibility in responding to and acquiring the advantages of improving computer technology.

This problem of technical paralysis is the flip side of the advantage of technological independence. Outsourcers want you to think of IS services like your other utilities. They'll ask, "You wouldn't build a power plant to get electricity, would you?" It's a good question. They have a point, but maybe the answer is no only because you can't fit a nuclear reactor on a desk-top.

THREE'S A CROWD WHEN TALKING LIABILITY

An outsourcing relationship can increase your risk of liability to third parties. The increased risks occur in two separate areas: liability to software vendors and liability to your customers.

Almost all software licensed for mainframes and mid-range systems is licensed pursuant to written license agreements. These license agreements contain numerous and differing restrictions on disclosure and transferability. A typical part of the outsourcing relationship is a transfer to the outsourcing vendor of existing licenses and disclosure of existing software. In most instances, the user's software license agreements will prohibit such transfers and disclosures. If you fail to obtain your software vendor's permission to outsource, you expose yourself to its claims of breach of contract, copyright infringement, and misappropriation of trade secrets. You may end up on the wrong side of an injunction, forbidden by a court to use the software until the matter is resolved.

If a software vendor (also called a licensor) will not permit you to use its software with your outsourcer, you have a number of unattractive alternatives available. First, you can pay the outsourcing vendor to acquire a license for your benefit. Occasionally an outsourcer will agree to pay for such a license if there is a problem in transferability. Be aware, though, that outsourcing vendors often intend to make money by employing the software licensed to one user for many of the outsourcer's other customers. Without sufficient authority for such use, the outsourcing vendor jeopardizes not only itself, but also the user who supplied the software.

A second option is for a user to negotiate with the licensor to modify the provisions of the software license agreement. Unfortunately, the licensor has all of the negotiating leverage once a user has made a commitment to the outsourcing transaction. Moreover, the licensor may not want to do business with the outsourcing vendor. There may be an existing dispute between the outsourcing vendor and the licensor. Outsourcer and software licensor disputes have generated much of the litigation related to outsourcing. Or the licensor may, reasonably or unreasonably, fear the vendor will allow unauthorized use by other outsourcing customers. Any or all of these issues may present obstacles to moving licensed software into an outsourcing relationship.

The third major alternative for an outsourcing customer is to use a different software package. The threshold problem in this approach is that use of a new package will require conversion from the old software to the new software. Since this user is about to enter into an outsourcing relationship, conversion probably cannot be accomplished prior to the initiation of that relationship. If conversion to the new software is the only alternative, then the user may have to delay the commencement of the outsourcing relationship. That delay may be very costly to both the user and the vendor.

On the other hand, you may be able to coordinate the conversion with your transition to outsourcing. In fact, the new relationship could provide a unique opportunity to run your old and new software in parallel before you switch. However, but for outsourcing, you would not have this problem to resolve.

An outsourcing relationship can exacerbate problems with the user's customers also. First, outsourcing inserts a stranger into the middle of the customer relationship. Whenever data processing causes a problem with a customer, the outsourcing user must coordinate the resolution of the problem with the outsourcing vendor and the customer. Second, the typical outsourcing agreement often shields the vendor against even the most egregious behavior. If so, liability for customer problems, even for damage to customers caused by the vendor, may fall on a user whose outsourcing contract lacks meaningful remedies. Thus the user becomes responsible for events not subject to its control.

Is this trip necessary?

The final disadvantage of outsourcing is that some outsourcing customers could have realized outsourcing's benefits with less cost and disruption by making changes in their IS department. For a full discussion of this idea see Chapter 7.

CHAPTER 5

HELP, I NEED SOMEBODY—NOT JUST ANYBODY!

You may be the CEO's offspring or a rich dilettante who enjoys dabbling in management, but that's not likely. You probably have your job because of many years of hard and smart work. You stick to well-lit streets because you're sensible, but if you have to go down a dark alley, you carry a lug wrench; they fear you and not the other way around. Much of your knowledge is self-taught by study, analysis, and experience. Over the years, you've "come up to speed" more times than you remember. In short, you're a top performer because you are always learning, thinking, and acting.

The most successful high achievers are on intimate terms with their own limitations. Chances are you would not be reading this book if you believed you already knew enough about outsourcing to proceed with a transaction on your own.

REALITY THERAPY

Part of being a top performer, nevertheless, is acknowledging reality. You don't want to hear this, but your ex-spouse was right: you need help, serious help. Of course, your ex was alluding to psychiatric assistance and not outsourcing therapy. While this may be rude to state, the ugly truth is that you probably know more about the northern spotted owl than you do about outsourcing. You are in good company, though. The typical executive has serious disadvantages, impediments, and disabilities in analyzing or considering an outsourcing transaction. He or she may be an expert in accounting, information systems, or manufacturing, but not in outsourcing. That lack of expertise may even be one of the reasons you are inclined to outsource in the first place, rather than accomplishing your goals in-house.

In most outsourcing relationships, a lot of money is at stake and a lot more than money is at stake. Perhaps your life, country, or sacred honor are not at risk, but the future viability of your company—that super-set of employment opportunities that includes your job—may be. In this "Information Age," you might expect gigabytes of advice just floating out there in cyber-space. In reality, until now almost nothing has been available to help you analyze a prospective outsourcing transaction. And while, in all modesty, the value of the information on these pages dwarfs whatever you paid, no book can completely substitute for the expertise you need.

In most full-outsourcing transactions, you will be transferring your entire IS function to the outsourcing vendor. Think for a moment of what your company would be like if it had no IS functions available to it at all. Could your business survive if your computer didn't handle accounting functions? Could your business survive if your computer didn't keep personnel files? How well would you manage inventory if you didn't have a computer? What if your company is a bank and the entire ATM network shuts down for five business days? (Remember those December 1993 storms?) How about if you take orders over WATS lines and each order taker has a computer terminal for entering orders. What if those terminals were down for two days—or even for an eight hour shift? How would your business continue?

If you presently have any IS functions, you are already exposed to these risks. However, the difference between having your IS function inside the company and outsourcing the IS function is that you have substantially more control when the function is in-house. If something goes wrong, you can make decisions immediately, implement contingency plans on the spot, and, if necessary, rid the company of the individuals who are responsible for the catastrophe in the first place. But when data processing is in the hands of an outsourcing vendor, you may not have the ability to deal with such problems as expeditiously and as dramatically as you would when those problems occurred inside. Therefore, the consequences of those problems would likely be greater when you have outsourced. In both outsourced and in-house operations you risk something, but with outsourcing there is a middleman between you and the solution. If possible, you need to structure your relationship with that outsourcer so that the outsourcer serves as an ally rather than as an impediment.

ONE SIZE DOES NOT FIT ALL

Outsourcing is not for everyone. Some companies, industries, and applications make poor outsourcing prospects. Also, there are better and worse points in a company's history and strategic plans to outsource operations. First investigate whether your company is a suitable prospect for any outsourcing. The next issue is whether to outsource some or all of your IS functions.

In an outsourcing transaction, business, technical, and legal issues are closely interrelated. Without some experienced players on your team, you'll probably take a beating. You need a first string to help you evaluate, structure, and execute an outsourcing transaction. As a prospective outsourcing customer, you need either to develop the talent in-house or to bring it in from the outside.

MAYBE YOU NEED AN OUT-SORCERER AFTER ALL

Part of analyzing an outsourcing transaction requires predicting the future, not only of your company, but also of its data processing needs. Additionally, you must predict information systems technology. A recent survey asked CIOs how far into the future they could predict their data processing costs and needs. The consensus answer was three years or less. Many outsourcing agreements, though, endure for ten years. Are the needs for seventy percent of those decade-long relationships a wild guess? Perhaps. Is an outsourcing contract of three years duration the answer for you? Perhaps. But in return for committing for ten years, many outsourcers can give you an irresistible deal. Whether and for how long you should sign up depends on many factors unique to your company.

If you feel comfortable flying solo in these areas, so much the better and good luck. The less confident and competent you are to make such a prediction, the greater your need for help.

Part of your prognostication involves a prediction of where your business will be five or ten years from now and how it's going to get there. If you are a financial services firm, will you require expanding on-line capabilities or distributed processing at various satellite offices nationally or internationally? Perhaps your business plans to grow through acquisitions over the next decade. How will those acquisitions fit into the outsourcing relationship? Will you expect to merge the data processing operations of those acquired businesses into your own data processing operations? Or will you expect them to remain separate? If they are to remain separate, should the acquired operations be subject to your existing outsourcing agreement? Likewise, if you divest a division during the next decade, how will that impact the outsourcing relationship? Will you allow that spin-off to piggyback onto your deal with the outsourcer? Or if you anticipate putting the whole division on the block, should you keep its IS center intact to offer a prospective buyer a self-contained, turnkey operation? How you answer that question and related ones could affect the marketability of the operations you might divest.

In fact, if you plan to outsource, you must consider all the issues of mergers, acquisitions, and takeovers and where your company might fit in. Restructuring will affect your outsourcing relationship, or the outsourcing relationships of an acquired or acquiring company. Your company might prefer the outsourcing arrangement of its acquirer—or vice versa. None of these questions are to suggest that before entering into an outsourcing agreement one must know absolutely everything about the next ten years, or at least must know about business and technology for the prospective term of the outsourcing agreement. Rather, the more you know about these issues, the better you can plan and negotiate for them—or at least incorporate appropriate flexibility in your outsourcing agreement.

HELP YOURSELF FIRST

This book will assist you considerably in the evaluation process. However, you are unlikely to have the time and the personnel to evaluate every one of these issues in an objective manner and to bring these evaluations to bear on the outsourcing transaction. At a minimum, you want to avoid outsourcing yourself into a legal, business, or technological corner.

SISYPHUS REVEALED

One person well known for footwork is Sisyphus. Allegedly he was a Greek. Born long before the invention of outsourcing, he gravely offended the oppressor-divinity establishment. For his "crimes," he was incarcerated for life in an Olympus-managed correctional facility known as Hades. His sentence contained some fine print. First, he would live forever. Second, his prison job was to push uphill a boulder which would roll back to the bottom whenever he reached the top.

Analyzing, structuring, and negotiating an outsourcing transaction may appear to be a "Sisyphian" project. The good news is that Sisyphus was a creation of tabloid journalism; he didn't even sell this story about a rock. He's a myth. You can't repeat a project that never existed, can you?

The bad news is that coping with outsourcing remains a formidable task. You may be tempted to charge in to solve these problems, but don't.

FORWARD HOOOOOOOOOOOOOO...............LD

The Horse Soldiers, She Wore A Yellow Ribbon, and *Fort Apache* are great movies. On the silver screen, there was no better leader of horse and human flesh than John Wayne. Keep in mind, though, that he always had scouts. He never led a charge without first reconnoitering. If you've forgotten the outcome in that canyon when Henry Fonda ignored Big John's advice, rest assured it was a massacre.

In evaluating outsourcing, you too need to reconnoiter. Discover the terrain on which you must fight, consider the condition of your troopers, and hire the right scouts.

R<small>EAD</small> <small>THE</small> M<small>APS</small> B<small>EFORE</small> <small>YOU</small> G<small>ET</small> <small>TO</small> <small>THE</small> E<small>NTRANCE</small> R<small>AMP</small>

One immutable law of the universe is that people rarely reach their destination if they don't know where they are going in the first place.

Learn about outsourcing, its advantages, disadvantages, how to manage the transition and the on-going relationship, and how to unwind the relationship. By reading this book you are halfway home. In addition, talk to your peers about their experiences and do some research in the trade press. In an unscientific survey (margin of error +/- 100%) conducted by your author over a three week period, at least one trade press article on outsourcing appeared every day.

L<small>OOK</small> <small>AT</small> <small>THE</small> T<small>EETH</small> <small>AND</small> T<small>HEN</small> <small>AT</small> <small>THE</small> H<small>EART</small>

To get help in evaluating an outsourcing transaction, the first place you will look is inside your company. And the first help to seek are people with the appropriate attitudes and abilities. Are your employees snails or eagles? The closer they are to mollusks, the less help they can provide. Talent, though, is randomly distributed throughout the population. So you, too, should have some top notch people working for you. After all, you hired them or you hired the people who hired them.

Since outsourcing is about data processing, you will undoubtedly look first at your IS employees. They can be valuable in deciding how to proceed. However, keep in mind that once consummated, the outsourcing transaction will put most, if not all, of these people out of work. These candidates for the unemployment line may be super competent, but can you trust them? Even if you trust them now, how long can you rely on their loyalty?

In an effort to reassure you, many vendors will promise to engage your displaced employees. Clearly this can help ease the pain and thereby ameliorate your personnel's morale problems. Even such a commitment, though, cannot eliminate several persistent, fundamental concerns. First, no outsourcer will agree to employ all of your IS employees forever. You may be able to negotiate a minimum period, but more than a year is unlikely. A year's job security is better than immediate bread lines, but not particularly reassuring.

You will have employees who do not want to work for the outsourcer. Some outsourcing companies have gained bad reputations as employers and their shops could be considered extremely undesirable places to work. These reputations are arguably unfair and antiquated, but your employees' perceptions will govern. You can't please everyone, you may say. True, but don't even think of relying on those you displease for expert, objective advice in approaching an outsourcing transaction.

You may need to surmount a "don't blame me" attitude. Unless you outsource only selected functions, the move to the outside suggests that your company no longer believes in its IS department. When enlisting employees to assist in your analysis, you will be asking them to criticize themselves and to evaluate how someone else can do a better job. In some societies this process has its virtues. You may even have some employees who tell you why they do such a bad job and how much better off the company will be without them. But with attitudes like that, these people probably hail from "Remulac, a small town in France," and may return home any time.

You must cope with resentment as well. Even your decision to consider outsourcing will deeply offend some of your workers. "Why aren't we good enough?" "All the company cares about is money." And so on. For better or worse, company loyalty to workers already has all but disappeared in the U.S. Yet many people refuse to read the handwriting on the wall. Poor readers good outsourcing advisors will not make.

TELL ME NO SECRETS AND I'LL TELL YOU NO LIES

Expecting to obtain all your expertise in-house presents another problem: confidentiality. Who is to know about the prospective outsourcing transaction and when will they know it? If you are worried about employees' loyalty, announcing a study to evaluate outsourcing will not enhance retention of employees. Quite the contrary, it will signal employees to pursue their careers elsewhere. Unfortunately, the first to go will be your most talented and perhaps most needed IS employees. So, there are good reasons to keep the lid on your outsourcing thoughts.

On the other hand, you should share your secret with someone. And someone really means several people, both up and down your chain of command. Unless you sit where the buck stops, you will be unable to proceed without top management's assent. Furthermore, failure to enlist certain other key people will set the stage for disaster.

Trying to leave the CIO or MIS manager, or whoever is the top IS executive, in the dark won't work. However, before you tell him or her what you are considering, dredge up those interpersonal skills focused on reassurance and give this person a good reason to pledge allegiance to the company. Even if you outsource everything with silicon in it, you will continue to need someone to look over the vendor's shoulder. Your CIO is a logical choice.

Before taking your CIO into your confidence, though, you need to evaluate that person's allegiance. Discuss with the CIO's boss, if you are not that person, the CIO's loyalty to the company. If the loyalty is in question, consider what can be done to enhance such loyalty. Can a promotion and a new title do the trick? A salary increase?

This actually will be the easiest part of outsourcing. The CIO's enlistment should be straightforward. Most individuals who have attained such a position already feel themselves more a part of top-level management than of the people they supervise. Nevertheless, they may have second thoughts about the wholesale eradication of the area that they manage. To some extent they may conclude that if the impetus for outsourcing comes from above, such a decision implicitly displays a lack of confidence in their performance as CIO.

On the other hand, your CIO's loyalty may not be an issue at all. Outsourcing ideas often spring from CIOs' crania. For a CIO on a career track to the top, controlling, rationalizing, and cutting data processing costs may be the springboard that propels his or her career upward.

Once the CIO is on board, top management and the CIO must decide who else, if anyone, should be involved in the decision-making process. Whether you require help from any other IS person will largely depend on the structure of the IS department. The more the department is decentralized and spread out across many physical locations, the more difficult it will be to avoid taking the managers of those decentralized units into your confidence. On the other hand, a CIO may be the only person you need from a very centralized IS department.

In addition to recruiting the CIO, you will need to consider whether to include the managers of those user departments—e.g., accounting, human resources, sales, manufacturing, etc.—where outsourcing will have the greatest impact. Can any of these individuals project unique experience or expertise into analyzing outsourcing?

There are many reasons to keep your outsourcing thoughts secret; there are nearly as many reasons to reveal them. Too many reasons exist to give a general rule, other than that you should tell people on a need-to-know basis only. Your dissemination of the outsourcing news should work like the ripples from a splash, spreading in ever-widening concentric circles to include those people you need. The following chart may be helpful as a suggestion:

Stage	*Who may need to know*
Early speculations	No one
Initial feasibility study	CIO Consultant
Full feasibility study	Necessary department heads Consultant

| Decision to search for outsourcing vendor | IS operations managers IS applications managers Consultant |
| Drafting and negotiating an outsourcing agreement | IS operations managers IS applications managers Consultant |

M.D. BY CORRESPONDENCE SCHOOL

You are going to need help in deciding whether and how much to outsource. One useful way to analyze your need for help is to list those corporate functions where outsourcing may have an impact. Then consider what that impact could be and what type of expertise you will require in evaluating that impact. For example, an outsourcing transaction may have consequences in at least one of the following functions within your company:

Financial

Outsourcing will impact financial functions in at least two ways. First of all, since the outsourcing transaction itself is likely to be of extreme financial significance to the enterprise, you will need financial people capable of assessing the transaction's impact. Secondly, the financial functions are one of the largest users of computer resources within a company. Your financial systems users must decide whether outsourced functions can meet their needs.

Plant and Property

Many outsourcing transactions involve either the sale or lease of the company's facilities to the outsourcer. In addition to the spreadsheet warriors, you will need real estate expertise.

Information Systems

Obviously, the more IS functions that you want to outsource, the greater the impact will be on the IS department's operations. In analyzing and deciding what IS functions you will transfer to the outsourcer, consider both business and technical issues.

Legal

Often an outsourcing transaction raises several fundamental legal issues for the outsourcing customer in addition to the specific provisions of the outsourcing agreement. For instance, should the outsourcing agreement be reported in the firm's 10(K) and 10(Q) reports to the Securities and Exchange Commission? Will outsourcing ruffle any secured creditors' feathers or, worse, put you in default? Finally, what happens under your existing software licenses when you open the doors to an outsourcer? This question presents vexing legal issues requiring significant attorney footwork.

If you believe that you can cope with an outsourcing transaction on your own, use the following checklist to help construct your own list of all the issues for which you will provide an answer. For those of you who refrain from self-surgery, the next chapter describes where to find some help.

CHECKLIST FOR EVALUATING YOUR NEED FOR HELP

I. In general, you may need assistance in the following areas:

    A. Strategic.

    B. Financial.

    C. Technical.

    D. Departmental.

    E. Legal.

    F. Miscellaneous.

II. Strategic issues for which you may need help.

    A. General strategic plans: in general where is your company headed?

    B. Specific strategies: what specific strategies should your company devise and is outsourcing one of those strategies?

C. Tactical considerations: to achieve your strategies
you need tactics—that is, the specific allocations
and dispositions of your resources. Among those tactics to evaluate are the following outsourcing possibilities:

   1. Outsourcing now.

   2. Outsourcing later.

   3. Full-outsourcing.

   4. Selective outsourcing.

D. Considering the prospective duration of an outsourcing relationship.

E. Intra-corporate considerations for which you may
need assistance if you are considering outsourcing.

   1. Impact of outsourcing on each corporate division.

   2. International ramifications when your divisions
   or operating units are in different countries.

      a. There may be local law issues to consider.

      b. There may be tax issues to consider.

      c. Software rights and protection may differ
      in each country.

F. Inter-corporate considerations if you want to outsource.

   1. If there are parent and subsidiary corporations
   involved, which ones participate and which
   one makes the outsourcing deal?

   2. Are corporations under common ownership
   with your company included in an outsourcing
   transaction?

   3. How do wholly-owned subsidiaries fit in the
   arrangements?

   4. Should there be a different consideration for
   partially-owned subsidiaries?

5. How will your company integrate acquisitions into outsourced IS operations?

6. If your company merges with another, how should that affect your IS and your merger partner's IS, if you have outsourced?

7. If your company makes a divestiture, where does the spin-off obtain its IS processing?

8. How would outsourcing affect your company as a takeover target?

   a. Does your company's attractiveness as a takeover matter?

   b. Does outsourcing enhance your desirability for an acquirer?

   c. Does outsourcing discourage an acquirer?

9. Should you acquire another entity that has already outsourced?

G. What realistic alternatives exist to outsourcing?

III. Financial issues related to outsourcing for which you may need help.

A. Identifying financial issues.

B. Evaluating financial issues.

C. Suggesting financial alternatives when considering outsourcing for financial reasons.

D. Evaluating proposed outsourcing fee structures and impact on company finances.

E. Suggesting alternative fee structures to the proposed fee structure with analysis of alternative structure.

IV. Technical issues related to outsourcing for which you may need help.

A. Identifying technical issues.

    B. Evaluating technical issues.

    C. Suggesting technical alternatives.

    D. Specific types of technical expertise that may be useful in evaluating outsourcing.

        1. IS top management—chief information officer.

        2. Operations management.

        3. Software management.

        4. Specific application knowledge.

        5. Systems programming management.

        6. Communications.

V. Departmental issues related to outsourcing where you may need help.

    A. Identifying departments affected by outsourcing.

    B. Determining the appropriate level of involvement of each department's top management.

    C. Coordinating the involvement of each department's top management.

    D. Investigating the issues within each affected department.

    E. Contributing specific knowledge of each department's applications.

VI. Legal issues related to outsourcing where you may need help.

    A. Negotiating and drafting the outsourcing agreement.

    B. Accommodating third-party software licenses.

    C. Evaluating and making SEC disclosures.

    D. Evaluating plant closing laws.

    E. Coping with employee termination issues.

        1. ERISA (Employee Retirement Income Security Act).

  2. EEOC (Equal Employment Opportunity Commission).
  3. ADA (Americans with Disabilities Act).
  4. COBRA (Consolidated Omnibus Budget Reconciliation Act of 1985).
  5. Fair Labor Standards Act.
  6. Age discrimination issues.
  7. State employment law.
  8. Employment contract issues.
  9. Union issues.
F. Evaluating antitrust issues.
G. Analyzing international concerns.
  1. Software issues.
  2. Trans-border data flow issues.
  3. Employment security issues.
H. Evaluating intellectual property issues.
I. Evaluating communications issues.
  1. FCC issues.
  2. Tariffs.
J. Analyzing industry specific regulatory issues.
  1. Health care administration.
  2. Third party claims administration.
  3. Electronic fund transfer.
  4. Financial institutions.
  5. Clearinghouses.
  6. Tax preparer business.
K. Evaluating taxation issues.

VII. Miscellaneous issues related to outsourcing for which you may need help.

A. Real estate transactions.

B. Human resource administration.

VIII. *Analyzing sources of assistance.*

  A. Help is potentially available from inside your company and/or outside your company.

  B. Available inside help.

    1. Existing IS employees.

    2. CFO.

    3. Corporate counsel.

  C. Available outside help.

    1. Consultants.

      a. IS consultants.

      b. General business consultants.

    2. Attorneys.

  D. Cost issues.

  E. Loyalty issues.

  F. Management and control issues.

  G. Coordination issues.

CHAPTER 6

THERE IS A CAVALRY FOR YOUR CALVARY

Its a sucker's bet that you will find all the help you need inside your company. Sooner or later you will call the cavalry. Make it sooner.

The sooner you involve professionals from outside the company the better. Two basic reasons support this approach. As you already know, your own employees may lack the objectivity you desperately need. Second, you need many different kinds of knowledgeable assistance. It takes time to locate the appropriate people, to evaluate their credentials, and to schedule their engagement with your company.

THERE'S NO FREE LAUNCH

Taking a reasonable amount of time and hiring outside professionals will cost something. Look at the money you spend up front in an outsourcing transaction from the feasibility study to the contract negotiation as a research expenditure. Resist the temptation to conclude that because you have expended significant monies up to each stage that you must proceed to the next stage. If after a stage you conclude that outsourcing is not for you, consider your money well-spent in avoiding a wrong move that would have likely cost millions. And, if you should proceed to the next stage, most of what you paid to learn in one stage will assist you in the next.

THE EXPEDIENCY OF GEORGE III

In 1776, H.R.M. George III had serious problems with one of his overseas divisions. What had once been a cash cow was mired in red ink because of labor problems. In fact, loyalty had deteriorated to the point where workers were destroying inventory and killing security guards. Local law enforcement had been unsuccessful in calming the situation. Reinforcements from the home office had been insufficient. And worse, internal politics at headquarters made reassigning additional security personnel problematic. So, like any good chief executive, he sought outside help. He hired security consultants known as Hessians. Ultimately, they could not turn around the North American operation, but their presence did delay the divestiture for several years and gave him time to restructure to save some assets.

Millions of written words have second guessed George III, but he clearly recognized that when you cannot get the help you need from within, you can hire outside consultants.

In addition to your own employees, you will also need technical computer expertise, legal expertise, and accounting expertise. You may also need management expertise. Your company probably is accustomed to seeking advice from attorneys and accountants. At any rate, the hiring of management and technical consultants may be the most problematic of the lot. After all, you have technical experts and managers in-house. How do you decide whether to hire someone from the outside? How do you find a consultant who can help you?

DIAL 1-800-CAN-HELP

The right consultant can aid your struggle with an outsourcing transaction.

There are a large number of consultants available. There are many types and levels of experience and proficiency available. If you are willing to look, you can find an individual or a consulting firm that fits your outsourcing needs. Often a consultant blows away the fog of confusion and the smoke of subjectivity. The right consultant can bring special skills to untangle perplexing problems and overcome the built-in biases possessed by your own staff.

There are consultants with much greater knowledge in the technical issues of outsourcing than you can find within your own organization. You should also be able to find this ability combined with experience in coping, not only with outsourcing's problems, but also with problems other companies have had that were similar to what your outsourcing problems may be.

If the consultant focuses on your company alone, he or she can concentrate on your project better than your employees can. Your existing personnel have other jobs to perform, and enlisting them in the cause could hurt their other work, or their commitment to the outsourcing project, or both.

In the outsourcing context, you may need the confidentiality that a consultant can provide. Your consultant can roam around the IS departments and other departments under any number of pretexts while keeping the prospective transaction secret.

A final advantage of consultants is that you can always use them as a target or a foil. Have the consultants propose something easy for you to trash and thereby reveal your omniscience. Or when something goes wrong, blame them. Use your consultants to test ideas with management and the masses. If people like the pitch, you can share in the glory; if they don't like it, it's the consultants' fault. In other words, let consultants pilot that trial balloon. If it gets shot down, only the consultants burn.

In sum, a consultant can give you objectivity, expertise, time, confidentiality, and a scapegoat.

DIAL 976-BULL

There are, however, several disadvantages to hiring a consultant. In deciding whether to engage a consultant to help with outsourcing, you should weigh these disadvantages.

There could be too many fish in the sea. The advantage of numerous consulting choices may create the disadvantage of too many choices. And the caliber of available consultants varies widely. Anyone can become a consultant—and anyone has. Unlike physicians, CPAs, and attorneys, consultants are not a licensed profession.

Moreover, in some areas the consulting business has become the last refuge of the downsized and unemployed. This has both good and bad aspects. The down side is that some consultants are people on a job hunt and do not have the sense of professional objectivity which is necessary for the best consulting relationships. On the other hand, because these people are unemployed does not necessarily mean they are unfit to be consultants. Indeed, you may be able to interview IS professionals who managed outsourcing transactions so well elsewhere that they now need a job. Nevertheless, there are many hungry people out there who will not think twice about overselling their talents.

If you don't have a clear picture of what you want your consultant to do, your consultant will not either. There are many excellent consultants, but none so good that they can read your mind when you can't.

Consultants cost money. If you're not careful, they can cost a fortune. So be careful. Set goals with associated budgets. One cause of consultant cost overruns is the failure to control the consultant in the first place. If you give a consultant a blank check, some will fill it out and cash it.

CONSULTANT MYTHOLOGY

Many of consulting's disadvantages arise out of preconceptions that surround consulting in general. If you believe these fables, retaining a consultant will at best disappoint you.

Most professions have their clichés and stereotypes, like all doctors are devoid of emotion, or all lawyers are friendly. (Ok, maybe the second one isn't so common.) Although some element of truth may give rise to a stereotype, reliance on stereotypes is an unsound basis for selecting friends—or consultants.

Stack all the consulting clichés and stereotypes and what you'll get is a mythology. Here are some of the more prevalent myths about consultants. Even if you don't believe them yourself, many other people, including some consultants, do.

Myth: *"Consultants are good, if not better, business people than you."*

If they were that good, more of them might be running their own businesses. This is not disparagement of the consulting profession in general. There are many sharp business people among consultants, but you cannot tell consultants' business acumen by eye-balling them. Nor can you take for granted that because a consultant belongs to a consulting firm he or she knows anything. The same is true for consultants who claim to be specialists. Your prospective consultants might be the best thing in computers since silicon chips, but that doesn't mean they understand your applications or needs in information technology.

Myth: *"Consultants can solve nearly any problem."*

The consulting profession would certainly like for you to believe this. As you know, though, not every problem has a solution and not every attempt to solve a problem will arrive at a solution.

Myth: *"Consultants can make any project happen faster."*

Some companies engage consultants thinking that consultants' problem-solving tactics, multiplied by their other advantages, equal abbreviated project timetables. They want to believe that a consultant can make a project happen no matter how short the fuse. This is not the case. Some things have their own time frames, and there is very little anyone can do to make them occur more quickly. Moreover, too many projects sacrifice wisdom for speed.

Myth: *"Consultants can readily convert ideas into actions."*

This is true only with consultants who have those skills. Not everyone who can analyze a problem can implement the solution to that problem.

Myth: *"Consultants have superior people skills so as to mesh well with your existing staff."*

All consultants would like you to think that they are personable and people-oriented and therefore will work well with your existing staff. While consultantcy may attract more affable individuals than exist in the general population, this is a very dangerous myth to rely upon without investigation. (Additionally, if you are trying to keep the consultant away from your existing staff, this may be an irrelevant consideration.)

Myth: *"You met the actual consultant."*

Many consulting engagements coalesce during the three martini lunches between top dogs at the consulting firm and their counterparts at your company. But never assume that whoever made the sales pitch will be the person doing the work. In fact, if the "consultant" who secured the engagement is effective in attracting business, his or her firm will fight to keep that person rain-making and not imprisoned somewhere working for you.

Myth: "Consultants only tell you what you already know."

If this were really true as often as people contend, there wouldn't be a consulting industry. Yet, the consulting industry is growing by leaps and bounds, leading only to one of two reasonable conclusions from such growth. Either corporate America is full of idiots who pay hundreds of millions of dollars in consulting fees and receive no value, except what they already knew in the first place. Or in the majority of engagements, consultants actually contribute something to their clients.

MYTH PROOFING

Now that you know the myths, you can cope with them. Your having been "de-myth-tesized" means they will not unduly influence your attitudes towards the consulting profession in general, or your decision concerning an outsourcing consultant in particular.

The myths are a disadvantage only in two senses. If you believe them, they can impair you and the usefulness of any consultant you engage. If your employees or senior management believe them, then you have another set of challenges. Yet, because they are myths, you can ensure that when you hire a consultant, you will rely on facts, not fables.

Consultant conquers computers—film at 11

In an outsourcing transaction, a consultant offers value in several potential tasks. The consultant can help you decide whether or not to outsource. To do this, a consultant can help define your existing problems and articulate your objectives. Then he or she could help you determine whether outsourcing will solve your existing problems or exacerbate them. Finally, the consultant can determine if some solution other than outsourcing exists.

If you decide to outsource, a consultant can assist you in contract negotiations and in the transition to outsourcing. Particularly useful will be competent help in evaluating the technical aspects of a vendor's proposal and in finding answers for technical questions that arise along the way to closing the deal. Your consultant can also assist your attorney in drafting certain exhibits to the outsourcing agreement, such as:

A. An inventory of existing hardware and software

B. A transition plan

C. A disaster recovery plan, and

D. Performance standards.

Prospecting for consultants

Once you have decided you want a consultant, you have to find one.

There are numerous ways to locate prospective consultants. You should explore them all. In a nutshell these avenues are:

- Solicit referrals from your industry
- Solicit referrals from companies outside your industry, but with similar IS requirements
- Research the trade press
- Research online databases
- Contact professional associations
- Contact computer consulting firms
- Contact big six accounting firms

You might know of another company that has made the decision to outsource its IS operations. If so, that is a good place to start. Talk to your peer at that company. Find out if he or she used a consultant, the consultant's identity, how your peer felt about the experience, and if he or she would recommend your doing the same.

If for competitive reasons you won't contact another company in your industry to discuss outsourcing, consider conferring with a company of similar size that has outsourced. CIOs often know of other companies with IS departments similar to their own.

Scanning the trade journals to uncover what companies are outsourcing and the identity of their consultants might yield a prospective consultant. You could stumble upon an article about outsourcing consultants that leads to pay dirt. Don't underestimate the value of online services such as the Internet, CompuServe, and Nexis for bulletin boards, online discussions, and information retrieval. These information avenues offer information, referrals, and discussions—all of which can lead you to a suitable consultant.

If you have tried all of these options and remain unable to find an IS consultant who has experience in outsourcing transactions, you can approach one of the large accounting firms or one of the large data processing consulting firms. Think very carefully, though, before engaging any firm that itself provides outsourcing services. Even though companies will assure you that they have no conflict of interest, and a wall separating their consultants and their outsourcing services, the potential for a conflict of interest is too great and you have too much at risk.

On the other hand, if the consultants you want to hire provide outsourcing services, they may have a unique perspective on your proposed transaction. If so, in your relationship with them, you'll have to establish some means of insulating your company from their inclination to recommend their own outsourcing services. You could decide that, no matter what, you will not engage your consultants for outsourcing services. Yet your ability to stick to that decision is questionable because the consultants could do such an in-depth analysis of your operations and needs so as to become the low cost outsourcing bidder. How effectively could you argue that you will ignore the lowest cost vendor because it was the same company that provided you consulting services, or because it is too familiar with your needs?

PICK A CONSULTANT, ANY CONSULTANT

Having performed some research, you should have a list of several prospective consultants. To evaluate these potential consultants in a useful manner, you need a framework. The remainder of this chapter provides such a framework. It's applicable to selecting any consultant whether for outsourcing or other tasks. If, however, you are already familiar with selecting consultants, skip to the next chapter.

The foundation of your framework is determining the consultant's tasks. For an outsourcing transaction, there are three major tasks: (1) Evaluating outsourcing, (2) negotiating an outsourcing transaction, and (3) managing the transition to outsourcing. Consultants would be useful in all three.

But not every consultant would be appropriate for all three tasks. A consultant may have skills useful in one task, but not in another. The evaluation of outsourcing will focus heavily on the strategic management of your company—an area where management consultants have more to offer than do people experienced in application conversions. Conversely, in the transition to outsourcing, a management consultant has little to offer on the technical problems of software conversions. In contract drafting and negotiations, you may need people with both skills, since technical and strategic thinking are relevant to the construction of an effective outsourcing agreement.

Consequently, while using the same consultant for evaluating outsourcing and for assisting in the subsequent tasks introduces a conflict of interest possibility, it may also mismatch the consultant and the task.

Consider engaging more than one consultant. Undoubtedly, multiple consultants will increase your consulting costs. At the same time, though, you will avoid the consultant's potential conflict of interests and better fit your task to the consultant's skills.

In all likelihood, you will ignore this advice because of the hassle and costs of selecting multiple consultants. Consider then a compromise. Engage a consultant with the full range of skills you need and have the consultant explain in detail how it will match its personnel's skills to each task.

Whether you will hire one or multiple consultants, you must winnow your list of prospective consultants.

YOU'VE GOT A LITTLE LIST

One way to proceed is by assigning a rank to each consultant candidate on your list based on a range of qualities described below. All of these qualities are desirable. The table below ranks a continuum of qualities in the order of increasing value to you. The more of these characteristics that a consultant possesses, the greater the likelihood that this consultant will prove useful. The qualities are as follows:

1. Knowledge of your business.

2. Experience with your company.

3. Experience in your industry.

4. Technical expertise in IS, particularly large scale systems.

5. Ability to speak English as opposed to computerese.

6. Ability to work with many different kinds of people.

7. A good reputation for this kind of work.

8. The ability to disagree with top management.

9. Objectivity.

10. Candor.

11. Experience in outsourcing engagements.

12. Experience in outsourcing engagements in your industry.

13. Specific, relevant prior engagements.

MAKE A CONNECTION

After building the ranked list of prospective consultants, you need to contact them. It makes sense to use the ranked list to determine the order in which you contact prospects, and later when evaluating the candidates.

In communicating with these consultants, stress the confidential nature of your inquiry and your proposed consulting engagement. Consider having candidates sign a non-disclosure agreement. Many consultants will be reluctant to do so at this stage, but it is worth asking. Possibly you could use an intermediary, like an accountant or an attorney, to make the contact.

Writing an RFP (Request for Proposal) to submit to these candidates is another useful way of making a connection, but companies rarely use RFPs to select consultants. Alternatively, consider writing a short (one- or two-page) questionnaire to submit to the consultant to obtain information that might help in your evaluation. Here is an example to stimulate your thinking:

SAMPLE
CONSULTANT'S QUESTIONNAIRE
CONFIDENTIAL

Consultant's name _____

Address _____

Telephone _____

Fax _____

Brief Description of company:

Consolidated XYZ, Inc. ("Conz") is a leading distributor of refrigerator magnets. It takes mail and telephone orders for its products and electronically notifies the warehouse closest to the customer to ship. It has three data centers located in different states. Conz has six mainframe and five mini-computers running a full range of financial, manufacturing, inventory, and related applications. Last year Conz's total revenue was approximately $190 million. Conz is considering outsourcing its entire IS function and is seeking a consultant with an appropriate skill portfolio.

Thank you for answering the following questions:

1. What relevant prior engagements or other knowledge do you possess that could benefit Conz and how?

2. What specific experience in outsourcing transactions in the refrigerator magnet industry do you possess?

3. What specific experience in outsourcing transactions do you possess, other than in the refrigerator magnet industry?

4. Please describe your technical expertise.

5. Please describe your experience in the refrigerator magnet industry.

6. Please describe any prior experience you have had with Conz.

7. Please list three references that Conz can contact.

8. Please list a dissatisfied client that Conz can contact.

9. What is your availability?

Before you send your questionnaire to a prospect, you ought to inform the consultant that you are considering a confidential engagement and that you require the consultant to maintain the confidentiality of your discussions and the questionnaire. If the consultant can't deal with your ground rules, move on.

I'VE GOT A SMALLER LIST

If you use the questionnaire approach, then you ought to be able to create a list of prospective candidates based on those answers. From that list, you can select the most promising. You should have an interview with the prospective candidates to ask any follow-up questions or clarify the consultant's answers. As part of that interview, if you decide to go to the next step with the consultant, ask for a written proposal from the consultant and give the consultant a reasonable time frame within which to prepare that proposal. You can give the consultant some guidelines for that proposal. They are, at a minimum, the following:

1. The objectives of the consultant in performing consulting services for your company.

2. The proposed schedule for performing those services.

3. The deliverables the consultant is going to provide, for example, a report.

4. The proposed fee structure, how it is calculated, and any cap on those fees.

5. Checkpoints the consultant can establish for both sides to monitor performance.

6. The project team member(s) and a resume or resumes of those people.

7. Assumptions the consultant is making in drafting its proposal.

8. The consultant's need for your company's resources.

    a. Human Resources.

    b. Information System Resources.

    c. Office Space, etc.

Undoubtedly, you evaluate proposals all the time. So, very likely, the manner in which you evaluate and select proposals in general is what you will apply in these circumstances. There is nothing wrong with such an approach. Keep in mind that the proposal is a consultant's best foot forward. They are not likely to do any better job in their consulting engagement than they did in making the proposal. Therefore, you may reasonably emphasize the quality of the proposal in selecting a candidate.

THE WINNERS ARE . . .

You should select several, probably no less than three top candidates for the consulting engagement and then interview the proposed project team members. Since the consultant who made the sales pitch to you is not likely to be a member of the project team, you need to size up the team members themselves. If your technical people are privy to the whole outsourcing possibility, then you can include them in your interview of the project team. Perhaps you can get comments from another of the consultant's clients concerning the specific team members to add to your dossier on this consultant. Of course, you need to make your own evaluation. Below are some additional guidelines to help you appraise candidates. The team member(s) should have these minimum skills:

1. Ability to define problems.

2. Ability to describe solutions—preferably more than one solution per problem.

3. Ability to research and find facts.

4. Listening and communicating ability.

5. Creative thinking.

6. Grounded in reality.

7. General "people skills."

In selecting a consultant, you will find that it may be advantageous to have the consultant rework the proposal until both sides are satisfied that the proposal clearly states the objectives, checkpoints, and fee structure of how the relationship is to transpire. This recursive process with the top two candidates will allow you to evaluate their ability to be flexible and to respond to your feedback. There is also the added benefit that as a result of such a process you and your consultant may actually be on the same wavelength.

THE PICK OF THE LITTER

Finally, when you make your selection, prepare a written agreement that incorporates your RFP, if you did one, and the consultant's proposal. Nothing needs to be too elaborate, but if it is not in writing, it is probably not part of the deal.

Even though you engage consultants as independent professionals, you should not give them free rein. They are a resource that you must nevertheless manage. In dealing with consultants, the following list of "Do's" and "Don't's" might help out:

Do's:

1. Do manage consultants in their performance of services for you.

2. Do check the consultant's performance against an agreed schedule.

3. Do be realistic about the consultant's capabilities.

4. Do constantly worry about the consultant's loyalty.

5. Do review the financial implications of the consultant's ideas.

6. Do provide those financial implications to the consultant as feedback.

Don'ts:

1. Don't give a consultant a free hand.

2. Don't let consultants incur fees without your knowing exactly what they are working on.

3. Don't fall for lofty promises.

4. Don't assume that a consultant is objective.

5. Don't let your personal affinity for the consultant impede that consultant's value by failing to focus efforts or by reducing the consultant's objectivity.

6. Don't allow consultants to spend too much of your fee-paying time on the start-up process. Let the consultant absorb most of the start-up costs.

7. Don't shoot the messenger. The best consultants should be like your spouse and your attorneys: they don't tell you what you want to hear; they tell you what you need to hear.

MISSILE TREATIES

While the cold war thrived, the Soviets took advantage of an American negotiating characteristic. Administrations of both political parties were frequently more concerned with reaching an agreement than they were with the implications of such agreements. This led to some very dubious treaties. We agreed not to develop a missile defense system; to allow our obsolete computers to be bought and installed as guidance systems in Soviet ICBMs; and so on.

Too many outsourcing customers fall into this trap of trying to reach a quick deal rather than the right deal. This tactic is self-defeating and plays into the outsourcer's hands. Always remember: the vendor is very experienced at negotiating outsourcing transactions; you are not.

A quick deal may be very tempting, but it forces you to take short-cuts. If you rush to the closing, you risk having an insufficient time to evaluate relevant issues, to react to vendor proposals, to counter-propose, to negotiate all parts of the contract, and to fully evaluate the outsourcer.

Even though this advice may differ significantly from the way you ordinarily do business, take your time to plan and to be prepared without rushing. Look very, very carefully before you leap. The ten-year term of your outsourcing agreement won't pass any more slowly for your having spent an adequate amount of time at the front end. Spend the time to evaluate if outsourcing really is for you. Then spend plenty of time preparing for the transaction. Think of how much time you spend looking for a new car in relation to its price. Give your outsourcing transaction at least the same ratio of time to price. And give your outside professionals enough time to help you.

CHAPTER 7

HAVE I GOT A DEAL FOR YOU

In evaluating and choosing outsourcing, the most important criteria is money. But you need to look beyond the dollars at several other significant issues. The decision to outsource will have long term and profound consequences for your company. Of course, saving a great deal of the stockholders' money will have long term consequences as well.

MIRROR, MIRROR ON THE WALL . . .

Before trying to decide if outsourcing is for your company, learn everything possible about your existing IS function. Unfortunately, those above the CIO level of management tend to look down their noses at IS. Yet, even if you think of DP personnel as glorified and overpaid electricians, you could make a serious mistake if you fail to do a self-examination.

Is the IS department as bad as you believe? Get someone to study your existing operations. Your consultant, if you have one, is a good candidate. Think of your IS broadly; companies often have IS functions outside their IS departments. Don't forget that little sales call tracking system they have on three PCs over in marketing, or the new voice mail system that can't stop telling you every available option. ("To leave a message, if today is Tuesday, press 1; to send your message on the fifth day of the month, press 2; to send an urgent message during leap years, press 3;" etc.)

Begin with your IS department and find out what it does. Even most CIOs have never catalogued all the functions and services that their domain entails. You can approach this task in several ways; if you have something in mind, use it and skip the next section on determining what you want out of outsourcing.

You can help yourself by imposing some kind of organizational structure on your catalog. One way is to allocate current IS functions into four major categories: IS operations; communications; software development and maintenance; and other IS services. Then add details to each category. Here's an example:

1. *Information systems operations*

   a. operate computer hardware.

   b. initiate the execution of application software (production runs).

   c. maintain system software.

   d. maintain hardware (unusual).

2. *Communications*

   a. maintain communications software and network software.

   b. monitor performance of communications circuits.

   c. re-route traffic around bottlenecks.

3. *Software development and maintenance*

   a. analyze and recommend application software.

   b. develop and install application software.

   c. maintain application software.

   d. resolve production problems caused by application software.

4. Other IS services

    a. train users.

    b. install and authorize user terminals and work stations.

    c. consult internally and perform hand-holding for departmental users of IS functions.

    d. monitor technological developments.

    e. IS services occurring outside the IS department.

Your catalog of services will help you in a number of ways. It will reveal the scope of both what's going on in IS and what services outsourcing might take over. Itemizing services helps in itemizing costs. It also helps differentiate areas for establishing performance standards.

Once you know what your IS department does, find out what it does well. Find out what it does not do well. If there are inefficiencies, find out where.

It's more than play money

As part of this self-examination, identify the cost for every service that your IS department currently provides. Unless your only motivation for outsourcing is to sell your assets in order to bring in cash for your company, you need excruciating detail on costs. How can you determine if outsourcing will save money if you don't know your costs? Moreover, knowing your costs may help in eliminating those costs without outsourcing.

While you're uncovering costs, determine the performance level of each of the IS department's services. You may have difficulty in assigning numbers to costs and performance levels in some areas. A consultant should be capable of helping out here. There is a checklist at the end of the chapter that suggests ways to measure costs and performance for the IS functions that you have identified.

If your internal billing system already involves charge-back mechanisms that incorporate your areas of IS operations, you may believe you already have costs detailed. But sometimes these internal charges are "funny money," or based on incentives other than pure cost. For instance, some charge-back arrangements inflate on-line charges to encourage users to shift daytime, on-line processing to off-line processing at night. When you consider paying an outside vendor, the money loses its sense of humor. Investigate. Don't assume your internal costs are the true costs to your company. You must compare apples to apples and not to Asian pears.

As Freud said: "What do users really want?"

Once you know what your IS operations are, you must determine what you want out of outsourcing. Which of outsourcing's advantages are the most important to you? Which of the disadvantages do you most need to avoid? Once again, here's the list of advantages and disadvantages of outsourcing:

Advantages:

1) Fix costs.
2) Control costs.
3) Pay as you go.
4) Extend useful life of equipment.
5) Obtain expertise.
6) Focus on your core business.
7) Minimize negotiations cycle.
8) Attain technological independence.
9) Minimize IS management responsibilities.
10) Reduce attention to computer technology changes.
11) Gain quick access to advanced technology.

Disadvantages:

1) Total dependence on outsourcing vendor.
2) Risk to third-party confidentiality.

3) Increased security risk.

4) Loss of control in fulfilling your IS needs.

5) Change in accountability.

6) Loss of expertise.

7) Risk of technical paralysis.

8) Constituent issues, such as employee issues.

If you see your own goals through a glass darkly, you cannot expect a vendor to understand, let alone meet, those goals. However, do not think that you must have goals set in concrete from the outset. Commence your decision-making process in one of two ways. Either intend to achieve specific benefits from outsourcing and decide whether outsourcing will let you achieve them, or inquire into the advantages and risks of outsourcing and decide if you want the expected benefits at their accompanying costs.

Whichever way you select, the clarification process should involve as much learning as it does decision making. You may begin by wanting outsourcing for one reason, but later reject your initial reason and discover others. Likewise, risks that threatened at first may later seem manageable. At the same time you are certain to uncover concerns that had never occurred to you before. Keep in mind that rather than carving things in stone, you are exploring poorly-charted territory. And, even though many other companies have outsourced, this is your first time in the big city. You have a right to be cautious and inquisitive.

If you have engaged consultants, try this exercise before you know the consultants' recommendation. Make a list of your expectations and concerns about outsourcing your IS. Don't show the list to the consultants until they have completed their analysis. Compare this list to the consultants' recommendations. Obtain the consultants' comments on your list and such discrepancies as exist between your conclusions and the consultants'. Don't be surprised if they differ significantly. The final product of this process, though, will be a more accurate summary than if you and the consultants had collaborated on the same list first.

Moreover, the reward for all this work should be the following:

- a detailed list of all your IS operations including those outside the IS department;
- a detailed cost associated with as many of these IS operations as possible;
- nascent performance standards for the IS operations;
- a list of goals you want outsourcing to achieve; and
- a list of outsourcing risks to avoid.

LOOK BEFORE YOU LEAP

Before looking for love in all the wrong places—or outsourcing for all the wrong reasons—consider alternatives. For every possible advantage of outsourcing, think of at least one alternative method of achieving the same goal. For every advantage of outsourcing you want, ask these questions:

Can my company obtain the advantage through means other than outsourcing?

Can we improve current operations sufficiently to realize advantages equivalent to those of outsourcing?

The answers to these questions would produce a list such as the one that follows, of outsourcing advantages and alternative means of obtaining those advantages:

Advantage—cash infusion.

Alternatives:

- sale and leaseback (or license back) of certain IS assets, such as equipment, company developed software, and data centers.
- drastic reduction in DP costs to save cash.
- corporate re-structuring.

Advantage—equity investment.

Alternatives:

- public or private offering of equity or debt.
- corporate restructuring, e.g. merger or divestiture.

Advantage—lower or control IS costs.

Alternatives:

- put your IS department on a diet.
- better control of internal costs.
- implement a charge-back method to encourage IS
resource conservation.
- let your IS department offset costs by becoming
someone else's outsourcer.
- set up your IS department as a separate entity that
your company owns and that is an exclusive outsourcer to your company.

Advantage—technical flexibility.

Alternatives:

- move to "open systems" such as UNIX.
- lease, don't buy.
- move to more third party software.

Advantage—increase available skills.

Alternatives:

- use consultants as needed.
- increase your IS department's skills.

Advantage—increased access to technical resources.

Alternatives:

- increase your own technical resources.
- contract for the necessary resource only, e.g.,
telecommunications network.
- conduct an audit to judge if existing resources are
under-used.

A SIMPLE NUMBERS GAME

In deciding whether to outsource, you must answer this fundamental question: "Will we receive all of our intended benefits without suffering the disadvantages of outsourcing?" Evaluate the issues below and determine whether the potential benefit outweighs or at least balances the potential disadvantage. You have probably guessed that this is a suggestion for a cost-benefit analysis. If you already have your own tried-and-true way to do such an analysis, use it. Then if you are still considering outsourcing, you may want to skip to the section of this chapter on selecting what to outsource.

Simplistic Test

While the decision to outsource requires an extremely complicated analysis and an in-depth decision-making process, you can use a simplistic test to determine whether or not to proceed to the more in-depth analysis. The basic structure of this simplistic test is to assign a certain number of points to your answers on the following questions:

1. How significant is the potential cash infusion from the outsourcer?

_____ A. If the cash that the outsourcer will provide is significant to your overall financial health, score one point.

_____ B. If it is irrelevant to your financial health, score zero.

_____ C. If it is deterimental to your financial health, score a negative one.

2. How significant is the potential equity contribution from the outsourcer?

_____ A. If the equity contribution that the outsourcer will provide is significant to your overall financial health, score one point.

_____ B. If it is irrelevant to your financial health, score zero.

_____ C. If it is deterimental to your financial health, score a negative one.

3. How important is the control of IS costs?

_____ A. If IS costs are a problem, and if you are willing to implement the necessary contractual provisions to actually control those costs, score one point.

_____ B. If you presently have good control of IS costs, score zero.

_____ C. If you are skeptical that IS costs can be controlled, even by an outsourcer, or if you need to have increasing IS costs to meet increasing business demands, score negative one.

4. Would a decision to outsource increase or decrease your technical flexibility?

_____ A. If outsourcing will add to your ability to switch to more useful technology as needed in the future, score one point.

_____ B. If it will not have an impact on your technical flexibility, score zero.

_____ C. If outsourcing will tend to lock you into a particular form of technology, score negative one.

5. Would a decision to outsource increase or decrease your business flexibility?

_____ A. If outsourcing increases your ability to "pay as you go" for using IS resources or enhances flexibility in other ways, score one point.

_____ B. If there will be no impact on your business flexibility, score zero.

_____ C. If, on the other hand, outsourcing will in some way limit your business flexibility, such as not providing for acquisitions and divestitures, score negative one.

6. Will outsourcing enable you to focus on your core business?

_____ A. If outsourcing will allow you to better focus on its core business, score one point.

_____ B. If IS will continue to consume substantial management time and energy even with outsourcing, score zero.

_____ C. If outsourcing will require more management time because of accountability and control problems, score negative one.

7. How difficult will leaving the vendor and returning to in-house operations (the turnback process) be?

_____ A. If the only thing you would need to do is to transfer the name on the door of the data center and replace a few top managers, then score one point.

_____ B. If in turnback there is no conversion between your current operations and the outsourcer's operations, then score one point.

_____ C. If you are uncertain as to how difficult it would be to take back your own operations, score zero or a negative one. The more uncertain you are the more you should score a negative one.

_____ D. If your operations are extremely complex and the transition from the outsourcer back to your own internal IS processing will be expensive and difficult, if not impossible, then score negative one.

8. What will be the duration of your outsourcing agreement?

_____ A. If your agreement with the outsourcer will be three years or fewer, score one point.

_____ B. If your agreement with the outsourcer will be three to five years, score zero.

_____ C. If your agreement with the outsourcer will be greater than five years, score a negative one.

AND THE WINNER IS . . .

Add your scores together. If you end up with a negative number or a zero, then the simplistic test for outsourcing indicates you are not a good candidate. If you proceed to additional, more thorough evaluations, you should investigate those issues where your answer was a negative one or a zero, and reexamine why that was your answer.

If your total score is a positive number, then you should move on and evaluate outsourcing in greater depth. Here as well, though, pay attention to your answers. Where your scores were negative one, try to structure your outsourcing relationship to eliminate or mitigate the reasons you answered with a negative one.

Even in those areas where you scored a positive one, challenge your reasoning. Were you making unwarranted assumptions? If after re-evaluating your logic you remain confident that you are not assuming too much, you can proceed to the next phase of analysis.

No matter what the initial outcome, your next step should be to assign a relevant weight to each question. For instance, does the need for a cash infusion outweigh the other elements? If so, you should multiply it by a number that reflects that increased weight. The cash infusion may be ten times more important than any other issue in the outsourcing decision. If so, it should have a weighing factor of ten. Go back and recalculate your answers to the simplistic test by multiplying by the weights that you assigned to each issue and totaling the weighted answers.

Question	Answer	Weight	Weighted answer
Cash infusion	_____	_____	_____
Equity contribution	_____	_____	_____
Cost control	_____	_____	_____
Technical flexibility	_____	_____	_____
Business flexibility	_____	_____	_____
Focus on core business	_____	_____	_____
Turnback problems	_____	_____	_____
Duration of relationship	_____	_____	_____

Complete dinner or à la carte?

There are few road maps to outsourcing because there are so many ways to get there. Determining whether to outsource all or some of your company's applications resembles the evaluation of whether to outsource any applications in the first place. The main difference is that you can reduce the enormity of the transaction when you are outsourcing one, or just a few, applications. Reducing the quantity of the task should reduce the qualitative issues and problems you must address.

Outsourcing one particular application is a good way to get your feet wet in outsourcing. It is also a good way to evaluate a particular vendor. Outsourcing a specific application works best when the outsourcing vendor is a specialist in that application. For instance, if you need a vendor to do your payroll and produce checks for your employees, then naturally an outsourcing vendor with that particular expertise would be an optimal choice. All things considered, payroll is one of the simpler applications around. There are outsourcers with software applications and related expertise unmatched anywhere else. For solving certain business problems, selective outsourcing could be the optimal or even the only solution.

Hit me with your best shot

Once you've decided to take the next step and research the outsourcing market offerings, you need to fashion an inquiry to vendors. A request for proposal (RFP) is an extremely useful tool in preparing for an outsourcing transaction. If you evaluated your existing operations as suggested in the first part of this chapter, you will have most of an RFP's building blocks.

First, drafting an RFP forces you to analyze and then articulate your needs in the transaction. Secondly, by providing the same RFP to all prospective vendors, you can more easily compare and contrast one vendor's proposal with others' proposals while you see how well the vendor plans to meet the requirements of your RFP. Circulating an RFP tends to place you in control of the outsourcing transaction, rather than leaving the driving to the vendor. With an RFP, you tell vendors what you want, rather than having vendors tell you what you need. Circulating an RFP tells the outsourcers that you have done your homework. Finally, if nothing else, the existence of an RFP shows vendors your intent to investigate their competition.

Details in your RFP will be dictated by whether you are contemplating full or selective outsourcing. The general contents of an RFP for outsourcing are as follows:

1. State your overall objectives. That statement should include not only the specific, concrete goals that you seek to achieve in outsourcing, but also the intended consequences of your outsourcing. If one of the primary reasons you are evaluating outsourcing is to reduce IS costs, say it in your statement of intent. On the other hand, if your objective is obtaining a specialized technology, say that. In other words, tell the outsourcers what you want and the relative priority of what you want. Don't make them guess. And state your goals, even if you're unsure whether those goals are attainable. The outsourcing vendors may be unable to give you all you want, but they may also propose some creative solutions.

This is also a good point at which to decide if you want the RFP to remain confidential. Keeping your competition in the dark is but one of the many possible reasons you might insist upon the vendor's non-disclosure of the RFP.

Also, if you plan to retain any part of your IS functions, personnel, or operations, this is the place to enumerate them.

2. Describe your current operations and your current applications. The description must be sufficiently detailed to give the prospective vendors a reasonable chance to understand how you do business in the IS area. In addition, give the vendors some statistics concerning your current operations: your hardware configuration, your communications configuration, the approximate number of on-line users, the size of your data storage capabilities, as well as general descriptions of how your data bases are constructed and what the relevant volumes are, etc. Also, you should describe a typical day's processing cycle. For instance, if batch processing is relegated to the third shift, tell the vendors that. If you run a

CICS shop and a CICS region has to be up from 7 A.M. EST to 7 P.M. PST, let the vendors know. If your business requires that you produce hard copy reports, don't keep it to yourself. Mention any reports of a particularly large volume. Were you running a building supply operation, your inventory list could be quite extensive and require frequent updates. Let the vendor know.

3. Specify for the vendors' benefit both your short-term and long-term IS goals. These goals may have but a loose relationship to your overall goals. You might be in the middle of implementing a particular application and you want that implementation to be completed by the time an outsourcer comes on board. Include that in your RFP. If you are contemplating selective outsourcing, and five years from now you expect to have replaced your mainframe with a distributed, client/server configuration, the vendors need to know. If you expect a vendor to provide all hardware at its site, focus more on the service you expect in five years and less on the actual hardware configuration.

4. Describe your short-term and long-term strategic business goals as clearly as possible. Do you plan to grow by acquisitions? Do you plan to grow by increased sales? The answers to these kinds of questions are relevant to how vendors will respond to your RFP.

5. Consider whether vendors must agree to maintain the confidentiality of the RFP's information. You will be revealing many things you might not want competitors to know.

6. Consider whether to include a proposed contract in your RFP. Computer-related RFPs increasingly include the user's proposed agreement. As a general rule, though, you should leave it out.

Your specific circumstances will determine the appropriate answer for your RFP. There are at least two advantages of including your proposed agreement. First, it helps you remain in control of both the negotiations and the ultimate agreement that will document your outsourcing relationship. Control of the process tends to translate into control over the outcome. Putting the vendor on notice of your requirements in the relationship is the second advantage you gain by using an RFP. One of the more difficult problems to manage in any kind of transaction is raising issues at the contract drafting stage long after the business deal has been settled. The sooner you raise issues in the overall process, the easier and more likely you are to resolve those issues to your satisfaction. If you can't resolve them, the sooner you discover that the better.

On the other hand, providing your contract in the RFP has some drawbacks. First of all, you may alert the vendor to your overall negotiation strategy. Whether you want the vendor to know your strategy is an issue that will vary depending upon the particulars of your transaction. Secondly, if you have failed to think through your outsourcing goals, it is unlikely that your proposed agreement articulates them. And in that instance, you are better off not providing the agreement in the RFP.

A third drawback is the time you take to develop an agreement to include in the RFP. That time is better spent refining the RFP. You can provide the agreement later, perhaps sometime during the negotiations, when you know more about what you want. Finally, placing the proposed agreement in the RFP locks you into that agreement's terms and conditions to some extent. You may want greater flexibility in your actual negotiations and avoid pinning yourself down too early.

In balance, you are probably better off omitting a proposed contract in your RFP for outsourcing. There is a middle ground, however. You can raise certain issues in your RFP that relate to the contract, but that also relate to other aspects of the transaction. Raise those issues in such a way that the vendor is put on notice. Articulate your intent and any specific goals, while at the same time you avoid a commitment to specific contract language.

The consultant's favorite outsourcer

If you are using a consultant and the consultant recommends that you outsource and is ready to provide those services, consider the source carefully. The consultant may even suggest that you skip the RFP process altogether. There is an obvious conflict of interest in the consultant's initial work and its vendor recommendation. This does not mean that the consultant is unfit to become the vendor, but tread very carefully. At least complete the RFP process and solicit proposals from other vendors.

If you received a consultant's recommendation not to outsource, investigate the consultant's approach. Ask why the consultant reached that conclusion and what alternative the consultant can recommend.

NEXT STEP

Even if you decide against outsourcing, all the work was valuable. Now you have a better handle on your IS department and can more easily justify its existence, if not its budget. A decision not to outsource now is not irrevocable. Your company can change its mind at any time.

If you decide to proceed with outsourcing, then you will need to select a vendor. Making the choice is as easy and as difficult as choosing the outsourcer that best meets all the requirements of your RFP. Your decision will involve both objective and subjective criteria. You asked for "X" and the vendor proposed "X," or you asked for "X" and the vendor proposed "Y." But in some areas, such as the vendor's reputation, you may have more difficulty articulating your preferences. Conferring with other customers of the vendors you're considering is one tactic to help with the subjective issues. Inquire into the outsourcers' good, bad, and ugly attributes. Unless your consultants also provide outsourcing services, they can help you with the decision too.

But decide you must. And while you should avoid changing your mind, until you actually sign your outsourcing contract, you still can. Occasionally a vendor treats its prospective customer badly enough during negotiations for the customer to select another vendor.

Once you have made a selection, you can begin negotiating your outsourcing agreement. The next chapter will help you with the negotiations.

1. IS operations

a. Possible cost measure

- CPU hours
- direct access storage required (Megabytes/ Gigabytes/Tetrabytes)
- lines printed
- total cost per hour of operation
- fixed costs
- variable costs

b. Possible performance measures

- response time
  - average
  - maximum acceptable
- uptime
  - daily
  - by shift
  - by software application
  - by communications region
- downtime
  - daily
  - by shift
  - by software application
  - by communications region
  - mean time between failure/downtime
  - adherence to production schedule
  - number of re-runs
  - reasons for re-runs

2. Communications

   a. Possible cost measure
- per hour
- by distance
- by path selected
- per line
- per switch

   b. Possible performance measures
- uptime/availability
  - daily
  - by shift
  - by software application
  - by communications region
- downtime
  - daily
  - by shift
  - by software application
  - mean time between failure/downtime
- circuit quality
- re-transmissions required
- reasons for re-transmissions

3. Software development and maintenance

   a. Possible cost measure
- development
- maintenance
- per person
- by job classification (manager, programmer, analyst, etc.)
- per application maintained

- per line of code (nearly worthless as a measure, but often used)
- hours spent by IS personnel
- computer system resources used to support development and maintenance

b. Possible performance measures (difficult to measure)
  - lines of code per day
  - ratio of personnel to applications
  - applications development time
  - adherence to development schedules
  - adherence to production schedules

4. Other services

a. Possible cost measure
  - per person
  - per application maintained
  - lines of code (still nearly worthless)
  - hours spent by IS personnel (often only maintained in shops using charge-back)
  - number of departmental (non-IS department) stand-alone systems maintained per IS person

b. Possible performance measures
  - difficult to measure
  - few good measures
  - ratio of personnel to applications
  - number of departmental (non-IS department) complaints per terminal/work-station

CHAPTER 8

BEWARE OF BARGAINS IN PARACHUTES AND OUTSOURCING AGREEMENTS

Having zeroed in on a vendor, you can begin negotiations. And one of the first things on which you are likely to concentrate is the economics of the transaction.

The money a user spends in an outsourcing relationship is very important, but it is not the only important element in the relationship. Numerous other issues are equally important. Many prospective outsourcing customers, however, focus only on the fees. Such a narrow focus is a mistake.

VENDOR BENDERS

As in any contract negotiation, vendors in outsourcing negotiations use various techniques to encourage a prospective customer to sign up. The following sections discuss some of the more common techniques.

A user should always remember that there is a choice. For general data processing services, there are several prospective outsourcing vendors available. The degree of choice for specialized technology from outsourcers is narrower, but options do exist, including the ultimate option to have the technology in-house.

ATTENTION OUTSOURCING SHOPPER!

The typical outsourcing vendor's pricing strategy is "We'll save you money in the first year." In this approach the vendor works with the user to determine how much the user's IS function costs. When the numbers are acceptable to both sides, the vendor promises to cut those costs by a fixed percentage, for instance ten percent, even for the first year.

You should consider several things when a vendor makes such a proposal. First, if the vendor can cut the cost by ten percent, or whatever percentage, why can't your organization? Second, is this cost reduction going to stay in place throughout the duration of the agreement? Or, is the vendor over time going to recoup the savings it gave you the first year? Third, is it wise to let the vendor know what your cost structure is? Wouldn't it make more sense to tell the vendor the services that you need and ask the vendor to formulate proposed fees based on the services you require? This really ought to be part of the RFP and proposal process. Then compare what you believe to be your costs to what the vendor proposes to charge for supporting the same data processing.

Chances are you need to motivate the vendor to price its proposal to you aggressively. Just because the vendor is going to save you money doesn't mean the vendor is giving you its best price, let alone a good price. What if the vendor could have really saved you fifty percent instead of ten percent? Wouldn't you have preferred to receive the larger discount? But when the vendor knows your cost structure before revealing its pricing, you lose the ability to find out what the vendor's best offer would have been. Instead, the vendor simply convinces you that it is making a good offer because it is comparing its proposal against what it knows you believe are your costs.

Finally, examine your own cost figures very carefully. Your figures may reflect the way your accountants have decided to make entries in the firm's books on costs and may understate or overstate the real cost to the company of having its own data processing function. Moreover, verify that in comparing your in-house costs to outsourcing costs, you don't include items on the in-house side that will remain as your costs even if you engage an outsourcer.

A vendor's cost reduction approach also assumes that your data processing costs would have remained constant or risen over time. In the very brief history of computing, the cost of each unit of computing power has actually declined, and declined drastically. Although staffing costs have increased, it's hard to predict the bottom line with different costs going up and down. As a result, basing a price formula on an assumption that your data processing costs will increase is a questionable bet. So, too, is assuming for your pricing formula that all increasing costs will not be offset by commensurately increased benefits.

DAMN THE TORPEDOES, FULL SPEED AHEAD

Another vendor strategy is glossing over the technical considerations that contra-indicate outsourcing.

Your prospective vendor may wallow in mainframe technology. If you have been a mainframe user, then transferring your applications to the vendor's system may superficially make sense. But if what you really need is a client-server environment, moving your applications to the outsourcer's legacy system might be technically inadvisable. The outsourcer though, in this instance, doesn't want you to choose the processing solution it doesn't offer. So, it will downplay alternative technical approaches, instead recommending the solution that favors itself as the prospective vendor.

Likewise, in an effort to divert your focus from performance standards, the vendor may claim there is no way to measure response time with its hardware and software configurations. Yet, if there will be no way to measure the vendor's performance, how will you be able to hold the vendor accountable when the vendor's actual performance dissatisfies you?

The vendor may breeze by other technical contra-indications for outsourcing, such as those situations where your in-house mainframe will vanish and all terminals and work-stations around your facility will have to function as remote terminals to the vendor's data center. Don't expect the vendor to point out that there is now a "middleman," the telephone company (or companies), between you and the mainframe and that by adding a link in your IS chain, you are adding an additional place where the chain can break. This is not to say that outsourcing would therefore be ill-advised, but rather that this should be an important consideration in your decision to outsource.

END AROUND ON THREE

Another common vendor strategy is to bypass all of the technical people in the IS department and go straight to top management—an end run on the IS professionals to top management. Top management may induce the outsourcer to do this in the first place, since often top management is the impetus to investigate outsourcing.

While outsourcing is a strategic decision and top management should oversee the evaluation, management should not ignore the issues that the company's IS professionals raise. By definition management is unaware of all the technical details. And, management may be more likely to believe the vendor's rosy scenarios in the absence of alternative viewpoints. Don't listen to the vendor's story without soliciting comments from your own professionals. If you are uncertain about the objectivity of your IS people, solicit your consultant's opinions.

THEY BLINDED ME WITH SCIENCE

The outsourcer is an outsourcing expert and you are not. Count on the vendor to exploit this discrepancy to the utmost.

Expect the vendor's promises of performance to fly fast and furiously with tales of how well it has done for its other customers and how much money it's saved those other customers. The vendor will unveil its superior technology, allowing you to forget for a moment that your intent is to become ignorant of computer technology.

Most of all, plan to hear how the vendor's personnel are superior performers. Phrases such as "we hit the ground running" and "we make it happen" will ring through your offices. Many of these vendor personnel are ex-military, so don't let a little flag waving surprise you either. Keep in mind, though, that the terrible risks and immense sacrifices of military life have no relevance whatsoever in determining who is a superior IS professional. The vendor's employees may be superior IS professionals, and they may not, but you are not in a good position to determine in either case.

Document whatever the vendor tells you about its performance. Try to put these representations in concrete terms and then make a further inquiry. For instance, when the vendor tells you how great its on-line response time will be, get some numbers. And then find out the vendor's definition of response time. As you document these representations, be sure to examine each one and see if it makes sense. The representations may have made sense to the vendor in another situation, but you need to see if it makes sense in your circumstances. For those representations that you consider valuable, put them in your proposed agreement with the vendor. If you don't get them in the contract, they won't mean very much.

We're at least as good as your IS idiots

Often a vendor will promise to perform at least as well as the customer's current IS department. If you are outsourcing to improve your IS function, this pitch seems strange. A reasonable translation would be, "We're not any worse than the IS department you are about to eliminate." Nevertheless, this approach often provides a level of comfort to the prospective customer.

If you are susceptible to this sales pitch, evaluate whether you are gaining a meaningful level of security. There are a number of reasons why this sense of security could be false.

First of all, why outsource if your service isn't guaranteed to improve? Second, even your current IS department can meet these performance goals. Better the devil you know. Third, if this promise is to mean anything, you will need to have precise performance standards that reflect how your current IS department performs and those standards must become part of the contract with the outsourcer. Of course, readers of previous chapters may already have gathered such information.

There are times when such a promise of performance is not unreasonable. For example, if your motivation in entering into outsourcing is to cut costs, control costs, or change your balance sheet, then the status quo in terms of performance may be satisfactory. But why not demand better performance?

WE'LL GIVE YOU STICKS IF YOU GIVE US CARROTS

Part of having meaningful performance standards is having a way to enforce those standards in addition to suing the vendor. If you have to sue the vendor for performance inadequacies, you are unlikely to litigate unless the vendor's performance is terrible. While atrocious vendor performance is possible, what is more likely to be a problem with some vendors is performance that is somewhere between atrocious and satisfactory. For example, the response time is slow, below the performance standards, but not so bad that you want to take the drastic step of declaring war on the vendor and suing.

One of the most common techniques to keep a vendor's performance at or above the performance standards is to attach financial consequences to substandard performance. In lay terms, you have penalties for poor performance.

A common vendor response to a request for penalties is to demand a bonus for performance that exceeds the performance standards. Most of the time this is a vendor smoke screen. The vendor either wants you to back off of the penalty path or is trying to increase its fees indirectly. Why should you pay more if the vendor performs better than it promised? After all, the vendor's performance in relation to the performance standards is under the vendor's control.

What these bonuses really amount to is a gratuity. Tips may be appropriate in a restaurant where the workers are low-paid, but tips seem very out of place in an impersonal business context. Moreover, the extra performance may not be of value to you. If one-second response time is what you need, why pay a bonus for one-half a second?

DON'T WORRY, THE TECHNICAL PEOPLE CAN WORK IT OUT

Yet another vendor strategy to encourage execution of the outsourcing agreement consists of trying to get you to do the deal before you have time to consider all of the important issues. What happens often in outsourcing negotiations is that the negotiations and the transaction take on a life of their own. Many top managers make the mistake of deciding that they have an outsourcing arrangement and it's only a matter of working out some insignificant details in a contract.

Those managers send the wrong message to their negotiators and to the outsourcing vendor. Once the outsourcing vendor knows that management has committed itself, the vendor also knows that the inertia of the relationship will begin. Meanwhile, the customer has lost substantial negotiating leverage, that is, the leverage of being able to walk away from the deal. A vendor that thinks management cannot walk away will start to dig its heels in on various issues in the negotiations. If you and the outsourcer have tentatively agreed to a schedule, then the vendor will chide that the longer the negotiations take, the harder it will be to meet the schedule.

If there are employee issues that must be resolved, then the longer the negotiations take, the more critical such employee issues may become. Your control over "Rumor Central" will become more and more tenuous as time goes by. And in every negotiating session the vendor who promised to cut your cost by ten percent will point out to you that a month without outsourcing is a month without the ten percent savings. "Sign up today and let the savings begin."

To some extent, this type of pressure will be unavoidable. There is no question that the tide of negotiations will start to turn on you once the financial aspects have been worked out. The best way to combat such a situation is through a two-fold strategy. First, do everything you can during the negotiations to dissuade the vendor from the notion that the deal is definite. Second, take the time and spend the money, prior to entering negotiations with the vendor, to have your attorney develop a contract. Present this agreement to the outsourcer along with supporting decisions and technical information. Then you can negotiate from the strongest possible position. Having done your homework and being fully prepared for the negotiations will greatly reduce the inertia that the vendor will try to create.

IT DOESN'T GET ANY BETTER THAN THIS

The best the vendor will ever treat you is when it wants your business, but does not yet have it. Keeping this incentive for the vendor as long as you can is a good idea. This is not to say that once the vendor gets your business it will treat you worse, but rather that it is unlikely to treat you better. This phenomenon is, of course, not limited to outsourcing transactions.

PART II

OUTSOURCING UNDERGOES MANAGEMENT TRAINING

Now you know outsourcing basics. To maximize your ability to contract for and to receive the benefits, you should have an appreciation for the issues in managing both the transition to outsourcing and the outsourcing relationship itself.

CHAPTER 9

THE VALUE OF MAPS IN MINE FIELDS: MANAGING THE TRANSITION TO OUTSOURCING

"We had to destroy the village to save it" has always seemed an odd strategy.

In full-outsourcing, a company sacrifices its entire in-house IS operations to obtain other strategic objectives for the enterprise. Because that's a little like calling in an air-strike on your own position, it can appear counter-intuitive. If poorly managed, administering the transition to and continuation of an outsourcing relationship can cause numerous self-inflicted casualties. The next three chapters explain a framework within which you can not only survive outsourcing, but prevail.

YOU HAVE TO GET FROM HERE TO THERE

Before realizing any benefits from outsourcing, you have to change from your current operations to the outsourced operations. This is an elementary concept whose implementation can require powerful tranquilizers. Whether you refer to the process as the transition, conversion, cut-over, or turnover, getting from "here" to "there" may be painful and difficult.

Your agreement with the outsourcer needs to include a plan to accomplish the turnover. This plan in the outsourcing contract will also serve as your map of the transition. The plan must answer the following four questions:

1. What do you intend to transfer to the outsourcer?
   A. What goes to the outsourcer?
   B. What remains with you?
   C. What goes to a third party such as an equipment lessor, hardware broker, charity, etc.?
2. Whom do you intend to transfer to the outsourcer?
3. When do you intend to make the transfer?
4. How do you intend for the transition to proceed?

WHAT'S ON SECOND?

Your company will do one of two kinds of outsourcing. Either it will outsource all IS functions, or it will outsource some IS functions. As discussed previously, you can call the first kind "full-outsourcing" and the second kind "selective outsourcing."

Within full-outsourcing, you can take one of two directions. Down one path, only the control of your existing IS operations transfers. The operations remain in the same building, with the same equipment, and often many of the same people, as before outsourcing. What has changed is that the outsourcer is now in charge and is managing your IS function, although using your facilities. In the other type of full-outsourcing, your IS operations relocate to a vendor facility. Each type of full-outsourcing requires a different turnover recipe. One is as easy as apple pie (or turnovers); the other requires probing the existential issues of *nouvelle cuisine.*

FLIP THE SWITCH

If your full-outsourcing involves only a change in management of the IS function, then your transition to outsourcing may be as easy as "flipping a switch." Describing a transition where the people remain, albeit with new management, the hardware and software remain, and the location of everything remains unchanged makes for a straightforward transition plan. The plan must identify your IS management personnel who will become "redundant" by virtue of the full-outsourcing, any familiarization period for the vendor, and some related details. Overall, though, in flip-the-switch transfers, the cut-over to outsourcing should be relatively smooth and seamless. You shouldn't have a problem answering the four questions at the beginning of this chapter. Nevertheless, if the outsourcer is to become your employees' new employer, you will have to address the relevant labor issues.

A RIVER RUNS THROUGH IT

If your full-outsourcing will not permit flipping a switch, then you must build a bridge. Assuredly, such minor details as not knowing what river you'll cross, or the exact location of the other side, shouldn't deter you. Moreover, the path across this bridge is a one-way path. You will be emigrating to a new land of IS. After your crossing, few, if any, data processing functions will remain with your company. The bridge will take the form of the transition plan.

WHAT DO YOU INTEND TO TRANSFER TO THE OUTSOURCER?

The short answer to the first question is "everything"— "well, almost everything." Someone in your organization must make a list of what you will and will not transfer to the out-sourcer. The list should answer the following question first:

What are all the IS resources, other than people, that the out-sourcing transaction could involve? That is, what do you have now?

   A. Hardware—make, model, serial number
      1. Owned
      2. Leased—include copy of lease

   B. Software—vendor, function, license and maintenance fees
      1. Owned—developed in-house
      2. Licensed from a software vendor—include copy of license

   3. Leased from a vendor—include copy of lease

C. Other property

D. Communications equipment

E. Services

   1. Hardware maintenance

   2. Software maintenance

   3. Software development

   4. Other services

WHAT GOES WHERE?

Every item on this "what" list will have implications for the transition. Therefore, the transition plan should connect every item on the list with the item's disposition. To do this, ask yourself the following question:

For each resource, what is its disposition?

A. What do you intend to transfer to the outsourcer?

   1. What do you intend that the vendor own?

   2. What do you intend that the vendor have authority from the owner/licensor to use?

      a. Leased hardware

      b. Licensed software

B. What gets left with you?

C. What goes to a third party?

This chapter concludes with a checklist of possible dispositions for you to consider. If you are transferring removable media such as tapes and disks, then for your own self-defense, you should transfer only possession and not ownership to the outsourcer. (See Chapter 11.) Also, for similar reasons, unless you have a powerful reason to do otherwise, be clear in your plan and with the vendor in your agreement that for any software you are transferring to the outsourcer for your use, you are not transferring your license to the outsourcer. (See Chapter 19.)

Sample Example

Here's an example of how your entries may appear after you merge your first list with each item's disposition information:

Hardware list:

1. Mainframe CPU (1) . . . : vendor is purchasing, moving to vendor data center, and will pay for removal costs. User pays for costs of restoring room to usable condition.

2. PC clones (300) . . . : vendor is purchasing, but all will remain at current installation locations of user.

3. Multiplexor units (15) . . . , leased: vendor is assuming lease obligations, vendor will replace with its own hardware, user to pay for removal costs, vendor to pay all costs of installing its hardware.

Software list:

1. Mainframe operating system software. Combined monthly license and maintenance fees $15,000.00. User will terminate its license because vendor has license for same operating system software. Vendor's license for the operating system gives vendor permission to use for outsourcing to user.

2. ABC Inc. database management system. Combined monthly license and maintenance fee $10,000.00. Vendor does not have license for the ABC Inc. software. Permission required from ABC Inc. to permit vendor to operate software at vendor's location for the benefit of user. No conversion required. Technical transition team will install a copy of software and related files in accordance with the master transition schedule.

3. XYZ Inc. accounts receivable application software: One-time fee of $134,000.00 paid, annual maintenance $10,000.00. Will not transfer this application to vendor, but will convert to ABC Inc.'s accounts receivable software to be installed by vendor. License fee of $65,000.00 to be paid to ABC Inc. by vendor. Conversion plan required. ABC Inc.'s software will be licensed

to user and contain permission for vendor to operate ABC Inc.'s software for user's benefit.

4. Payroll application: One time fee of $20,000.00 paid and currently maintained by IS staff. Will not transfer, but will convert to vendor's payroll application. No license fee. Conversion plan required.

Whom do you intend to transfer to the outsourcer?

Describing the "what" of a turnover provision may be straightforward or extremely complicated. The same ease or difficulties arise when describing who is changing in the outsourcing relationship.

Just as in the last section you listed what resources you had, and assigned a disposition to each, now you must list whom you employ. Listing employees by function rather than by name is sufficient at this point. Then you must decide one of three dispositions for each IS employee:

1. The employee continues to work for your company; or

2. The outsourcer offers the employee a job; or

3. You throw the employee into the street.

In other words, you retain, transfer, or terminate. This section suggests principles to use in making these determinations.

Keep the applications people

For the cyberspeak-disadvantaged, the IS function on corporate organization charts usually consists of two areas: systems and applications. The systems area is divided into operators and systems programmers. The systems programmers are the people who are involved in writing or maintaining operating systems-type software. Operations personnel are those people who actually run your computer operations on a daily basis. Operators run the computers, load paper into printers, change the cartridges on laser printers, mount tapes on tape drives, and monitor your IS department's actual data processing production.

Most applications departments have two subdivisions: software development and software maintenance. Applications development personnel are systems analysts, programmers, and project leaders. Over the years, these people have translated your business needs into computer software solutions. Maintenance personnel are programmers and systems analysts whose main task involves fixing applications software problems as they arise and making software updates to keep your software current and useful to you.

As previously discussed, it is possible to make a transition to outsourcing without changing any of your personnel. In flip-the-switch transitions to full-outsourcing, your outsourcing relationship may simply provide a layer of management on top of your existing IS management and give the new managers appropriate authority to accomplish the objectives of outsourcing. Slightly more likely in a flip-the-switch transition to full-outsourcing is replacement of the IS management with the vendor's people, but no other personnel shifts. Or, sometimes your employees transfer en masse to the outsourcer. The most common transition to full-outsourcing, however, gives vendor meal tickets to your worker bees in operations and pink slips to your operations managers.

In most instances of full-outsourcing, the user wants the outsourcing vendor to hire the bulk, if not all, of the user's operations and systems programming staff, and the vendor agrees. In general, the more an employee talks to computers, the more the user may want that person to find another discussion group. On the other hand, the more an employee works with other employees, i.e., talks to people instead of machines, the more a user may want to retain that person. Thus if an outsourcing vendor should offer to hire your applications personnel, you should probably refuse the offer.

MAINTENANCE WORKERS KNOW WHAT AND WHERE TO REPAIR

There are many reasons for your company to retain at least its applications maintenance personnel. The main reason is control over resolution of production software problems and control over modifications to your software.

When your production software terminates abnormally, two things should happen. You need someone to discover the cause of the termination and you need someone to make changes to correct the software. In other words you need a "fix for the bug." Maintenance programmers are the usual detectives for software problems. They are also the problem solvers. Your maintenance personnel find and fix the software bugs.

The other main use for software maintenance people is updating your software. You need one kind of update because your software will over time need revisions. If you license software from third parties, the third party software company may issue a software release: an error correction, update, or enhancement. Software maintenance personnel are usually the ones to install applications software releases. You will need another kind of update when a user department wants a software modification. Perhaps income tax brackets have changed and payroll tax withholding requires a new computation, or maybe your accountants want a new category of aged receivables. Once again your software maintenance personnel will perform this task.

If you are an IS professional, none of this is news to you. When you outsource software maintenance, you will continue to have access to people who can find and fix your software problems. The difference is that those people will belong to the outsourcer. You will pay for those software maintenance services either way. But when you retain software maintenance people, you pay at "wholesale" prices; the cost of maintenance is the cost of employing those IS professionals. When you have outsourced software maintenance, you pay retail: probably an hourly rate that includes the outsourcer's overhead and profit. If your software maintenance needs are modest, then retail prices on a pay-as-you-need basis may not be too bad. If your maintenance needs are extensive, your lowest cost will be performing software maintenance in-house.

APPLICATION FOLK WISDOM

Another reason to keep the maintenance staff is that they are the best repository of knowledge of your applications. Your maintenance personnel will work only on your applications. They are or will become experts in your applications. If you have outsourced software maintenance, the vendor's staff will do their work for whatever customer needs assistance. The likelihood of the vendor's maintenance personnel having a level of expertise equal to your own staff's is slim. The less someone maintaining an application knows about the application, the more time that person will require to perform the maintenance. And more vendor time equals higher charges for you. So, in general, having your own applications maintenance people can save you money and time. Of course, as with every such generality, don't assume it's true for you, but review your own situation carefully.

The reasons for keeping your own applications development personnel parallel those for keeping maintenance personnel. You should pay less to develop your own software than to hire the outsourcer to do it. Since an in-house development staff should be better acquainted with your business than outsiders, in-house development should proceed faster than outside development. Also, the relationship between your applications people and user departments will likely facilitate better communication than would a user department to outsider link. Better communication will lead to better results.

This discussion assumes that you have a competent staff and use efficient techniques for development. If you don't, you may find that your outsourcing vendor does and could really be the better choice. In fact, you may be leaning toward outsourcing because you want to get rid of incompetent, inefficient employees.

RE-INVENTING WHEELS HAS LOW ROI

In addition, this discussion assumes that your or the vendor's developing software are the right choices for you. Before committing inside or outside resources to a large scale development project, evaluate the existing software product offerings. If a third party application could do the job, then you can avoid re-inventing the wheel as well as paying for it.

On the other hand, if the proposed application may have broad use for a number of the outsourcing vendor's customers, you may be able to persuade the vendor to exchange its software development services in return for your application expertise. You could both benefit. You get the application for a song; and the vendor gets an application to market with its services.

MAKING THE CUT

The result of listing your employees and determining what to do with them will be a list similar to the example below. Of course, actual title and job responsibilities vary considerably between companies, so make your decisions based on functions. Most importantly, let your plans for outsourcing be your guide. For example, for selective outsourcing, which applications go and which stay will greatly affect whom you need to keep. Finally, you may want to single out employees to stay when others with their job title go, or vice-versa.

Job Title	_Disposition_
Information Systems Manager	Retain
Operations Manager	Transfer
Computer Operator	Transfer
I/O Control	Transfer
Related clerical positions	Transfer
Systems Programming Manager	Transfer
Systems Programmer	Transfer
Applications Software Manager	Retain
Systems Analyst	Retain
Applications Programmer	Retain
Documentation Control	Transfer
Database Administrator	Transfer
Database Manager	Retain
Database Programmer	Transfer

Help Desk	Transfer
Communications Department	Transfer
Communications Software Personnel	Transfer
Chief Information Officer*	Retain

Establishing such a list of who is changing is the simplest part of managing the personnel issues in outsourcing. You can run, but you can't hide from the myriad other employee issues and problems that are likely to arise before the outsourcing relationship formally begins and during the transition.

Your first set of issues can be complicated, but generally do not have an emotional content. These are issues such as transferring employee benefits, pension and ERISA (Employee Retirement Income Security Act) questions, continuation of terminated employees' benefits under COBRA (Consolidated Omnibus Budget Reconciliation Act of 1985) issues, and possibly dealing with unions or plant closing laws. All of these issues will have to be addressed, just as if your company were either laying off these people or transferring them to a new subsidiary. Each of these issues require specialized legal skills and you should seek such specialized legal advice.

FEELINGS, NOTHING MORE THAN FEELINGS

As complicated as some of those issues might be, they are probably more manageable than some of the emotional issues.

Secrecy is the first issue with emotional content. Will consideration of outsourcing and negotiation of the prospective relationship remain a secret? If so, to which employees? Clearly, some employees need to know or they will be unable to advise you. But whether everyone should know is an issue that requires considering your particular company, the employees, and the prospective vendor.

---

*And reward with a seat on the Board of Directors if outsourcing is successful.

In the early stages, keep your lips sealed. But as consideration of outsourcing progresses within your company, the word will spread. At some point you will want to appear on a talk show and confess. Once you make that disclosure, however, expect many things to happen. Not the least of these is that the outsourcing vendor will interpret your announcement as a commitment. When the outsourcer believes you are committed, your negotiating leverage declines. Also, when the word gets out internally, chaos could ensue. So nail down as many issues as possible before telling the world.

Another issue with emotional content is a moral issue: an instant conversion to free market job economics is not very caring and probably insincere. You can look at treating your employees well as an act of generosity and as good business. To some extent, what goes around, comes around. Your company may never shake a reputation for treating its DP employees badly. Moreover, the fewer disputes you have with existing employees, the less troublesome the entire process will be.

A third emotional issue is convincing your employees to go along with your plan. For those you want to retain, you'll need speeches about great futures, both for your company and for the retained employees. Explain how someday they may even get your job. Then inject into the jawboning some financial incentives, such as bonuses after the conversion.

Calming and persuading the people you want to trade to the outsourcer may be a little more difficult. Some managers may pull out the "things are tough all over" speech they give during performance reviews without pay raises. They may even shed a few crocodile tears over employees' departing after twenty years of loyalty to the company. But the transparency of this approach could dissipate whatever goodwill remains with the staff. What you should do is reveal the facts; listen to people's concerns, even if you cannot remedy them; and elaborate on the opportunities with the outsourcing vendor.

THE BAD NEWS

Some employees, including those who cannot accept being transferred, are likely to lose their jobs in the transition.

The real questions will be who gets axed and when. Even the vendor who will hire most of your employees cannot guarantee lifetime jobs. The economics of outsourcing, largely economies of scale, generally demand eliminating redundancies—and that means layoffs. Almost every full-outsourcing transaction ultimately reduces the number of IS personnel doing your work.

The outsourcer is taking a risk in hiring large numbers of IS personnel from you. The vendor wants your employees' help toward a successful conversion. It also wants to make a better sales pitch to you by solving both your DP problems and your personnel problems. Beyond that, the vendor will reserve judgment about your transfers. Probably you outsourced because you did not believe these same IS employees could do the job as efficiently as the outsourcer. It goes without saying that the worker bees were the problem, not you and your managers. So your former employees may not be a good match with the outsourcer. Some of them, for whatever reasons, will experience terminal disappointment in their new jobs.

SMART RATS TAKE A NUMBER

The more astute members of your work force will understand how their jobs have slid onto shaky ground. Once the news gets out, some of your workers will jump ship. Probably the first rats overboard will be among the most talented. Don't be surprised if these include systems programmers, not known for predictable behavior. They will be the ones who can most easily find another job, and they will. The most talented employees, unfortunately, are just the people that you or the outsourcing vendor would have most wanted to retain, at least through the transition process. You may end up with employees who have more loyalty than talent.

Of those employees who stay and wait to find out what will happen or rely on your promises of what will happen, some will resent the move and feel betrayed. Expect to see anonymous memos about being "sold down the river" or whatever colorful metaphors those disgruntled employees can create. Each individual will wonder, "What's going to happen to me? Why wasn't I good enough? Why couldn't the company have treated me better?" Unhealthy competition and back-stabbing may develop in futile attempts to retain jobs. Once in a while, employees even think they can prevent your outsourcing. They will erode morale intentionally, if not turn to covert sabotage, in order to thwart your plans. In any of these scenarios, expect productivity to plummet.

INFECTIOUS ENTHUSIASM CAN MAKE YOU ILL

A problem almost as serious as the nay-sayers are the enthusiasts. Some of those employees who stay will soon begin to identify with the outsourcer. There are a number of reasons for this. First, the outsourcing vendor is their prospective employer. If the vendor offers jobs to your soon-to-be-unemployed, whom do you think these employees will try to impress? Your company, the one that took strained beets out of their children's mouths, or the only company standing between them and the unemployment line? You don't need a degree in psychology to figure this out. Also, the vendor likely represents a larger and better managed operation than does your company. DP is the vendor's business. The outsourcer may seem more technologically advanced and superior in a number of other ways, both real and imagined.

If some of the people upon whom your company must rely are among those who begin to think more highly of the vendor than they do of your company, they can pose serious problems when you attempt to manage the transition to the vendor. On the bright side, these people will still whistle while they work for you because they know the world is not coming to an end. On the dark side, these enthusiasts can cause a lot of problems. At best, their loyalties will be divided; worst case, they simply will have gone over to the other side while remaining on your payroll. Their lips may loosen around your confidential information. Some of them, in planning their future jobs, may increase your company's burdens in the transition in order to decrease their burdens in working for the outsourcer.

No magic bullets, just suggestions

The personnel problems inherent in an outsourcing transaction are very similar to those arising in mergers, acquisitions, and divestitures, and in plant closings and other downsizings. There are no magic bullets to deal with employee problems, but some of the following ideas may be useful:

• Problem: Talented or key employees may jump ship.

Possible solution: Identify employees whose talent or presence you require for making the transition to outsourcing. Most IS managers and CIOs can name these people quickly. Prepare an incentive package to entice them to stay during the transition. A salary increase, a completion bonus, company-paid skills enhancement, and company stock are all among typical and successful inducements.

• Problem: Many employees are anxious about transferring to the vendor's employ.

Possible solution: Negotiate with the vendor to obtain an attractive package for the transferring personnel. Obtain a vendor commitment for a minimum period of "guaranteed employment, except for cause." Have the vendor make a sales pitch to your employees about its employment opportunities.

• Problem: Some of your employees' loyalties are divided.

Possible solution: Be aware and beware. Forbid contact with the outsourcer except through approved channels, such as your liaisons.

• Problem: Some of your employees are trying to sabotage the decision to outsource.

Possible solution: Fire them, but after you have decided to proceed with outsourcing. Until then, these people could articulate significant reasons not to outsource, and you need to hear both sides of all issues.

Consider all these elements when thinking through the problems of the transition. You may not be able to provide for all of them in the agreement, but, nevertheless, someone has to think about the consequences for your company. All of these employee issues can have an impact on the entire transaction and particularly the transition.

WHEN DO YOU INTEND TO MAKE THE TRANSITION?

What is the schedule for transferring to the outsourcer? In a flip-the-switch transition, you pick a day, but other transitions to full-outsourcing are more complicated. You may want to cut-over everything at once. Chances are that this approach is risky, like trying to swallow a cantaloupe whole: humanly possible—maybe—but very tough on the esophagus. In addition, your top management, as well as the vendor, will endlessly remind you that every day of transition is a day your company could have been saving IS expense.

When possible, a phased transition, application by application, is the easiest to manage. Note that an application is not necessarily easily defined. All interrelated systems probably have to cut-over together. While order entry and inventory or accounts receivable may be obvious candidates for overlap, they are probably not alone. In essence, you must arrange for all applications that access the same data base or files. With the trend toward integrated data bases, some shops could find themselves unable to do a phased transition.

It is helpful to think of and treat the transition as a series of application conversions. Here's one possible transition schedule:

• First phase. Applications that require no more conversion than re-compilation or rewriting operating system instructions (job control).

First phase completion: successful test of the first phase applications.

- Second phase. New applications provided by either the vendor or you. There is nothing to convert, but you will require training.

Second phase completion: successful installation of second phase applications and completion of training for second phase applications. This training can occur while phase three is in progress.

- Third phase. Applications that require a full conversion to run on outsourcer's system.

Third phase completion: successful test of all third phase applications. These are the applications for which the "how" determines the "when" to make the transition. Of course, these would be the more common type of application.

HOW DO YOU INTEND THE TRANSITION TO PROCEED?

"How" refers to what procedures you will use to get from in-house to outsourced operations. There are a number of ways for you to proceed. You could follow the sample schedule suggested above and move from one phase to another in sequence. You could perform the schedule in reverse order and begin with the third phase, based on a desire to do the tough things first. Or, you could perform all phases simultaneously. What will work best for you will depend on a combination of your management and technical resources, as well as how much the vendor will assist.

You can structure each phase in your transition schedule as a separate project. The only hitch is that the third phase, the phase where you do all the conversions, will itself have a number of projects—every conversion is a project in itself. Each phase, and if necessary each project within a phase, should be a checkpoint in the transition to outsourcing. Each checkpoint should be tied to a calendar. If you have the vendor performing much of the work, the checkpoints and schedule are good measures of the vendor's performance.

You will rely heavily on your own DP staff, especially your software maintenance people, in planning how to make the transition. They know your systems, including interdependencies and quirks. Chances are that your major applications have survived several conversions in the past to new or substantially improved software. So don't feel too overwhelmed by this task. You have—or at least used to have—employees who can tell you what's required, unless they've jumped both your and the vendor's ships.

Finally, consider whether parallel operation of any applications would be useful. In parallel operation you perform work and run applications in a redundant manner. An application would run at both yours and the outsourcer's facilities. For example, say payroll applications are running parallel. Your company runs its payroll and the outsourcer runs the same payroll. (Unless you are really feeling guilty, only one run actually cuts checks.)

The advantage of parallel operation is in comparing the converted application to the old one: how the payroll ran on your IS system versus the vendor's. You don't cut-over to the new application until the results parallel the old.

PAVING AN EXPRESSWAY TO THE UNDERWORLD

The biggest disadvantage of parallel operation is that it is often impossible, or at least impracticable. It's possible to parallel the operation of an on-line order entry system that receives 100,000 orders a day, but does it make any sense to have order-takers use two terminals to enter everything twice into two different systems?

On the other hand, you can make a transition that resembles parallel operation involving simultaneous uses of the old and converted applications on different data. For instance, in the order entry example, route all orders from a single state to the converted application at the vendor while all other orders continue to your facility. As the converted application proves its mettle with orders from one state, add states. While this type of phased conversion might not work if your inventory control application can't cooperate, you might try the same tactics for other applications.

Expense is the second big problem with parallel operation and testing. You will be running two data centers and possibly increasing your costs in the short run.

And of course, if the outsourcing relationship is a facilities management, then there may be no point in even considering a parallel operation because there is nothing to run in parallel. There are no new data centers and no new machines. You may decide to add extra equipment or further burden your existing equipment to facilitate the transition, but it will cost you.

Conversions are not a religious experience, but should be

Using standard application conversion procedures is one approach to moving from an existing application to an outsourced application. Standard conversions usually involve five major steps. You must perform each step for each application that you want to convert.

(1) Research the basis of the conversion. What is the existing application and what are its attributes? This research is often more difficult than it looks: documentation may be missing or incomplete if the application has not required attention for years. Do some digging for someone who is a fount of information for this application. Get every bit of that information out of this person as fast as you can. These "old timers" often feel most threatened by a transition to outsourcing. You can't assume they'll stick around for the turnover.

(2) Define the target of the conversion. To what will you convert the existing application? If your outsourcer is supplying the application, it should provide all the information that you'll need to know.

(3) Define what, if anything, you want to convert. There may be nothing to convert for several reasons. Your current application and the new application could be so unrelated that converting data from the old to the new is impossible or impractical. Also, if you have an application whose data has a short life-span, the conversion effort may be inefficient. For

instance, if the application tracks health claims under your self-insured health plan, you may want to put only new claims on the new application. You can run the old application until the existing claims are resolved, rather than converting the existing claims to the new application.

(4) If you have an application that merits conversion, define the conversion process. That may be difficult or simple to describe. It depends on how much of a change there will be between the two applications. The definition you need is not only what happens in the computer software sense, but what are the corollary procedures and other interfaces upon which this conversion will have an impact.

(5) Define and determine what you will consider a successful conversion. This, too, is an area that can appear deceptively easy. For instance, assume your company wishes to convert from an existing general ledger accounting system to the general ledger accounting provided by your outsourcer. What definition of a successful conversion will you employ? Do all the numbers have to equal each other on both sides of the conversion? In other words, do the totals and the breakdown of accounts on the existing application have to come out exactly the same as totals and breakdowns in the outsourced application?

Take another example. Imagine that what you are converting is the time and billing system of a consulting firm, including work in progress, from the firm's existing system to an outsourcer's time and billing system. What if the different time and billing systems do not have comparable totals or do not treat balances in the same way?

Moreover, who is going to do what if those totals don't agree? How will you reconcile those differences? All of these considerations must go into the game plans for any conversion, as well as for a transition to selective outsourcing.

FROM NOTHING TO SOMETHING

If, on the other hand, there is no existing application, then a data processing type of conversion will be unnecessary.

Instead, treat the transition to the outsourcer's application like a standard IS software acquisition. You will want specifications, an evaluation and acceptance process, and training. Even under these circumstances there may be an element of conversion, but the process should remain as straightforward as any software acquisition can be.

When there is no existing application, you are either replacing a manual system (functions performed by people and not computers) or the new functions were not previously performed at all. In replacing a manual system, there is a "conversion" element. Nevertheless, the process has much more to do with the management of the people who performed the manual tasks than with IS considerations. The IS issues are centered on your re-training the manual workers to step into the computer age, rather than experiencing accounting migraines from discrepancies in results.

In addition, a number of your applications may require minimal conversion or perhaps no conversion at all. In these instances, your company should consider abandoning the application, simply taking the plunge on an entirely new way of doing some data processing function, or not even turning that particular application over to the outsourcer, but keep it in-house and continuing to run it. In other words, perhaps you don't outsource that particular application. Such alternatives should never be discarded without at least thinking them through.

MANAGING THE TRANSITION TO SELECTIVE OUTSOURCING

Not all outsourcing is full-outsourcing. Frequently outsourcing involves something that is less comprehensive. You can outsource to obtain one or more particular applications or technologies. This is partial or selective outsourcing.

In selective outsourcing, you need to determine if there is an existing application that outsourcing will replace. If there is, then you need to plan a transition for that existing application.

Selective outsourcing is just a subset of full- or comprehensive outsourcing. You can also view full-outsourcing as a collection of selective outsourcings. When your company and the outsourcing vendor agree to make a phased or gradual transition from the existing IS operations to the outsourcer even in a full-outsourcing relationship, you can view each phase of that process as an incident of selective outsourcing.

THE VENDOR WANTS YOUR TRANSITION TO SUCCEED

The vendor could assist you in managing the transition. Many outsourcers have considerable experience and expertise in turnovers. In the preliminary negotiations, discuss with the vendor in detail how it can aid you in the transition. At that time, neither side may have a definite idea of what work will be necessary, but you will learn the possibilities. The vendor should tell you specifically what it can do in response to each situation. The outsourcing vendor should also be willing to arrange for you to hear transition testimonials from its other customers. Take very good notes.

However, your outsourcer's experience may not be appropriate to your circumstances. Every company is different, and so is every transition. Yours may differ significantly from most. Don't be persuaded simply by a formula or glossy set of manuals that describe how the vendor will do the transition. You may hear, "We have this methodology developed by 1,000 Ph.D.s to make the transition seamless." Don't confuse a method with results. You need to make sure that the outsourcer's approach will accommodate your company's particular needs.

On the other hand, don't ignore what the vendor has to offer either. The vendor's methodology, even if not a good fit, may help you construct your company's transition plan.

Bottom line, you need a transition plan. The vendor may be able to help. The transition plan should be incorporated in your agreement with the outsourcer. Determine who is going to control the transition process and who is going to be responsible for what in that process. Even if the vendor is going to control all of it and be responsible for all of it, you should not leave everything up to the vendor. You should at least establish guidelines, timetables, and checkpoints for the turnover process. Then you can monitor each element of the process in light of the master schedule and your needs.

I. Owned property.

    A. Title to property transferred.

        1. Sold to vendor.

        2. Remains on user's premises.

        3. Moved to vendor's premises.

        4. Moved to other location as vendor directs.

    B. Sold or otherwise transferred to third party (e.g., buyer of used computers or charity).

        1. Moved to third party's premises.

        2. Moved to other location as third party directs.

        3. Remains on user's premises.

    C. Title to property not transferred.

        1. Remains on user's premises.

        2. Moved to vendor's premises.

        3. Moved to other location as vendor directs.

    D. Existing maintenance agreements have the following dispositions:

        1. Assumed by vendor.

        2. Not renewed.

        3. Terminated/canceled.

II. Leased property.

    A. Leases assumed by vendor.

        1. Remains on user's premises.

    2. Moved to vendor's premises.

    3. Moved to other location as vendor directs.

B. Leases assumed by third party or hardware sub-leased to third party.

    1. Remains on user's premises.

    2. Moved to third party's premises.

    3. Moved to other location as third party directs.

C. Leased hardware is purchased and then disposed of like purchased hardware.

D. Leases terminated early by paying cancellation fee; hardware returned to lessor.

E. Existing maintenance agreements for leased property.

    1. Assumed by vendor or third party.

    2. Not renewed.

    3. Terminated/canceled.

III. Software.

A. For existing software licenses, obtain authorization for use in outsourcing.

B. Software to be licensed from the vendor.

C. User-developed or owned software to be provided to vendor.

D. Software for which there will be a conversion.

    1. Software conversion from existing hardware to vendor hardware.

    2. Software conversion from existing operating system to different version of existing operating system.

    3. Software conversion from existing operating system to new operating system.

4. Software conversion from existing application to new version of same software.

5. Software conversion from existing application to new application.

6. Conversion from existing manual system to new software application.

7. Entirely new application installed at vendor, requiring no conversion.

IV. Communications.

A. Reroute existing communications.

B. Connect existing networks to vendor's data centers.

C. Change existing networks to conform to vendor network's topology and link to vendor's network.

D. Network protocol conversion.

1. Unnecessary.

2. Accomplished by hardware.

3. Accomplished by software.

E. Establish new set of communication links from user to outsourcer.

CHAPTER 10

No Bad Dogs: Managing the Relationship After the Transition

In a sense the transition never ends. Even though all of your IS processing is in the hands of the outsourcing vendor, you still have work to do. You might have hoped that by outsourcing you need never consider your IS function again. Wrong. You no longer have to monitor the details of data processing, but you must continue to monitor the outsourcing vendor. Every user should always keep tabs on its outsourcing relationship.

There's always something there to remind you

How you approach the post-transition relationship with your vendor depends on where you and your company now are in the overall life cycle of your outsourcing transaction. Where you are in the relationship determines your options.

As you read this chapter you are probably in one of the following situations:

1. You are investigating outsourcing.

2. You have decided to outsource, but have not signed a contract with a vendor yet.

3. You have signed an agreement and you participated in the negotiations.

4. You inherited a relationship and an agreement that someone else negotiated.

5. You are related to the author.

In situations 1 and 2, you have many options yet available. In situations 3 and 4, you have but a few options. This chapter will try to help you in whichever of these situations you find yourself (except for situation 5 which is hopeless). For situations 3 and 4, this chapter does address existing relationships throughout and especially in the final section. Nevertheless, the chapter focuses on situations 1 and 2, and contracting based on anticipated problems.

THE BEST DEFENSE IS A GOOD OFFENSE

What do the following activities have in common?

- Installing a good roof.
- Moving out of a flood plain.
- Regularly backing up your software and data.
- Installing surge protectors for your PCs.

The answer is, they are all ways of avoiding a problem by preparing in advance for the possibility of the problem's occurrence.

Two tactics when used before outsourcing can minimize problems in an ongoing outsourcing relationship: careful selection of the right vendor for you, as discussed in Part I, and negotiation of an outsourcing agreement that anticipates likely turnover and post-transition problems and provides workable solutions. This chapter discusses generally how your contract can help you, while Part III details legal issues and contractual language. Check the corresponding text there for further information.

For your contract to assist you in managing the relationship, you should include several key areas in your outsourcing agreement:

- Performance Standards

- Obedience School
- Liaisons
- Dispute Resolution
- Buy-out
- Merger/Divestment Provisions

Performance Standards

Performance standards are an effective way to measure how well the outsourcing vendor is adhering to the spirit and the letter of the outsourcing agreement. These standards are general measures, assigned specific values by which you can evaluate the vendor's performance. A number of different performance standards could be relevant. Some of the more common performance standard measures are as follows:

- Response Time: The time consumed in processing an on-line transaction.
- Uptime: The time the outsourcer's computers are available for your company's use.
- Delivery: Adherence to output delivery schedule.
- Throughput: The number or volume of transactions that the outsourcer processes within a unit of time.
- Cost Savings: The cost savings the outsourcer promised.

If an agreement is otherwise silent on the performance expectations, you may find to your surprise that the vendor's opinion of an appropriate level of performance and your opinion of an appropriate level differ substantially. That is why specific, articulated performance standards must be in the agreement in the first place.

Last Things First

Differing approaches to software development projects present a good analogy to when and how to develop performance standards.

For the reader unfamiliar with IS, many software development projects proceed in the following way:

1. The user department, that is the prospective "consumer" of the software to be developed, suggests the development of a software application.

2. A systems analyst interviews the user and prepares a document describing the proposed application. The document is in essence a proposal. It contains no detailed specifications.

3. The user and systems analyst go through one or more cycles of commenting and revising the proposal document.

4. The analyst prepares programming specifications from the proposal document.

5. Programmers program the application and test it.

6. After programming and during testing, the user sees the detailed functioning of the software for the first time.

7. Often the user discovers that one or more vital functions or critical data elements are missing.

8. Additional design and reprogramming continue until the user finally obtains an approximation of its request.

9. The analyst or programmer writes the user manual, which is the instruction manual for the user on how to use the software.

Another approach for developing software starts with writing a draft of the user manual. This allows the user to visualize the results before there is even one line of programming. A user who is unfamiliar with the technical aspects of the proposed software, or how software development proceeds, can preview the proposed software's functions and how to access them. The user is, after all, the ultimate consumer of the software. Before a company has spent a lot of time, energy, and money on software development, the prospective user will have a meaningful basis upon which to make comments and ask questions. Once the draft manual is acceptable to the user, software development can proceed with a level of confidence that the result will be something that the user not only wants, but understands how to use.

Likewise, creating prototype performance standards before even making the final decision to outsource will be beneficial in assuring that you know what you want and how to get it.

EVERY WHICH WAY BUT LOOSE

Choose performance standards that reflect meaningful ways to measure the relationship. For example, if you have few on-line transactions, then overall response time may not be a good measure of the vendor's performance. On the other hand, if your management must always have certain reports every day by 9:00 A.M., then timely delivery of those reports could be an effective measure. Whatever standards you choose, though, assign specific, quantitative measures. Loose words like "best efforts" or "acceptable" won't cut the *moutarde*.

Make sure you provide myriad ways to monitor the vendor's performance. It is hard to tell in advance which measure will be the most significant to your particular outsourcing relationship. So even if you have few on-line transactions, think about your response time performance standard. If your operations follow current trends, within a few years your on-line transactions could mushroom.

TIE ME UP; TIE ME DOWN

The three most important principles of performance standards are to monitor, monitor, and monitor. There is no point having the standards if you have no intention to evaluate actual performance in light of those standards. Over time, most users find that some standards provide better measures than others.

You must weave your monitoring procedures into your daily production runs produced by the outsourcer. Consider having the option to receive daily, weekly, and monthly reports that compare actual performance to the performance standards.

As the relationship develops, you may find no need for such frequent reporting. Few vendors will complain if you reduce reporting frequency, but many will balk at requests for increased reporting. Let the computer do the work of monitoring. Use software to calculate averages and produce exception reports. Identify the software monitoring tools in your contract. You want a monitor and not the *Titanic*.

Any time and every time the vendor fails to meet the performance standards, you should make a note and inform the vendor of such failure. This is a good way to let the vendor know you are watching over its shoulder. Also, failure to inform the vendor of substandard performance could constitute a waiver of the vendor's deficiency. If you ever want to evict the vendor, you will be in a much better position if you have documented its failures all along.

Having performance standards and monitoring them are not enough by themselves. You need means to enforce those standards. Enforcement equals the ability to discipline and that means obedience school for vendors.

OBEDIENCE SCHOOL

In the beginning of your outsourcing relationship there will be a lot of enthusiasm and emotion. What both vendor and user need is a stable, steady and, inasmuch as possible, predictable relationship. The vendor will undoubtedly try to assert itself and control the terms of that relationship.

If you follow this chapter's advice, your outsourcing contract will contain performance standards. Unfortunately, not everyone complies with the written terms of their agreements. Just because the standards are in the agreement doesn't mean the vendor will comply with them. You should try to avoid situations where you have only two choices: either accept the vendor's substandard performance or sue the vendor for breach of the agreement. What you want is some middle ground, some mechanism by which the relationship automatically gives the vendor an incentive to perform and a disincentive to fail in its performance. In other words, you need to train the vendor to meet the performance standards.

HEEL

When you take your dog to obedience school, you don't take it there to punish it; you don't take it there to reward it; you take it there to train it. Likewise, your outsourcing agreement needs a way to take your vendor to obedience school.

The optimal way your contract can create compliance is through certain incentives that are not rewards for the vendor. These are incentives the vendor receives for meeting the performance standards. What you want is to make the vendor's receiving payment contingent upon the vendor's meeting the performance standards. This is a dinner versus dessert type of incentive: Feed the vendor, but don't let it grow fat. You pay the agreed upon fees for meeting the performance standards, but you don't pay a bonus for meeting or exceeding those standards.

In a sense, you exert control by withholding full payment. Yet you structure the payment not as a withholding, but rather as a rule that you don't pay for services that you don't receive. Thus you structure the payment without a punitive factor.

To be effective this approach must dovetail with the charging method, by which fees are calculated, in your outsourcing relationship. For example, if you pay for usage, usage fees automatically decrease if there is no usage, unless of course there is a minimum usage fee. So if the vendor's computers are on the blink for two days, you will not pay usage fees for those two days. Generally, though, not having to pay for services that you never received will be little consolation. After all, you have contracted for the services because you need them.

You can always get a rebate on the minimum usage fee. But you want more than that. You want to give the vendor an incentive greater than the two days' revenue it lost.

You want to "reward" the vendor for having kept the system up those two days. What you need in your payment and performance structure is an interrelationship that makes the vendor want to meet the performance standards in order to get paid. In terms of the canine construct, you cease to feed your pup in the old way, but rather Rover gets nutrition by timely performance of specific chores and tricks. Returning with the newspaper intact merits supper. Failing to retrieve it results in a hungry night of howling at the moon.

A variation on this theme is not paying for any substandard performance. In the first example, the vendor provided no services at all for two days—an extreme and unlikely case in the real world. More common are those situations where the vendor performs, but performs inadequately for a period of time. If you pay based on usage, the usage charges adjust automatically. If the outsourcing services are available part of the time, you pay only for the time you used those services. Yet, it is very unlikely you would have engaged this vendor if you couldn't rely on full-time service at a certain level of performance. Think of it this way: would you hire someone full time and then adjust that employee's wages when actual performance was part-time? Labor laws permitting, you would either not pay that person at all, or hand out a pink slip.

The outsourcing vendor wants you to think of it as you used to think of the phone company. But now with long distance telephone competition, you are not likely to tolerate consistently poor service. Instead you'll switch carriers. Unfortunately switching outsourcing vendors is not as easy. If it were, you could use the threat of their competition to motivate vendors. Once you have signed up with a particular outsourcing vendor, however, switching to another may replay all the transition agonies you suffered in turnover to the original vendor. To some extent, you're stuck.

Remember, for outsourcing relationships, it's hard to live together without benefit of clergy. Given that outsourcing divorces, like real ones, are expensive, nasty, and destructive, you have a better argument for refusing to pay for inadequate services. If your company could switch from one vendor to another easily, then your solution to poor service would be as easy. Yet, since you wed your outsourcer, you are stuck with it for quite some time. If you pay for poor service, then you subsidize it.

Your vendor will undoubtedly argue that you received some value even from inadequate service. So what? Why pay for poor service even if you did receive some value from it? It's a little like giving your newspaper-fetching dog a bone for bringing the paper to your driveway rather than to your easy chair. Sure, Rover saved you some steps, but you expected full performance from your canine retrieval unit. Full newspaper retrieval should be a condition for biscuit distribution.

Don't be surprised if your vendor rejects this type of approach. The outsourcer may see the absence of a payment as punitive anyway and will argue for more common remedies.

CHOKE COLLARS HAVE THEIR USES

The other side of incentives are sanctions. "Sanctions" is a better word to use than "penalties." Sanctions are penalties that went to college. Calling punishment a sanction rather than a penalty not only is far more diplomatic, but it also circumvents a minor problem: penalties in most contracts are unlawful. Under standard contract law, a penalty cannot intend to punish. And penalty sounds too much like punishment. Both words begin with "p," and that rhymes with "t," and that stands for trouble, tension, and tough times.

The legal euphemism for penalties is liquidated damages. For several hundred dollars, you can pay an attorney to explain the differences between penalties and liquidated damages. For only the price of this book, here is the important difference. If one can reasonably calculate the damages one would suffer by a breach of contract, then a contract cannot have a penalty amount that differs significantly from that calculated amount.

Courts allow contractual penalties when the calculation of damages would be too difficult or uncertain. The difficulty and uncertainty of calculating damages transform a penalty into liquidated damages. The parties to a contract agree to a specific dollar figure to compensate the injured party for damages which they could not otherwise measure. So structure your sanctions as liquidated damages and not as penalties. Then hope a court will not consider your liquidated damage provision to be a constructive penalty and rule it illegal anyway.

Having the vendor pay sanctions in cash to you would certainly be very effective. Yet even if the vendor would agree to this approach, which is not likely, it puts the vendor in a difficult position from a business and economic sense. A vendor is far more likely to agree to issue a credit than it is to cut a check. Therefore, one common way to establish a sanction is for the vendor to issue a credit against future payment obligations of the user. Psychologically, issuing a credit will be easier for a vendor than making a direct payment to a user. If you get the right to offset in your agreement, you can effectively issue yourself the credit.

More than anything else, the vendor wants your money. It doesn't want your approval; it doesn't want your affection; and it can live without your testimonials. Your having sanctions available to you, such as withholding money directly or through offsets, is likely to get the vendor's rapid attention. Unless the agreement is structured to permit the user to take these steps, withholding money from the vendor could be a breach of the outsourcing agreement. Worse yet, your breaching the outsourcing agreement could give the vendor a basis to terminate it.

You need not punish the vendor for all transgressions. Not every failure to meet a performance standard should mean the vendor loses money. The occasional minor slip-up is to be expected in all IS functions. Your attitude should be one of occasional forgiveness. However, forgive but don't forget. Record the failure and communicate it to the vendor, but think before invoking the sanctions. Keep the vendor on a short leash, but pull it with discretion.

Tough love, though, is definitely the way to go. Ignoring a vendor's "faux paws" is useful to neither you nor the vendor. Without your raising the issue, the vendor may not have realized there was a problem in the first place or realized that you knew there was a problem. It wouldn't be the first business to have as a slogan, "What the customer doesn't know, won't hurt us." Unless you illuminate the problem, the level of management that can actually do something about it may never intervene. Many forest fires start as a spark. Small problems have a way of festering and mushrooming into large, serious problems.

The steady drip, drip, drip . . .

A closely related problem that you must confront are those situations when the vendor uses water torture on you. One drop of water never hurt anyone, but a drop every few seconds will drive you insane if it continues long enough. Likewise, one little problem that recurs may create a big problem and may blossom into a true crisis.

The typical outsourcing torture consists of repeated small transgressions of the performance standards. No one failure is by itself significant, but multiple occurrences become significant. For instance, assume your business is banking and all teller terminals lock-up for thirty seconds. If this thirty-second glitch happens only once a year, few people would lose sleep over it. If it happens every day, you will start to notice. If it happens every two hours or several times a day, this small glitch will start undermining your tellers' productivity.

For computer problems, there are millions of possible permutations of durations and frequencies, but few guidelines to assist in determining when the little problems become serious ones. You will either have to discover this on your own or make an educated guess.

Appropriate attention to small problems and snuffing them out quickly may prevent a later conflagration. Or if the forest does catch fire, at least you'll have some evidence of the cause and probably have someone whom you can blame. This is not to say you should nickel and dime the vendor to death, but don't let the vendor do it to you either.

Moreover, the frequency of any vendor failure to meet performance standards is not an issue only for small problems. The performance standards should contain an escalation of sanctions when more than one failure of any type occurs within a specified period of time.

No dangerous liaisons

Both sides in an outsourcing relationship should have a liaison. This person has the authority to act for his or her respective employer and serves as a point of contact through which user and vendor funnel all communications, especially complaints. Liaisons are intended to establish a permanent line of communication between vendor and user.

Your outsourcing contract should have provisions for liaisons that identify the people and describe their authority. User and vendor liaisons do not always have the same authority.

Good liaisons, for your purposes, should have the following qualifications:

- They will have extensive data processing experience.
- They will have extensive data processing knowledge.
- They will know how managers think and work.
- They will be diplomatic, but no wimps need apply.
- They will know your IS needs thoroughly.
- They will be conversant with the letter and the intent of the outsourcing agreement.
- They will be methodical and attentive to detail.
- They will be level-headed.
- They will be tight-lipped.
- They should have career paths within your company, to be successful over the long haul.
- They should be able to leap tall buildings in a single bound.

A user will often benefit by giving the vendor liaison an office in the user's facility. This will enhance access to the vendor's liaison. Moreover, there is no substitute for combat. From your trenches, the vendor's liaison can observe what is really going on at your end. Most liaisons are human and will try to avoid criticism and seek your approval. This kind of behavior might translate into doing that little bit extra in resolving problems. The resolutions are generally going to benefit you. You may be able to get the vendor's liaison to be "simpatico" with you, that is, to identify with you and your objectives.

On the other hand, avoid having your liaison office at the vendor's offices for the same reasons that you want the vendor's liaison office at your premises.

In a successful outsourcing relationship, a liaison's responsibilities may decrease over time. The highest hurdle for the liaison is the transition, and the toughest time in the relationship will be during the transition and the early part of the relationship after the transition. This will be a time of great stress and great responsibility for the liaison.

User and vendor liaisons should communicate frequently. The bigger the relationship, the more frequent the communication. Consider establishing regularly-scheduled meetings between liaisons. Also consider establishing backup liaisons who have the same authority and can act when the primary liaisons are unavailable.

If you expect the relationship to last for a number of years and involve many complicated IS applications, you should consider having a primary liaison with understudies. The understudies may help reduce the workload and decrease the stress. Such an arrangement would also allow the liaison to flex his or her management skills, and to train replacements and substitutes. If and when there are problems, assistant liaisons can do any detailed follow-up the problems require. In turn, the chief liaison will be free to concentrate on the status of the entire outsourcing relationship; to determine the level of the problem's severity; and to push along the process of solving problems—without being bogged down in the details of every problem.

Whether you have one or several liaisons, you need to monitor them. Even a liaison at your premises may go over to the other side. The best person to fill your liaison position is exactly the kind of person the vendor would like to have as its employee—perhaps even as its liaison.

If your liaison considers a future in IS more desirable than a future in your company, then the vendor represents a career path. Your liaison will probably have more in common with the vendor's personnel than with your company's personnel. As a result, your liaison may be tempted to relate to the vendor's personnel better than he or she relates to yours. The vendor will be the active party, the provider, the one in charge. Your company, as a user, is at the receiving end, i.e., the passive, consumer, dependent role. Your liaison may relate to the characteristics of the vendor's role better than to the characteristics of the user's role.

Also, don't discount the possibility that your liaison may have some lingering hostility toward your company. Perhaps he or she disagreed with the decision to outsource. Your liaison may have considered your company callous in the way that it treated its employees, perhaps the liaison's friends, when terminating them as part of the outsourcing project. Your liaison may understand that your company's definition of loyalty to its employees extends only to those whose jobs cannot be outsourced.

THE LIAISON MUST BE ON YOUR SIDE

Make your liaison recite your pledge of allegiance every day. On a frequent basis, stress the importance of the liaison's job. The job really is important, so you need not be patronizing. Reinforce your exhortations and praise with concrete rewards such as bonuses, vacations, and time off.

Don't ever let the liaison believe he or she can do so well that the liaison's job will become non-existent. If the outsourcing relationship is going well, the liaison's role will decrease. If the liaison's role does become less significant, add to the job's responsibility. For example, have the liaison study future technology. Have the liaison study how to reduce dependency on outsourcing. Have the liaison start training its replacement and substitute liaisons for the time when the liaison will move up the management ladder.

You want your liaison to be honest with you about where problems lie. Yet, if your liaison always takes the vendor's side, raise some red flags. Ask yourself whether your performance is really that bad. Also ask yourself whether your outsourcing agreement is so inadequate that every service failure is your fault under the agreement.

Frequent stress and continuous difficulty are the hallmarks of many liaisons' job descriptions. These combine readily with many liaisons' tendency to side with the vendor. But the liaison works for you; never let the liaison forget it. Do what you can to bind the liaison to you and to ensure the liaison's loyalty. Most companies cannot secure employee loyalty by ordering that employees be loyal, but rather companies must earn the loyalty of their employees. Since the liaison's loyalty is so important, your earning that loyalty will be commensurately important. The liaison's managers must work continually and vigorously to keep the liaison's allegiance. This is best accomplished by doing things to communicate to the liaison his or her value to your business, and by having the liaison do things to demonstrate loyalty to your company.

DISPUTE RESOLUTION

It's a good idea for your outsourcing agreement to both anticipate likely areas for strife and agree on methods of resolution.

In any long and complicated relationship, disputes are likely. One of the most useful strategies in handling disputes is to deal with them. In other words, do not let disputes fester. Bring the source of conflict to the attention of the vendor. The tendency of many businesses in disputes is to pitch and yaw from one or the other extreme. Some businesses will ignore a lit match until it sets the plant on fire. Others take every minor disagreement and "make a federal case" of it.

There is a happy medium. You should give peace a chance. When a dispute arises, do not expect to always get your own way. Consider a peace proposal that costs you nothing, but gives the vendor a face-saving way to agree with you. Talk about the expansion of your business and how that will require the use of the outsourcer's services. Stress that you are still in the planning stage. You may find the outsourcer reacts positively and resolves the dispute accordingly.

If the vendor wants something of value, you may have some things to trade that will cost you little out-of-pocket. For instance, remember all those credits you've been accumulating? You can offer to give some of them back, in return for some concrete promises specified in writing. And in that writing, get a commitment to a timetable for implementation that everyone agrees will likely solve the problem.

Keep in mind, too, that while the vendor is in business to make money, it also wants a satisfied customer. If some situation develops that is bad in a business sense, but not necessarily provided for in the contract, communicate it to the vendor.

Approach the vendor even if the contract resolves the issue in the vendor's favor. The worst the vendor will say is no. It is also important to understand how the vendor has priced the outsourcing relationship and use that knowledge to mutual advantage. Because the vendor usually makes most of its money at the back end, it will want the relationship to last long enough to reach the lucrative stage. Even if the vendor says no, if you have tried the reasonable business person approach, you will have a psychological and legal advantage in any ensuing dispute. Most people believe that being reasonable is good. So do most judges and juries.

WHEN THE GOING GETS TOUGH, THE LOVE GETS TOUGHER

If your peace feelers are unsuccessful, then the love must get tougher and you must escalate. First of all, keep the liaisons talking while you escalate the level of management that is involved. Few outsourcing executives want to ruminate on a steady diet of problems or to meet endlessly over crises. So, climbing the ladder of vendor management in problem resolution may get results. Eventually you may have to escalate the problem to your top management and have your top management attempt to meet with the vendor's top management. Top management at the outsourcer does not want to meet with your top management if they can avoid it. Consequently, hitting that level gives you some advantage.

Don't be surprised, however, if your own top management resists having such a meeting. Your executives will remind you that outsourcing was supposed to relieve them of information systems problems. Your job, as long as it remains yours, will be to explain how diligent and persistent attention to the problem at hand will reap benefits in the long run.

Sessions between top executives may be deadlocks resolved only by who blinks first. If your management will not persist, try another strategy. Nevertheless, the time spent in escalation and the time spent by your upper management will show how serious your company considers the problem. That in itself is a significant accomplishment.

Last stop before the courthouse

The best way to protect yourself with your outsourcing agreement is to know what you want from the relationship and specify that in the agreement. Then you have a tool for bringing your vendor in line. Unfortunately, even reading this book can't ensure against unforeseen problems or undesirable solutions. Disputes happen, and your agreement with the outsourcer should include a mechanism that offers you and the vendor a way to resolve disputes without going to court.

The general label for resolving disputes short of litigation is ADR, for Alternative Dispute Resolution. ADR processes are usually non-binding, referred to as mediation, or binding, referred to as arbitration. As a business person, you probably are somewhat familiar with ADR concepts. But do you want your dispute resolution provisions to require mediation or arbitration? Probably, but read on.

Possible advantages to you of ADR over litigation include the following:

1. Faster resolution of the dispute.

2. Less expensive.

3. Fairer, by emphasizing resolving the problems rather than technical legal considerations.

4. Conducted in private, away from public scrutiny.

5. Dispute resolved with minimum of acrimony and residual ill-will.

On the other hand, ADR isn't perfect. It may have these disadvantages:

1. Failure to achieve the advantages.
2. Rules of evidence, such as the exclusion of hearsay testimony, may not apply.
3. If your position depends on a technical, legal consideration, you may fare better in court.
4. Mediators and arbitrators can ignore the law with impunity.
5. If you are in binding arbitration, there is no realistic appeal from an arbitrator's decision.
6. You can avoid the courthouse, but you cannot avoid lawyers.

Whether to have binding ADR in an outsourcing agreement is almost a personal decision. The answer really depends on your view of the legal system. When you're ready to butt heads with someone, do you really want to fight—take no prisoners, winner take all—and do you want your adversary to know that? Or do you want a lower key approach that will probably result in a compromise?

By providing for non-binding ADR, you can secure many of ADR's advantages without giving up the option of litigation. Non-binding mediation is almost always worth the effort because it is relatively inexpensive, it brings both sides together, and both parties benefit from the comments and opinions of an objective observer. Mediation may not resolve the dispute, but it will be a useful last attempt before a declaration of war.

WHEN IT'S JUST NOT FAIR

You have "rights" in every business relationship that are not necessarily stated in the contract. These are your "moral rights," or "human rights," or "good business rights." You should act to preserve those rights. A court of law may not enforce these rights, but many business people will respond positively to your assertion of those rights. For instance, many business people believe that a long-term business relationship where one side takes advantage of the other, is a bad relationship and headed for trouble. And, right next door to that view, is the "win win" school of thought; your vendor may be a graduate.

If you have a problem unaddressed by your contract, convey it to the vendor. Without your communication, the vendor remains unaware. If you fail to raise the issue, the vendor can pretend that it was unaware. You never know; the vendor may have a solution. Or discussions with the vendor may suggest a solution that you can propose. Of course, if you are willing to spend some money, solutions may suggest themselves.

DUST IN THE WIND

The only certainty in life is that things will change. No matter how much you plan, over time your business will change in ways you thought very unlikely.

Nevertheless, your outsourcing agreement should anticipate certain changes no matter how unlikely they now seem. During the life of your outsourcing agreement, your company may merge with another company, divest itself of a division or business, or acquire a business. Your contract with the outsourcer needs to provide for these possibilities.

To accommodate these potential changes, you need, at a minimum, to be able to increase and decrease your use of the outsourcer's services. Better yet would be the ability to renegotiate or terminate the outsourcing agreement if one of these changes occurs. The ability to renegotiate means little unless you can terminate altogether if the renegotiation is unsuccessful. Even when a change in your business occurs, don't expect the vendor to accept termination without some compensation. Again, the outsourcer makes most of its money on the back end, so some compensatory payment to the vendor is reasonable. The question is, how much? That answer is best left to your negotiating skills.

A contract provision to allow termination upon corporate re-structuring could prove useful in managing the post-transition relationship. Anything that gives you leverage to force a change in your relationship with the vendor will help encourage the vendor's attention to providing quality service. If the widget division of THINGAMAJIG, Inc. would make for a strategic fit with your other businesses, and your outsourcer has failed to perform satisfactorily, maybe you can accomplish two objectives at once.

It may seem extraordinary to consider a corporate restructuring merely to pressure the outsourcing vendor to change your relationship, but if and when the time ever comes, you will want numerous alternatives. Keep in mind, though, that just as it is usually not a good idea to enter into an outsourcing relationship merely to change the company balance sheet, it is equally inadvisable to exit an outsourcing relationship by changing the company balance sheet. You need to have a significant business and technological reason to make a merger or divestment, and your sole reason should not be to get out of your outsourcing deal.

STEPPIN' OUT AT THE DANCE HALL

In a city whose name shall remain unspoken to protect the guilty, there is a country-western dance hall. Weekdays, after lunch, many people take advantage of the dance hall's offerings. The typical afternoon patron is either a stay-at-home parent, or other worker whose job allows him or her to take some time off in the afternoon. Undoubtedly, some customers attend in order to research the infinite thematic variations of the dances known as the "Texas Two-Step," or the "Cotton-Eyed Joe." As for the others who show up, who knows their real motivations? Perhaps they like to dance; perhaps they are bored; perhaps they are lonely; or perhaps they want to meet somebody new. It's a safe bet that most of these people are married to people not then present at the dance hall. But they spend an afternoon dancing, maybe having a few beers, laughing, and in general trying to enjoy themselves. The first group leaves in time to beat the school buses to their houses, and by 5 P.M. everyone has scurried to be home before their spouses' estimated time of arrival.

For those who are there to meet someone new, the dance hall offers a test drive. And by "steppin' out," as the phenomenon is known at the dance hall, they do not, at least in theory, jeopardize their existing domestic relationships. What their spouses don't know, their spouses cannot use against them in divorce proceedings. These individuals can explore new relationships without terminating their existing ones. If the grass is not really greener, they go home to the tried and true.

As you now know, outsourcing relationships resemble marriages—intensive commitments for a long period of time. However, if your outsourcing relationship has soured, then maybe your company needs to try the analogy of the dance hall. You will not have any problem with steppin' out on your outsourcing vendor, as long as your agreement does not have an exclusivity provision. Exclusivity provisions are those that require your company to obtain all of its data processing services from the outsourcing vendor. You should never agree to one in the first place.

If, in fact, your agreement lacks such a provision, then your company can shift some or all of its data processing operations to another vendor. You can also consider bringing some operations in-house. When all you are trying to do is to discipline your vendor, sometimes even the mere suggestion of your intentions will be enough to get the vendor to improve its performance. On the other hand, you may have to go ahead and do a few trials with other service providers before you get a response out of the vendor. Such trials would not be a bad way to find out if there is another outsourcer who could better meet your requirements. One decided advantage of your test-driving with other vendors, unlike the dance hall scene, is that outsourcers—even in Texas—do not carry shotguns in the company pick-ups.

Bringing IS processing in-house, or turning IS processing over to another service provider, hits the vendor where it hurts the most: its pocketbook. Sometimes your best dispute resolution procedure, your best way to get the vendor's attention, will be not to argue or enter into any ADR process, but rather to begin to take your business elsewhere. Any vendor who fails to respond to this is failing to respond to normal business motivations and should alarm you considerably.

I HAVE NOT YET BEGUN TO FIGHT

If you inherited your outsourcing agreement, or it's already a done deal, you may think you're a crew member on an unseaworthy ship. You may or may not be right. Perhaps you have a contract that assists your management of the relationship. Or you may have an agreement that provides little assistance. Worse yet, your contract could be a monkey-wrench that actually inhibits or impedes the vendor-user alliance.

You probably recognize the immortal words of John Paul Jones, but do you remember the story? His ship, *Le Bon Homme Richard*, was fighting the British ship Serapis and taking a beating. After British broadsides battered the Richard—in fact she was sinking—the British captain demanded that the Richard surrender. This was, under the circumstances, a logical and humane gesture. Jones, however, was not ready to give up. He uttered his immortal words, rallied his crew, and finally, hours later, the Serapis surrendered. By dawn Jones had transferred his command to the Serapis because the Richard sank.

The moral is, don't give up easily. While your outsourcing contract may not be the mother lode, you may still be able to mine it. Start by determining if the agreement contains any of the provisions already discussed in this chapter: Performance Standards, Obedience School, Liaisons, Dispute Resolution, Buy Out, and Merger/Divestment provisions. If it does, commence vendor training under these provisions. For example, can you force the vendor to resolve the dispute without a lawsuit? Or is there a buy-out provision, to terminate the outsourcing relationship upon divestment, merger, or acquisition? If so, you may consider drawing the vendor's attention to such a provision and, if necessary, starting a process of invoking such provision to bring the vendor's performance in line.

If your agreement does not have helpful provisions, then reread the earlier section "When it's just not fair." Also, consider having your attorney review the outsourcing agreement. A little professional nit-picking can go a long way. And, remember the dance hall.

CHAPTER 11

"FIFTY" WAYS TO LEAVE YOUR VENDOR

All outsourcing relationships will end. In planning your outsourcing deal, negotiating your outsourcing relationship, and drafting the outsourcing contract, you must plan for this inevitability. If the relationship goes according to that plan, it will terminate at the expiration of the outsourcing agreement. If there are serious problems during the outsourcing relationship, then the relationship may terminate prematurely.

Few of the people who made the deal will be around at the end of the relationship. Outsourcing agreements typically plan for a five to ten-year term. During that time, most, if not all, of the people involved in initiating the relationship will have moved on. Moreover, the technology of information systems processing is likely to have changed greatly as well.

NOTHING LASTS FOREVER BUT THE EARTH AND SKY

You owe it to your company to think ahead. Even if the relationship lasts for the full contract term, something will have to happen at the expiration of that term. And even if the contract calls for a ten-year term, the deal could sour before then. In both cases, you need a plan for what to do when the relationship ends.

You owe it to yourself as well to think ahead. Perhaps when you make the deal, you are the CIO or CFO. Perhaps at the expiration of the deal, you will be President or CEO. Any plan established at the dawn of the relationship may be the plan you have to execute at sunset. If the deal unravels before you make it to the top, your career may detour. On the other hand, if you have armed the company with a plan for this contingency, you could save the company, as well as your own hide. You will have demonstrated a long-term vision, which seems in such short supply these days.

THE DAY AFTER

If you believe that you can let your outsourcing agreement end without planning, buy those tickets to Rio now and wire your savings to Switzerland. There will be a day after your agreement expires, when you will want to have already left the country. Unless that day after is to initiate months of total chaos, you must commence an exit strategy several months before the actual date of expiration. You cannot allow your outsourcing agreement to expire without having a plan and a means to continue processing the first day after expiration.

Admittedly, only an institutionalized CIO would allow such an unplanned expiration to occur. Much more likely, though, is that the planning for expiration begins only a few months before the anticipated date.

You should begin planning for expiration before you sign your outsourcing agreement. Your detailed planning and execution will need to start many months before the date of expiration.

EVEN OUTSOURCING CUSTOMERS GET THE BLUES

So you have planned for your agreement's expiration. Unfortunately, that planning is only half the battle. The other half is planning for termination which is unscheduled. You can characterize the end of an outsourcing agreement as being scheduled or unscheduled. You can schedule an agreement's expiration at the end of its term, whereas you will experience considerable difficulty in trying to schedule terminations instead of expirations.

You should plan at the outset for both expiration and termination. The first relies on the vendor's cooperation, while the second relies on your self-defense strategy when the vendor will not cooperate. Even if your contract lasts for its full term, and you anticipate an expiration rather than termination, you may need to invoke some of your termination strategies if the vendor fails to cooperate.

Consider this scenario. Your vendor's performance has been substandard. In fact, each day the vendor seems to find a new way to miss the performance standards. The vendor's liaison seems to be in non-stop meetings, but not with your liaison. As your complaints increase, you get less and less cooperation. Things are so bad that your users have threatened your person; earlier today you had an intimate conversation with your CEO. Bottom line is that your company wants to leave the vendor, and the company expects you to tell them how.

Assume that there is no dispute that your vendor has breached your outsourcing contract. The question is what you are going to do about it. Of course, you can sue the outsourcer. When your local sheriff delivers a copy of your lawsuit to the vendor, do you think the vendor's cooperation will increase? How much are you willing to bet on that outcome?

Without a plan to navigate you through an unscheduled termination, you will be at the mercy of the outsourcer. Some vendors might improve their performance in an effort to persuade you that litigation is unnecessary. Others may decide that you would not have sued unless you thought the situation unrecoverable; these vendors have no incentive to improve. Another possibility is that your outsourcer may have gone to the withhold-water-from-a-thirsty-person school of negotiation and may decide to decrease, rather than improve, its performance. Such a decision may be based on the vendor's theory that you cannot afford to be without IS, and that if your IS deteriorates sufficiently, you'll "come to your senses" about the lawsuit. You think no reputable company would ever do that? You don't ever want to find out. In all probability, when you and the vendor get to court two or three years later, the judge and jury will vindicate your position. But what did you do for IS in the meantime?

This discussion is not to suggest that you should not sue your vendor in the appropriate circumstances, but rather that you need a means to forestall a vendor's retaliation or evasion. Those means should be based on your turnback plan and built into your outsourcing agreement.

HAVE A PLAN, STAN

There is simply no excuse to enter into an outsourcing relationship without having a plan for getting out. This doesn't mean the plan will cover absolutely everything that might happen. This doesn't mean the plan will execute as perfectly in real life as it will on paper. This does mean that you have been warned.

To develop such a plan, consider two aspects of the end of an outsourcing relationship, while you are negotiating or participating in one:

1. The reason the relationship is over.

2. How your company meets its IS needs when the relationship ends.

WHY ASK WHY?

There are many reasons why your company's relationship with the outsourcing vendor may end. It is important to consider these various scenarios as early as possible in the relationship to ensure that you provide for and then look out for the following situations:

1. Expiration: The contract with the vendor may expire by its own terms. In other words, the agreement states that it lasts for five years, and five years are up.

2. Termination for breach: One party breaches the agreement, thereby allowing the other party to terminate. For example, you fail to pay your bills even though you don't question their accuracy. You breach and they terminate.

3. Termination for convenience: Some contracts allow premature termination, even though neither vendor nor user have

breached. An agreement might allow the user to terminate for a specific termination fee. Government contracts often must allow the government to terminate the relationship for convenience.

4. Termination for special circumstances: The basis for this termination can be almost anything. A common termination for special circumstances would be the ability to terminate if the user is acquired by another company.

NO-FAULT DIVORCES FOR CONTRACTS

In a termination for convenience, the vendor's breach is not the basis for the termination. Instead, the termination occurs because the user decides that it no longer wants to be in the outsourcing relationship.

There may be many reasons why a user would arrive at such a decision. There may be a breach that the user knows it will not be able to prove, but believes is significant enough to want to terminate the relationship. Or the performance standards included in the agreement could be insufficient to obtain the vendor performance that the user requires. In other words, the vendor's performance is poor, but not so poor that it amounts to a breach of the agreement.

Another reason to terminate for convenience would be if there is a radical change in data processing technology, something equivalent to enabling you to replace a mainframe with a PC. Such radical changes in technology become more likely the longer the agreement is expected to continue. Therefore, the longer the term of the agreement, the more you want to be able to get out of it for unforeseen—and unspecified—reasons.

Do not expect the vendor to permit termination for convenience at no cost. First of all, the vendor entered into a long-term outsourcing agreement expecting to get revenues for a long time. Secondly, many vendors price their outsourcing agreements to profit most at the back end of the affiliation. Thus, termination before the complete term of the agreement has transpired means the vendor could suffer a loss commensurably larger than pro rata for the remaining years of the term.

In other words, terminating a ten year agreement that would pay the vendor one dollar a year after the end of the eighth year could mean more than a two dollar loss to the outsourcer.

Contract provisions that allow termination for special circumstances, on the other hand, are not open-ended like termination for convenience provisions, but instead list the circumstances allowing termination. Among these special circumstances, you are most likely to specify mergers and acquisitions by either side, along with financial problems of the vendor.

There could be a change in control of your company. Or, your company may acquire another company. If that acquisition has substantial data processing resources, your company may be able to piggyback its IS needs onto the acquired company's resources. On the other hand, the acquired company may have such significant additional data processing needs that the combined companies can strike a better deal with another outsourcing vendor, or can realize sufficient economies of scale without outsourcing.

Your company also could divest one or more divisions, causing its data processing needs to decline substantially. You might no longer have sufficient volume to make the outsourcing relationship worthwhile for you or the vendor. And you certainly would not want to continue paying a minimum fee based on your previous IS requirements.

There could be similar corporate restructuring on the outsourcer's side. The outsourcer may acquire another outsourcer, divest itself of some of its operations, or acquire a company unrelated to its outsourcing business. Any of those changes in the vendor may be a reason that your company would want to terminate the outsourcing relationship. For instance, what if a competitor of your company acquired the outsourcer? You may not want to be sharing your information systems with the outsourcer. Guarding the confidential nature of your information, that is, keeping it from the outsourcer's new owner, might be quite difficult.

Another circumstance that may lead you to want to terminate your agreement is if the vendor gets into financial trouble. What you don't want to do is wait until the vendor is in bankruptcy or otherwise insolvent to try to extricate yourself. Prior to formal bankruptcy, you would be well-advised to start, if not complete, transition away from that vendor. Once the bankruptcy is filed, disentangling yourself will be a lot more difficult. Under bankruptcy law, the bankruptcy court's and the bankruptcy trustee's decisions prevail over the terms of your contract.

From your standpoint, you want the agreement to make termination for convenience and special circumstances available to you, but not to the vendor. Also, expect a lot of haggling in trying to arrive at a dollar figure to "buy yourself out" under these options. Don't forget that although the vendor may lose anticipated profits, it should not suffer out-of-pocket losses.

Get back to where you once belonged

The second component to planning for the end is determining how your company will meet its needs without the vendor. Turnback is a way of referring to both the procedures for accomplishing the transition back to in-house IS processing and the procedures for transferring your IS processing from your current outsourcing vendor to another outsourcer.

As in the transition to outsourcing, discussed in Chapter 9, there are flip-the-switch transfers from outsourcing. If your turnback will be flip-the-switch, then the turnback provisions in your outsourcing agreement, as well as the practical procedures for accomplishing those provisions, will be relatively straightforward. In fact, anticipating a turnback might cause you to select a facilities management relationship over a service bureau relationship, all other things being equal and you have a choice between these two. In the facilities management relationship, the outsourcer is on your premises, managing your facilities. So, if things get really tough and you need to regain control, you might be able to "storm" the IS facility and retake control of your operations. On the other, and more probable, hand, if the turnback is not flip-the-switch, but instead is best described as a disentanglement, your negotiations and outsourcing agreement must address many issues. Almost all turnback situations, since few can be flip-the-switch turnbacks, will require unraveling many complicated aspects of the existing relationship.

First you need a plan. At a minimum, your detailed plan for expiration or termination, that is your turnback plan, should address the following issues:

1. Where will you be processing the day after your outsourcing relationship ends?

2. Do you have an option to remain with the vendor after expiration or termination, and how much will it cost?

3. If you are moving to a new outsourcer, will you need to convert any applications? If so, how? (Your turnback plan will require considerations similar to a turnover plan, which Chapter 9 discusses.)

4. If you are bringing your IS processing back in-house, what resources do you need? Will you need to convert any applications under this approach? If so, how? (see Chapter 9.)

5. What is the vendor supposed to return to you and vice versa?

The turnback procedures may accomplish the transfer from outsourcer to user (or to another outsourcing vendor) of the following:

- Hardware
- Software
- Software licenses
- Hardware leases
- Hardware maintenance agreements
- Software maintenance agreements
- Real estate, such as the building in which the IS center is located
- Operations personnel
- Data

- Run-time documentation
- Software maintenance personnel
- Software development personnel
- Communications hardware
- Communications software
- Communications circuits
- Communications agreements
- Data entry connections to the IS center
- Disaster recovery arrangements

Most of these will require both a physical and a legal transfer, especially the licenses, leases, and other agreements.

Although your plan is likely to change over the course of the relationship, you are better served by having a plan to keep current than by expecting to create a plan only when needed. Moreover, the act of creating an exit plan prior to entering into an outsourcing relationship will alert you to many of the legal and practical strategies for which you must provide. Notice, too, that you may need to make turnback arrangements with third parties, such as obtaining licenses from software vendors and rehiring operations personnel.

WRITE THE DIVORCE DECREE BEFORE GETTING MARRIED

Avoiding marriage is easier than divorcing. If you disbelieve, ask your spouse. Prenuptial agreements attempt to help by planning a possible disentanglement. Prenuptial agreements are really divorce decrees written in advance.

Similarly, the time to plan for the turnback is before you enter the outsourcing relationship. It is a little bit like planning a divorce when you get married, but the big difference is that in an outsourcing agreement you know you will get divorced. You'll get the best terms for divorce before you get married. If you cannot negotiate reasonable turnback provisions in your outsourcing contract, there is still time to walk away from the deal. Merely trying to negotiate turnback provisions will increase the vendor's respect for you.

Therefore, your contract with an outsourcing vendor is the next issue in dealing with turnback. In that agreement, you need to establish two things: a legal process by which you can leave the relationship; and a workable procedure that will allow you to leave with a minimum of disruption. A smooth transition should be the goal of all turnback provisions.

TWO SIDES OF THE SAME COIN

Turnback provisions in your contract need to address both the legal and practical strategies that will be necessary.

For the legal side, you need the muscle to force the vendor to get you through the turnover crisis. The legal strategies must address many issues, including those described in the checklist at the end of this chapter. Especially important for turnback is to establish your right to the following:

1. Your data on magnetic media and the descriptions of the data's layout.

2. Your software.

3. The vendor's cooperation.

4. The vendor's assistance.

5. The vendor's disclosure of technical information necessary and useful for the transition back.

6. A license for software owned by the outsourcing vendor for which you will have a continuing need.

7. A license for software from a third party, but supplied by the outsourcing vendor, for which you will have a continuing need.

All of these are reasonable requests of the vendor. If your agreement does not provide for them, you will have to seek the vendor's cooperation for what you don't have when the time comes. For the technical information, for example, your best option is to keep it in your company's hands all along; next best is for your contract to compel the vendor to keep the information in escrow throughout the relationship.

Recognize that planning a turnback is not an exact science. Your agreement needs to establish a flexible reverse transition, i.e., turnback, period. This period commences no later than upon the expiration or termination of the outsourcing agreement, but should allow you to continue to use the outsourcing vendor's services for an indefinite length of time. Most vendors will not allow you to go on forever. Yet, there is little reason you should not get at least six months of services after the agreement is over. Try to get up to eighteen months.

The turnback period is likely to take at least as long as you expect the turnover, that is, the transition to outsourcing, to last. You will, of course, have to pay the vendor for those services. Negotiate the rates at the front end, because that is when you will have the leverage to support your arguments that the contract's rates, not "market rates," should continue during the turnback period. In fact, one of the reasons you may contemplate turnback will be if you are unable to renew your outsourcing agreement on terms that you consider favorable.

Also like turnover, turnback may require software conversions. Analyze whether you will need to go through any conversions to transfer from outsourcing back to in-house IS processing. If one or more conversions are possible, your contract provisions for turnback need conversion provisions just like your turnover provisions did.

PRACTICAL PRACTICES

Squirrels are practical strategists. That's why there are so many of them. They plan for the time when their food is in short supply. They don't wait until Christmas to begin storing acorns; they start in the summer and continue throughout the fall. They store many more acorns than they are likely to need and they store them in a variety of places. When the rodent equivalent of fast food restaurants freezes over, squirrels can still eat because they have a cache. If squirrels were in the army, they would call it a redoubt.

DON'T DOUBT A REDOUBT

A redoubt is first on the list of practical strategies to deal in advance with termination. A redoubt gives you the maximum ability to leave the vendor and commence your IS operations somewhere else, even if the vendor refuses to cooperate. In other words, it serves as a practical means of moving your IS processing elsewhere.

Not every outsourcer holds your company's interests above its self-interest. There is at least one report of an outsourcer that considered shutting down a customer's computers to gain leverage in resolving a dispute. The outsourcer claims it never seriously considered the suggestion. Though it may seem far-fetched that a vendor would even let the thought become words, you and your company certainly do not want to be the test case. Therefore you must have a means to defend your company. In other words, you need a user's analog to the Second Amendment to the U.S. Constitution, also known as the right to arm bears. Properly configured, you can be a very well-armed bear.

A successful redoubt requires planning and periodic priming. At a minimum, the redoubt consists of your software, your data, and your run-time documentation. You need enough so that you can hit the ground running at another location. While during the term of your agreement you may change your prospective location, you do need to have a prospective location. The outsourcing vendor will have a disaster recovery site that is in a different location from where it provides you services. Having yet another back-up site may seem needlessly repetitive. Your own back-up site is needlessly repetitive only if you never have to use it. Access to multiple back-up sites is a strategy worth considering. For periodic priming, as part of your normal backup process, make frequent copies of your data, software, run-time documentation, and any related materials necessary to perform your processing. These copies do not differ significantly from what you would need in the event of a disaster at the vendor's facilities. Your vendor, however, will be in charge of disaster recovery. Your redoubt should differ from your normal and disaster backups in that your redoubt should never be under the outsourcer's control. Your redoubt must be under your control both physically and legally. You will need to obtain your copies frequently and move them to a place outside of the vendor's control. This, of course, entails extra expense, but the expense is worth it.

Constructing a redoubt will not always be realistic or even sensible. But you don't necessarily need a duplicate of everything to benefit from the concept. Even if a complete and separate set of backups is irrational in your particular situation, perhaps at least a copy of your "mission-critical" database would still be worthwhile.

Keeping up with the phones

A second practical turnback strategy is to accommodate changes in your IS processing during the outsourcing relationship. Over time, your applications will change. Over time, the technology used to run your applications will change. Both of those considerations are relevant to your practical strategies.

You may enter outsourcing relying on available mainframe technology. Yet it's a safe bet that current technology will be obsolete in just a few years. Some changes will not touch your processing, but others could have a radical impact. Imagine that your company had entered into an outsourcing relationship in the early 1980s. The mainframe was king and PCs were thought by many to be expensive video games. A decade later though, client/server technology had become the fastest growing IS strategy and threatened the mainframe's very existence. Few doubt that an equally significant change will occur within the next decade. Wireless LANs are already knocking on the door. All of this means that your redoubt strategy at the beginning of the outsourcing relationship must keep up with the technical changes that occur during the relationship.

When the vendor has been very, very bad

There may come a point in the outsourcing relationship where the vendor's performance is so egregious your company can no longer tolerate it. If you are still the CIO, then undoubtedly managers and executives from every department and division will know your name. They will also know your home telephone number. They will know the address of your voice-mail box. You will be hearing complaints high and low. There may be threats on your life. There certainly will be threats on your employment tenure. You will undoubtedly learn first-hand the overlap between the science of scatology and the performance of propellers in wind tunnels.

No one will blame you for having thoughts that could get you 10 to life. But, alas, you'd be in jail and the outsourcer would still have its agreement in place. You need a legal remedy to your problem.

Chances are you had some warning about this problem with the outsourcing vendor. Quite likely, it's a problem that has remained unresolved since the inception of the relationship. In any event, it is unlikely that you went home on Friday without any inkling that Monday morning there would be a serious problem with the outsourcer.

The best advice for this situation resembles much of the advice in this book—plan ahead. Don't wait to complain about the outsourcer's conduct when the outsourcer hasn't bothered to process anything for two weeks. The time to complain is when the outsourcer does something you don't want it to do. However serious the problem, you should always follow the three most important principles of preparing for litigation: document, communicate, and follow-up on the first two. When there is a problem, make a record of it, notify the vendor, and give a time frame within which to resolve the problem.

There are many good reasons to do this. First, don't assume that the vendor knows there is a problem without your reporting one. Second, don't assume that the right people at the vendor know there is a problem if you don't tell them. For any number of reasons, the vendor's grunts in the operation trenches may, understandably, have refrained from alerting upper management. Also, even if the proper level of vendor management is aware of the problem, that level may choose to ignore it if you fail to remind them.

While going through this process may seem laborious and petty, you will establish a paper trail of problems with the vendor. The trail should serve as evidence that you brought problems to the vendor's attention. This could go a long way in convincing a judge and a jury that you were serious about problems that occurred, and that you took some action to communicate the seriousness to the vendor. Otherwise, should you have to sue without this paper trail, you will have what attorneys call a "swearing contest." Your people will swear how bad the vendor has been. The vendor's employees will swear that there was no problem or that they never knew anything was amiss, and that, if they only had known, they would have rushed to provide a solution. It will be your credibility versus the vendor's credibility.

You can understand why in such situations a jury would just throw its hands in the air and not decide for either party. The vendor knows this, too, and so documenting, communicating, and following up may keep the vendor on its best behavior. If the serious problems arise nonetheless, you will have a record of your attempts to get the vendor's attention.

Even with the documentation and communication cycle that you must follow with the vendor, you cannot wait forever to resolve all problems. If there is a serious unresolved problem, you must act within two time frames.

You must act within the appropriate statute of limitations. Get legal advice on this issue because the period of time varies under state law. Furthermore, the contract may have established its own period of limitations that is shorter than the state statute of limitations.

Don't let the statute of limitations or the contractual period of limitations be your only guide. You also must act within a reasonable time. Even if legally you have seven years within which to act on a particular breach by the vendor, suing the vendor at six years and 11 months, just under the statute of limitations, is not likely to get you very far. Yes, you will be in the right, technically, but reasonable jurors may ask why, if your problem was so terrible, you waited so long before you sued. And they will be right. So, you must act within a reasonable time. Use your business judgment to determine what is a reasonable time: When should you have known that the problem existed and that you could not resolve it without bringing suit? Part of this process is to give legal notice to the vendor.

Generally, your agreement with the vendor will establish how to give that notice. Usually you will send notice in writing to a specified title or person. Send such a notice certified mail, return receipt requested, to prove that you sent it and that it was received.

Generally, the contract will also provide an opportunity for the vendor to cure. That means the vendor gets an opportunity to remedy the problem for which you gave the vendor notice. The vendor may cure the problem within that cure period. Even if the agreement specifies no cure period, give the vendor some reasonable period of time. Courts will expect you to have done so, and so will most jurors. Also, the vendor may resolve the problem, and the short period of time during which you persevered will be less expensive than going to court.

CRYING WOLF

You may decide to file a lawsuit to persuade a vendor to mend its ways. There are at least two schools of thought on this strategy. One believes that filing a lawsuit without intending to go through with it is all right because it puts a lot of pressure on the defendant. This is often true.

The second school, however, believes such a suit is not a wise policy in general. First of all, the vendor may not roll over and die, but instead may fight. If the vendor fights, your company cannot go to the vendor or the judge and say, "Sorry, we didn't mean it," and expect that to be the end of things. The court could sanction your company for filing a lawsuit under such circumstances.

The second problem with this strategy is that if you do fight, and you weren't prepared to fight, you will actually have reduced a lot of the leverage and morale that you had going into the lawsuit. In other words, if you expected to spend only $10,000, when you start to spend tens or hundreds of thousands of dollars, your enthusiasm and your desire to win will decline. Moreover, the vendor may be able to detect that filing the lawsuit was only a stratagem, and not a serious attempt to proceed with litigation. If so, the vendor will fight you as hard as if you actually wanted to proceed to litigation, in the hope you will crumble quickly. In other words, the outsourcer may call your bluff.

If you're going to sue the vendor, prepare to really sue them. Prepare for a protracted battle. Prepare for a great deal of expense.

If you have your redoubt provisions in the agreement and the practical strategies resulting from the presence of the redoubt, then you may not have to remain at the vendor's mercy, but may be able to seek alternatives while you fight things out in the courtroom. If you do not have the redoubt, then you will probably have to rely on the vendor to continue to service you while you sue them, a strategy not calculated to be very successful. Or perhaps, as a last resort, you may be able to invoke your disaster recovery plan to leave your vendor. Using the disaster recovery alternative can be very expensive. If your disaster recovery is through the vendor, or a company closely affiliated with the vendor, then you're out of luck.

Not Every Inheritance Will Make You Rich

If you have inherited an outsourcing relationship, and you want to get out, do not despair. Look for ways to extricate yourself.

First on your to-do list is reading your current outsourcing agreement. Go over it with a fine-toothed comb. Find any modifications to it. Having an attorney scrutinize it is worth the time and the money. What you are looking for are legal safety valves and loopholes and other ways to get out of the agreement. Consider also having an IS consultant scrutinize the agreement, looking for practical and technical means of decreasing your reliance on the outsourcing vendor.

Then appraise your plan for alternative IS services. You may be able to take your processing somewhere else, or to move an application one at a time in-house or to another vendor. Another strategy worth considering is installing a new technology and bringing up new applications on that new technology. In other words, don't try to move an existing application from the outsourcer in-house or to another vendor, but rather duplicate, in a functional sense, the same application in-house. Moreover, if you have a resource-based charging mechanism, you can hurt the outsourcing vendor where it counts—in the pocketbook. Pocketbook trauma is an effective way to get the vendor's attention.

All good things must end someday

Perhaps by getting the vendor's attention, you will be able to solve the problems in the relationship. If not, you will still reduce your reliance on, and your payments to, the vendor if you have, or can establish, an alternative way of meeting your IS needs. That is why you must plan in advance for the timely, or untimely, demise of your outsourcing relationship.

Checklist for Preparing to Leave Your Vendor

I. Threshold issues.

A. Nothing lasts forever.

1. Every outsourcing relationship will end.
2. You should plan for the end at the beginning.
3. Your leverage is best at the beginning.
4. Draw up the divorce decree before the marriage.

B. The great data and software hostage crisis.

1. There are vendors who will hold your data and software hostage.
2. If you are without either a practical or a legal lever to recover your data and your software, the outsourcing vendor has the advantage over you.

C. Uncooperative vendors.

1. Even an outsourcer who doesn't hold hostages may not be very cooperative.
2. Obtaining the vendor's cooperation can save you much money, heartache, and grief.

D. Bring outsourced items in-house.

   1. Will this be realistic?

   2. How long a lead time will be necessary?

   3. Third-party software license issues (see Chapter 19).

   4. How will you actually accomplish this turnback?

E. Transfer to another outsourcer.

   1. New outsourcing agreement (but, of course).

   2. What is the timetable?

   3. Is former outsourcer a competitor of new outsourcer?

   4. Third-party software license issues (see Chapter 19).

F. Plan for the reasonably likely scenarios.

   1. Plan ahead.

   2. When establishing outsourcing relationship, try to provide for turnback.

II. *Turnback triggering events.*

A. Termination for breach.

   1. "Major."

   2. "Minor."

   3. Material breach.

   4. Chronic minor breaches.

   5. Violations of performance standards evolving into breaches.

B. Expiration of agreement.

   1. Outsourcing agreements are supposed to end someday.

   2. Many of the original players will be long gone.

    C. Economic failure of either party.

    D. Change in control.

        1. User.

        2. Vendor.

    E. Merger/acquisition/divestiture

        1. User.

        2. Vendor.

    F. Termination for convenience.

III. Establish legal procedures.

    A. Establish your right to the following:

        1. Your data on magnetic media and the descriptions of the data's layout.

        2. Your software.

        3. The magnetic or optical media upon which the vendor will return your software and your data.

        4. The vendor's cooperation.

        5. The vendor's assistance.

        6. The vendor's disclosure of technical information necessary and useful for the transition back.

        7. Licenses for software owned by the outsourcing vendor for which you will have a continuing need.

        8. Licenses for software provided, but not owned, by the outsourcing vendor for which you will have a continuing need.

    B. Breaches.

        1. Minor breaches.

        2. Repeated breaches.

        3. Serious breaches.

C. Notice.

    1. Of termination, if applicable.

    2. Of your intent to continue to use the vendor's services during the turnback period.

    3. Of any other relevant provision for which your agreement requires notice.

D. Opportunity to cure.

E. Injunctive relief.

F. Change in control.

G. Reduced usage of vendor's services.

H. Associated fees for the vendor's services.

I. The repurchase of the things sold to the vendor, such as hardware.

J. The retransfer of things transferred to the vendor, such as software licenses and software maintenance agreements assigned to the outsourcer.

IV. Establish technical and business procedures.

A. Be prepared—*semper paratus.*

B. Have a plan and the means to activate the plan.

    1. Schedule for the significant turnback events.

    2. Training of your personnel.

        a. In operating your applications.

        b. In maintaining the vendor-provided applications you choose to continue using.

C. Where.

    1. Hot-site.

    2. Your site.

D. Telecommunications.

E. Have a copy of the current backups.

    1. Know what you will need.

2. System software.

3. Packaged applications software.

4. Custom software.

5. Parameter files.

6. Catalogued procedures.

7. Data.

F. Technological weaning.

1. Can you reduce the amount of the out-sourcer's services you need by changing the technology that you require, e.g., moving from a centralized mainframe environment to a distributed environment?

2. Does your outsourcing agreement permit this possibility?

PART III

OUTSOURCING GOES TO LAW SCHOOL

The following chapters provide sample contract provisions that will assist you in constructing an outsourcing agreement. These provisions should be easy for you to read and understand. However, don't think you can copy these into one document and thereby write an outsourcing contract appropriate to your circumstances. You need to engage the appropriate legal assistance, also known as an attorney, to draft your agreement. The intent of these sample contract provisions is to give you and your attorney a place to start.

Each chapter in this part also discusses subjects related to the provisions. Many of the sections contain checklists to help you identify considerations relevant to the sample contract provisions. The checklists often contain issues that do not appear in the sample provisions. This is because the checklists contain business and technical issues in addition to legal issues. To construct an effective outsourcing agreement, you must evaluate contract provisions in the business and technical context of your specific transaction.

CHAPTER 12

DESCRIPTION OF SERVICES

CONTRACT PROVISIONS FOR DISCUSSION:

DESCRIPTION OF VENDOR SERVICES. With the exception of the Excluded Services, as hereinafter defined, Vendor agrees to perform the following services (the "Vendor Services"):

A. All the services provided by User's IS department prior to the Effective Date (the "Prior Services") and more specifically defined in Exhibit __, except the services specified in Exhibit __ (the "Excluded Services");

B. All the services specified in Exhibit __ (the "New Services");

C. All services for converting the Prior Services to the Vendor Services and more specifically described in Exhibit __ (the "Turnover Services"); and

D. The services specified in Exhibit __ for converting the Vendor Services to the User's or another vendor's operation (the "Turnback Services").

OMISSION IN VENDOR SERVICES. If a service provided by User's IS department prior to the Effective Date is omitted from both the Prior Services and the Excluded Services, then such omitted service shall be deemed to be included within the scope of Vendor Services.

GROWTH IN SERVICES. At no additional charge, Vendor shall acquire the necessary hardware and software to perform the Vendor Services irrespective of the volume of User's use of the Vendor Services. Any services that User requires from Vendor because of increases in User's volume that are not specified as Vendor Services shall be performed pursuant to the Section entitled "ADDITIONAL SERVICES."

GENERAL DISCUSSION OF DESCRIPTION OF SERVICES PROVISIONS:

A description of services provision in an outsourcing agreement describes generally and specifically the services that the outsourcer will provide. In many respects it resembles the software and hardware specifications in an acquisition agreement. Yet, in an acquisition agreement, the products may be off-the-shelf, customized off-the-shelf, or complete custom development. In an outsourcing agreement, though, you should always tailor the description of services to your specific circumstances.

In preparing the description of services, the threshold issue is defining the general nature of the outsourcing services. Will this agreement provide full or selective outsourcing services? What will outsourcing change in your existing IS function?

Many other provisions will revolve around the description of services and the issues that provision will raise. So try to articulate and negotiate the specific vendor services as early in the process as possible.

Usually the minimum goal in full outsourcing is replacement of all existing IS processing. Unfortunately, your contract should not just say, "Vendor does everything User did before the Effective Date," because there will be many qualifications and exceptions to that description. Therefore, your first task in writing a description of services will be to describe your company's existing IS services.

BECOME AN ARCHEOLOGIST AND START DIGGING

Uncovering your existing services will require research. This is not a function for which an attorney is well-suited. The existing IS department personnel, and in particular IS management, can be an invaluable resource in formulating the description. Of course, use of your IS personnel presupposes that they are privy to the outsourcing transaction. If for some reason the existing personnel are unavailable or undesirable, then a consultant is your next logical choice. One or more consultants can provide additional value if they bring an impartial perspective which your own IS management lacks. Moreover, your managers must perform their day-to-day jobs and may have neither the time nor inclination to assist in eliminating those jobs. If you have the appropriate consulting contract, your consultant will enjoy the "luxury" of having only one task. Also a consultant will display undivided loyalty to whoever is paying the bills.

To identify the existing services you are transferring to the outsourcer a good place to start is describing your intent and the vendor's intent, as well as your IS department's current services overall. In addition, however, you will require an itemized list of all the services that the IS department provides now, prior to the outsourcing transaction. You need the detailed list, in part because the general description will leave room for ambiguity, and in part because it is important that nothing gets overlooked. The detailed description of the existing services also will provide additional information on what is to be outsourced. Once you prepare the detailed list, you may want further negotiation on what services the outsourcer will provide and what services your company will retain.

ADD OR DELETE?

Preparing a description of your existing services is not the final task in describing the vendor's services. Next on your task list is composing a roll of necessary modifications to the services description.

First, specify those duties that are in addition to the existing services. A number of other services can fall into this category. Some of the services will be new functions that you want. Others will be services you need because there is an outsourcing transaction. For example, if your transaction will dismantle your existing computer center and you will receive computer services remotely through telecommunications links, then someone must provide those circuits. Usually the outsourcer does so as part of its services.

Second, specify any services that your IS department currently provides that you will not receive from the outsourcer. From the outsourcer's standpoint, these are to be deleted from existing services. These services will include any services you want to retain or to discontinue.

Part of the difficulty in drafting the description of existing services is determining the inter-relationship between existing services, services that you will add, and services you want to discard.

In describing new services, you are likely to encounter various problems. Part of those problems arise from trying to deal with what is unknown. You can treat acquiring the new services in a manner similar to other acquisitions. In that case, you would want detailed specifications. You would want to have evaluated institutions similar to your company for whom the vendor is providing these services. You may require customization of these services too. If so, specify the particulars of the customization. Altogether too often, though, users don't specify these new services in great detail, but rather describe them in some general manner. If you have insufficiently researched the new services, and how to transfer current operations to those new services, this omission could be damaging.

AND ONE TO GROW ON

In any description of services, existing or new, you should provide for growth. Your use of IS services can expand for a number of reasons. Your business could grow. You might add some applications. You could acquire another business. You may move into new lines of business. Whatever the reason, you must account for the evolution of your company's service needs.

The description should provide for at least two types of growth. In one type, your company needs more of the vendor's computer resources. Over time you may want augmented DASD or more CPU power. When increasing the quantity of resources available to you is insufficient, you need to have the other avenue of growth available. You may require added services or a qualitative increase in the sophistication of services to help you maximize the vendor's computer resources. You may not be able to specify what potential supplementary services you might want, but you can establish a framework for the acquisition of those services as well as some control on their cost.

INCLUDED AT NO EXTRA CHARGE

The sample provisions refer to exhibits where you would actually itemize and describe the services in detail. There are several ways to describe services, whether they are existing services or new services. You can describe the services in terms of generic resource availability. That is, you can describe specific information systems resources that are not particular to you, and are not particular to specific software applications. A generic resource description, for instance, might describe the number of CPU hours that the outsourcer will provide. It might describe the amount of direct access storage that is available on-line. Depending on the type of computer system involved, it may describe other system resources and their availability.

To a description of available resources, you should add the services you expect from the vendor to assist your using those resources. Usually there is no additional charge for these services. The following list is a sample:

1. Vendor initiates your production batch processing.
2. Vendor promptly informs your production manager of abnormal job terminations.
3. Vendor cooperates with your software maintenance personnel in finding and correcting reason for abnormal termination.
4. Vendor re-starts production processing.
5. Vendor starts CICS or IMS/DC regions.

6. Vendor applies software maintenance for system software and third party applications.

Another way to describe a vendor's services is via applications' results. For a retail sales summary application, the description would indicate the vendor's obligation to produce daily reports of all sales by product and by store and to gather the requisite sales data from each store daily. A user may not care how the vendor accomplishes these functions as long as the reports are accurate. In another example, the outsourcer might agree to provide all of your payroll services for a fixed price or a price per employee.

DESCRIBING HOW SERVICES SERVE YOUR BOTTOM LINE

You also can describe a vendor's services in terms of their value to you. This type of description is still in its infancy. But, generally, you could describe the value your company expects to receive from the vendor's services. For instance, an outsourcing service that processed and administered the collection of delinquent accounts could promise to increase the collection rate by ten percent each year, or to recover for your company a certain dollar amount from collected delinquent accounts each year. If your outsourcer's services include credit card verification, you could describe its services in terms of a decrease in the number of fraudulently used cards, or in charges over the credit limits.

Don't forget there may be several services you have to describe that exist only because of the outsourcing relationship. These may not add any particular value to your company, but are nevertheless essential in receiving the outsourcing services. You must describe those services in detail and account for them as thoroughly as any other services, even if you are describing other services in terms of their bottom line value to you. Those services you need in order to backup the vendor's operations are another example.

Another approach to the description of services in full outsourcing is to construct the full-outsourcing description as multiple selective outsourcing descriptions. The next section contains suggestions for writing a description of services in selective outsourcing situations.

DESCRIBING SERVICES FOR SELECTIVE OUTSOURCING

The main difference between selective outsourcing and full outsourcing is that in selective outsourcing you are dependent on the vendor not for all IS processing, but rather for only a subset. In fact, you may have alternative methods of performing an outsourced function. Even if you selectively outsource payroll, for example, you may remain capable of producing your own if necessary.

In writing a description of services for selective outsourcing, determine whether there is some existing analog in your business to the proposed service. Again payroll is an easy example. Describe your existing IS payroll services. Then add and delete as necessary to arrive at what the vendor will provide.

You must also describe how the new service will relate to the existing services. In the payroll example, the application needs information concerning employees, their pay scales, and in many cases their hours of work, their sick days, their vacation days, the number of dependents and so on. That kind of information is usually not static, but changes frequently. Somehow that data must be available to the outsourcer in preparing the payroll. Such information often resides in either a payroll database, or in a human resource database, or both. If the information is in your existing human resource system, the outsourcer's system needs an interface to your system. If your payroll system contains the data, but your existing human resource system needs some of the information for its processing, either you or the vendor will still need an interface. Your description of services must state who provides it.

Another approach is to describe the new service for selective outsourcing in terms of its specifications. Use the specifications concepts the way you would do in any other acquisition. Describe the vendor's offering in terms of the functions that the vendor is to perform and the functions, if any, you are to perform.

The description of services provision is important. You can approach it from a number of directions. One, or a combination, of the above approaches may work for you. At a minimum, both user and outsourcer should know their obligations. But don't be satisfied with that. Strive to articulate all obligations so that someone unfamiliar with the transaction and negotiations could read the description and understand those obligations.

DESCRIPTION OF SERVICES

CHECKLIST FOR CONTRACT PROVISIONS AND RELATED ISSUES

I. Threshold issue — general nature of outsourcing services.

  A. Full or selective outsourcing.

  B. Who and what are changing.

  C. Draft and negotiate early in the relationship.

II. Full outsourcing.

  A. Examples of full outsourcing:

    1. Full-service service bureau.

    2. Facilities management.

  B. Existing services.

    1. Existing Information Systems department or function.

    2. No existing Information Systems department or function.

  C. Description of existing services.

    1. Research existing services.

    2. Value of existing Information Systems management.

    3. Value of consultant.

    4. In general.

    5. Itemized.

D. Variants to description of existing services.

    1. New services.

        a. Difficult to deal with the unknown.

        b. Could describe new services in terms of functions.

    2. Services to be excluded or deleted.

    3. Interrelationship with existing services.

E. Provide room for growth in describing existing or new services.

    1. Possible reasons for growth.

        a. Business growth.

        b. Business expansion into new lines.

        c. Adding applications.

    2. Additional needs triggered by growth.

        a. Increased quantities of resources.

        b. Increased quantity and quality of services.

F. Have a way to ensure that prior services omitted by mistake are included as vendor services automatically.

G. Ways to describe vendor services.

    1. Generic resource availability description. Examples:

        a. Available CPU hours per day.

        b. DASD per month.

    2. Services adjunct to providing the resources. Examples:

        a. Production batch processing initiation.

        b. Communication of abnormal job terminations.

   c. Assistance in finding and correcting reasons for abnormal termination.

   d. Scheduling and initiating production reruns.

   e. Applying software maintenance for system software and third-party applications.

  3. Value resource description.

  4. Application resource description.

 H. Services required because of the outsourcing relationship.

  1. Such services may not add value to the user.

  2. Examples:

   a. Telecommunications to the outsourcer.

   b. Back-up of the outsourcer.

   c. The paper shuffle exchanging documents with outsourcer.

III. *Selective outsourcing.*

 A. Specific applications examples:

  1. Payroll.

  2. Medical insurance claims.

  3. Invoice printing.

 B. Specific technology examples:

  1. Point of sale credit card approval.

  2. Automated teller machine network.

  3. Voice and data communications network.

 C. Is there an existing analogue to the proposed service?

 D. How will the new service relate to the existing service?

 E. Describing the new service in terms of specifications.

IV. Important connections to other parts of the outsourcing relationship.

    A. Additional services.

    B. Fees.

    C. Performance standards.

    D. Growth.

    E. Contraction.

    F. Technological developments.

    G. Turnover of operations.

    H. Turnback of operations.

CHAPTER 13

ADDITIONAL SERVICES

CONTRACT PROVISION FOR DISCUSSION:

ADDITIONAL SERVICES. Vendor shall perform all services requested by User that are not Vendor Services (the "Additional Services") on a time and materials basis at the rates specified in Exhibit ___.

A. User shall not pay Vendor for Additional Services except in accordance with the following:

> (1) User requests Additional Services in writing; and
>
> (2) Vendor gives User a written estimate of the total cost of performing the Additional Services (the "Task Estimate"); and
>
> (3) User gives Vendor written authorization to perform the Additional Services.

B. User shall have no liability to pay any fees that exceed the Task Estimate by more than ten percent.

C. Vendor shall maintain time records for all time expended on the Additional Services and provide User with a copy of such records relating to each invoice.

General discussion of Additional Services provisions:

The outsourcer will label any services that you omitted in the description of services provisions as "additional services." The vendor will expect you to pay for additional services on a time and materials basis at the vendor's current rates.

Additional services provisions are inevitable, but you should try to corral their potential negative impact. First, do your job on the description of services so that the least amount falls through the cracks into the additional services category. Second, insist that your company provide written authorization before the vendor performs any additional services. Third, try to negotiate fixed rates in advance for additional services. Fourth, get a written estimate that requires your written approval before work commences. Finally, permit a modest overrun in the actual time and materials fees. The estimate would be meaningless if the vendor could charge whatever it wants, but requiring pinpoint accuracy of the vendor's estimate is unreasonable.

Additional Services

Checklist for contract provisions and related issues

I. Controlling additional services costs.

A. Draft a comprehensive description of services provision.

B. Establish the time and materials rates for additional services in the outsourcing agreement.

C. Require everything in writing.

1. Request for additional services.

2. Estimate of additional services fees.

3. Authorization to provide additional services.

D. Estimate of fees for additional services.

1. Estimate, rather than fixed price, is usually the most reasonable approach unless the additional services will be recurring.
2. A "not to exceed" amount is a viable alternative to an estimate.
3. If truly time and materials, vendor should include copies of time records with invoice.
4. Examine time records to determine authenticity of actual fees.
5. Have a maximum amount which the estimated fees cannot exceed.

II. Important connections to other parts of the outsourcing relationship.

A. Description of services.
B. Fees and charges.
C. Performance standards.
D. Growth.
E. Contraction.
F. Technological developments.
G. Turnover of operations.
H. Turnback of operations.

CHAPTER 14

FEES

CONTRACT PROVISIONS FOR DISCUSSION:

FIXED FEE. For the Vendor Services, User shall pay Vendor a fixed fee of $_____ per month in advance.

FIXED FEE ADJUSTMENT. User and Vendor agree that the fixed fee shall increase if User's transaction count exceeds 100,000 transactions in a given month. In such event, the fixed fee shall increase by $_____ for each transaction more than 100,000 transactions in a month.

USAGE FEES. Vendor and User agree that User shall pay Vendor a monthly fee based on usage of the Vendor's resources specified in this Section.

A. Vendor's resources for which there are specified usage fees are as follows:

Resource	Fee per unit
CPU (central processing unit)	$_____ per CPU hour
Tape mount	$_____ per mount
Lines printed	$_____ per line
Storage (DASD)	$_____ per gigabyte
Consulting	$_____ per hour

B. The fee due and payable to Vendor shall be the product of the units of resource consumed by User multiplied by the fee per unit.

C. Each month Vendor shall send User an invoice showing the units consumed for each resource and the related fees. User agrees to pay invoices within fifteen days of receipt.

D. There are no additional fees for the usage of other Vendor resources associated with the resources described in this Section.

FEES FROM SHARED SAVINGS. Vendor and User shall establish User's monthly medical costs by calculating User's average monthly medical costs for the twelve months immediately preceding the Effective Date (the "Prior Average Cost").

A. Each month after the Effective Date, User shall calculate its medical costs for the prior month (the "New Monthly Cost").

B. For every month for which the Prior Average Cost exceeds the New Monthly Cost, User shall pay Vendor _____ percent of the difference between the Prior Average Cost and the New Monthly Cost (the "Shared Savings Fee").

C. If for any month the New Monthly Cost exceeds the Prior Average Cost, there are no fees due to Vendor for such month.

D. There are no fees payable to Vendor for the Vendor Services other than the Shared Savings Fee.

FEES FROM SHARED REVENUE. For each month after the Effective Date, User shall pay Vendor _____ percent of User's revenue from each customer order that User shipped at or within twenty-four hours of User's receipt of such customer's order (the "Shared Revenue Fee").

A. Taxes and shipping charges are not included in User's revenue.

B. There are no fees payable to Vendor for the Vendor Services other than the Shared Revenue Fee.

C. There are no fees payable to Vendor for User's revenue from orders not shipped at or within twenty-fours hours of User's receipt of such order.

GENERAL DISCUSSION OF FEES PROVISIONS:

In general, the fees that users pay to outsourcers can be divided into one of six categories: fixed price, resource usage, shared savings, shared revenue, bottom line, and combinations.

- Fixed Fee Structures

Outsourcing vendors charging a fixed fee often charge on one of two measurements. One measure is a fixed fee per unit of output. The outsourcer may do your company's payroll and charge your company a fixed fee for each payroll check it produces or for each employee paid. An outsourcer that provides an automated teller machine (ATM) network, may charge your company for each ATM transaction.

The other common fixed price structure outsourcers use is to charge a fixed price for all of the services that the outsourcer provides. In other words, the outsourcer promises to provide all of the data processing services required by your company, as described in the agreement, for a set price, usually per month. Generally this fixed price assumes some maximum level of usage the user might require.

Some IS functions lend themselves better to fixed pricing than do others.

- Usage Fees

Some outsourcing vendors charge by the quantity and type of resources that a user consumes. Generally there is a definition of what resources the vendor will measure, such as CPU hours, tape mounts, and gigabytes of DASD. The vendor calculates the user's fee by multiplying the number of units consumed times the price per unit.

A variant of usage fee charging schemes are cost-plus approaches. Cost-plus is the vendor's cost of providing outsourcing services plus a profit percentage. The profit percentage can vary or remain fixed. The most difficult part of the cost-plus structure is in defining and monitoring the outsourcer's costs.

- Shared Savings

Sometimes outsourcing vendors share in the reduction of the user's IS costs instead of charging a fee. For instance, if your company's IS cost has been a million dollars a month, some outsourcing vendors might propose this: Your outsourcing cost will not be more than a million per month; the vendor will charge you its actual cost; and the vendor expects to get 30% of any savings below a million dollars a month that you realize. This kind of structure is very attractive to many users because it controls their data processing costs, offers at least the possibility of lowered costs, and builds in an incentive for the vendor to reduce costs.

Some vendors offer shared savings as a percentage not of IS cost savings, but rather of savings in other types of costs. An outsourcer processing medical claims may take its fees as a percentage of its customer's reduction in health care costs, for example.

- Shared Revenue

Shared revenue is another means by which a user may compensate a vendor. For instance, a system that processes traffic tickets and collects fines for those tickets could be structured such that the vendor shares some of the revenue of the fines from the tickets. Some property tax collection engagements work in such a manner.

- Bottom Line Approaches

An increasing number of users are approaching outsourcing fees with a fresh look and are trying to link their fees to their overall financial performance. You might, for example, offer to pay your outsourcer a percentage of your net profits. This type of fee approach remains in its infancy. It is not likely to spread except where vendors and users can ascertain how the outsourcer's performance correlates to the user's overall performance.

• Mix and Match

A specific transaction may use any permutation or combination of these approaches to establish and calculate fees.

FEES

CHECKLIST FOR CONTRACT PROVISIONS AND RELATED ISSUES

I. In general.

    A. How is fee calculated?

    B. Is there a minimum fee?

    C. Is there a maximum fee?

    D. Are there adjustments to fee structure?

II. Type of fee.

    A. Fixed.

    B. Resource usage.

    C. Cost-plus usage.

    D. Shared savings.

    E. Shared revenue.

    F. Bottom line.

    G. Combination.

III. Adjustments to fee structure.

    A. Fixed fee for change in volume.

        1. Increase in volume above a "ceiling."

        2. Decrease in volume beneath a "floor."

    B. Variable fee for change in volume.

    C. Self-adjusting fee for change in volume: fee based on usage alone.

D. For inflation or deflation.

    1. Consumer price index.

        a. Overall.

        b. Urban versus rural.

        c. Industry specific.

        d. Regional.

    2. Gross national product deflator.

E. For change in cost of computer technology.

    1. Do fees decrease if cost of underlying technology decreases?

    2. Can vendor impose an increase in a resource cost if vendor acquires more expensive resource?

F. Pass through of vendor's costs.

    1. Increase.

    2. Decrease.

    3. Must user approve vendor acquisition of hardware or software for which vendor may increase costs?

    4. Must vendor retain less expensive but obsolete hardware and software?

IV. Important connections to other parts of the outsourcing relationship.

A. Description of services.

B. Additional services.

C. Growth.

D. Contraction.

E. Payment.

F. Turnover.

G. Turnback.

CHAPTER 15

TURNOVER

CONTRACT PROVISION FOR DISCUSSION:

TURNOVER TO VENDOR OPERATIONS. User and Vendor agree that User's transition to the use of all the Vendor Services shall proceed in accordance with Exhibit __ (the "Turnover Plan"). The Turnover Plan describes the User's and Vendor's respective obligations as well as the schedule for accomplishing the Turnover Plan. Until the completion of the transition period, Vendor expressly agrees that User shall have no obligation to pay for the Vendor Services consumed by User except in accordance with the section of the Turnover Plan entitled "Phase-in of Fees."

GENERAL DISCUSSION OF TURNOVER PROVISIONS:

Turnover is how you get from here to there—how you transfer your current operations to the outsourcer. The turnover will involve at least the following issues:

1. Decisions about your existing employees.

2. Decisions about your existing software and hardware.

Every turnover is a customized project. Also, turnover may involve considerable negotiation. Leave the details of the turnover to exhibits in your outsourcing agreement. Your turnover plan consists of those details. Chapter 9 discusses planning and managing the turnover in detail.

Depending upon your planned charging mechanism, you will want to specify when you start paying for what during the turnover. You may want to include in your turnover plan a phased fee schedule that provides an incentive for the vendor by allowing full charges only if the vendor is on schedule in the turnover process.

TURNOVER

CHECKLIST FOR CONTRACT PROVISIONS AND RELATED ISSUES

I. *Threshold issues.*

    A. What is changing?

    B. Who is changing?

    C. When is the change?

    D. Transfer of control versus transfer of operations.

II. *Full-outsourcing.*

    A. Gradual transfer.

    B. "Flip the switch" transfer.

    C. Location.

    D. Platforms.

    E. Networks.

    F. Connecting to the outsourcer.

    G. Standard conversion procedures.

        1. Researching the source of the conversion.

        2. Defining the source.

        3. Defining the target.

        4. Defining the transition processes.

        5. Determining and defining the meaning of a successful conversion.

    H. Treated as a series of selective outsourcings.

III. Selective outsourcing.

   A. An application and a technology.

   B. Phased full-outsourcing.

   C. Existing application considerations.

   D. "Standard" conversion procedures.

   E. No existing application considerations.

   F. "Standard" acquisition procedures.

IV. Who is changing: personnel matters.

   A. Management.

   B. Operations personnel.

   C. Software development personnel.

   D. Software maintenance personnel.

   E. Secrecy, sorrow, and sedition.

V. Organizing the turnover.

   A. Despite vendor's experience in turnover, every turnover is different.

   B. Examine what the vendor has to offer.

   C. Work backwards from vendor's offering to determine user's required participation.

   D. Employ user's in-house expertise in conversions.

   E. Determine who should control.

   F. Consider application conversion teams.

   G. Consider minimal or no conversion for certain applications.

   H. Consider parallel operation.

VI. Important connections to other parts of the outsourcing relationship.

   A. Description of services.

B. Fees.

C. Schedules.

D. Software maintenance.

E. Software development.

F. Technological developments.

G. Employee considerations.

H. Third-party agreements.

    1. Existing software agreements.

    2. Existing hardware-related agreements.

I. Turnback of operations.

Chapter 16

Schedules

Contract provisions for discussion:

SCHEDULE OF EVENTS. Vendor and User agree to perform their respective obligations in accordance with Exhibit __ (the "Schedule of Events"). The Schedule of Events can be modified only with the written consent of both parties.

PRODUCTION SCHEDULE. Vendor shall perform User's daily, weekly, and monthly production processing in accordance with Exhibit __ (the "Production Schedule"). User may modify the Production Schedule upon thirty days written notice.

RESOURCE SCHEDULE. Vendor agrees to provide the resources and facilities described in Exhibit ___ (the "Resource Schedule") at the times specified in the Resource Schedule. The Resource Schedule can be modified only with the written consent of both parties.

General discussion of Schedules provisions:

Unless the timing of the Vendor's performance is never an issue, you need schedules. A general schedule of events, a production schedule, and a resource availability schedule are the most common. This is not to say that these three are the only relevant schedules. Your transaction may require others.

The schedule of events is most applicable to the turnover phase of the outsourcing relationship. It should contain milestones and associated dates.

The production schedule specifies the recurring cycles of vendor processing for your company. Like most schedules, a production schedule describes an event and when the event occurs. The vendor may want to add some of its own events to this schedule and make its own performance contingent upon the occurrence of those events. For instance, the vendor may require that you have all your data entered on schedule before starting a particular application. Your agreement should anticipate delays in the production schedule and provide solutions.

A resource availability schedule communicates when certain vendor services, hardware, or software will be available on a daily basis. The vendor may operate a help desk during business hours. On-line applications may be available only from 7:30 A.M. to 4:00 P.M. Central time. Or the vendor and user may choose to limit testing to a defined third shift.

SCHEDULES

CHECKLIST FOR CONTRACT PROVISIONS AND RELATED ISSUES

I. Schedules.

    A. Schedule of events.

    B. Production schedule.

    C. Resource schedule.

II. Schedule of events.

    A. Events.

        1. Major.

        2. Minor.

    B. Date on which event is to occur.

        1. Hard dates, e.g., June 19, 2017.

        2. Relative dates, e.g., 100 days after the effective date.

III. Major events.

    A. Effective date.

    B. Baseline measurement period, if any.

    C. Commencement of turnover.

    D. Application installations/conversions.

    E. Completion of turnover.

    F. Transfer of personnel.

    G. Commencement of processing at outsourcing vendor facility.

IV. Production Schedule.

    A. Schedule for each batch application.

    B. May include events to be performed prior to production.

V. Resource schedule.

    A. On-line regions available.

    B. Help desk available.

    C. Test time available.

VI. Important connections to other parts of the outsourcing relationship.

    A. Force Majeure.

    B. Turnover.

    C. Turnback.

    D. Performance standards.

CHAPTER 17

LIAISONS

CONTRACT PROVISION FOR DISCUSSION:

LIAISONS. Vendor and User hereby agree that the following individuals shall serve as their respective liaisons. The liaisons shall serve as a point of contact by which the parties may communicate on a frequent basis. Either party may change its liaison upon written notice to the other party. User acknowledges that the User Liaison may accept goods and services provided under this agreement and thereby bind User. Vendor expressly agrees that Vendor Liaison may obligate the Vendor in all matters pertaining to this agreement.

A. Vendor Liaison: _____.

B. User Liaison: _____.

GENERAL DISCUSSION OF LIAISONS PROVISION:

The liaisons are the individuals who serve as the communications conduit between the vendor and the user. Both will find that designating specific liaisons in their agreement will serve to mutual advantage. The major concern in drafting the liaison provisions is what authority the liaisons shall have. Both vendor and user should carefully consider what authority to give their respective liaisons.

On one hand, if a liaison has too much authority, the liaison can obligate its employer to contract modifications — even unintentionally. If the user liaison may accept goods and services delivered by the vendor, he or she might accept substandard goods or services. A vendor liaison who has the authority to issue a bid may underbid or overbid if not adequately trained.

On the other hand a liaison needs enough authority to facilitate the transaction. For instance, if the user's liaison has the authority to request a bid for additional vendor services, the vendor will receive such a request much faster than if the liaison needed approval from several management layers. Likewise, if the vendor liaison does not have the authority to quote a price upon request, then the entire request and bid process rolls to a stop.

Not as significant, but nevertheless important, is the issue of what happens when the designated liaison is unavailable. There may be different answers for "out of the office," illness, and vacation situations. One possible answer is to designate alternate liaisons in the agreement as well.

While there is value in having an alternate liaison designated in the agreement, the presence of such liaison may precipitate unnecessary confusion. Alternate liaisons will work well unless the alternates are unfamiliar with the transaction and what has transpired up to the point where their involvement is required. Also, some additional confusion may result from using an alternate liaison when the principal liaison is unavailable for a relatively short period of time.

Perhaps a better approach would be to designate an alternate liaison informally who is in essence a liaison in training. In those instances when a designated liaison is unavailable, the parties either act at a higher level without one of the liaisons, simply wait for that liaison to become available, or, if necessary, the party whose liaison is unavailable designates in writing an alternate or a new liaison for a short period of time or until the regular liaison is available.

Chapter 10 discusses liaisons at length.

Liaisons

Checklist for contract provisions and related issues

I. Authority.

   A. Issues relating to authority of user liaison to obligate user to vendor.

      1. Issue request for bids.

      2. Evaluate goods.

      3. Accept and reject goods.

      4. Evaluate services.

      5. Accept and reject services.

   B. Performance monitoring.

      1. Review vendor performance reports.

      2. Meet with user department heads.

      3. Follow-up on performance issues.

      4. Forward serious performance issues up the chain of command.

   C. Complaint/problem management.

      1. Management of complaints/problems identified by user.

         a. Field complaints/problem reports internally.

         b. Notify user management.

         c. Notify vendor.

         d. Follow up with vendor.

         e. Evaluate resolution of complaints/problems.

         f. Accept and reject solutions.

      2. Management of complaints/problems identified by vendor.

         a. Investigate.

         b. Notify user management.

        c. Respond to vendor.

        d. Coordinate solutions.

II. *Number of liaisons.*

    A. Minimum of one each for user and vendor.

    B. Alternates and multiple liaisons possibly required.

        1. Large transaction with numerous liaison activities.

        2. When primary liaison unavailable.

            a. Sick.

            b. Prolonged illness.

            c. Vacation.

            d. Otherwise engaged in office.

            e. Otherwise engaged out of office.

        3. When liaison-in-training is required.

            a. To keep existing liaison motivated by promising career path and demonstrating the intention to promote liaison-in-training to liaison.

            b. To keep existing liaison motivated by competition for liaison job.

        4. To prove to primary liaison that his or her position is managerial.

    C. Problems of multiple liaisons.

        1. Keeping all liaisons apprised of relationship developments.

        2. Inconsistencies: giving multiple answers internally and to vendor.

        3. Overlap in problemsolving.

        4. Primary liaison must be a liaison and manager.

D. Need mechanism for replacement of liaison with notice to other party.

III. Liaisons' ordinary communications.

A. Telephone usually suitable.

1. Should there be a written confirmation?

2. Should liaison maintain telephone log?

B. Occasionally more formal means required.

1. Letter, fax, and other written forms of communications.

2. Courier service deliveries.

3. Coordinate with contract's notice provisions.

IV. Liaisons' meetings.

A. Extremely important in turnover stage.

B. Frequency.

1. During turnover.

2. During continuing relationship.

3. During turnback.

C. Location.

1. Vendor's premises.

2. User's premises.

3. "Neutral" premises.

4. Alternate between premises.

D. Means.

1. In person.

2. Via telephone.

3. Video conference.

4. Mixed.

5. Dependent on circumstances.

V. Office location.

   A. User should keep its liaison at its facilities.

      1. Keeps liaison in touch with user problems.

      2. Helps prevent conflicting loyalties.

   B. User should try to persuade vendor liaison to maintain an office at user premises.

      1. Helps keep vendor liaison in touch with user problems.

      2. May increase vendor liaison's responsiveness to user.

VI. Liaison loyalty.

   A. User liaison's position is critical to user.

      1. Liaison may have substantial authority.

      2. Liaison likely to have most knowledge concerning vendor's performance.

      3. Liaison likely to have best ability to keep continuing relationship smooth.

      4. Liaison's diplomatic skills may keep small problems from exploding.

      5. To serve as the user's advocate and representative and to watch over vendor, liaison should not have conflicting loyalties.

   B. Issues with user liaison.

      1. May be one of few IS professionals left at user.

      2. May resent decision to outsource.

      3. May dislike confrontation.

      4. May identify more with vendor personnel than with user personnel.

      5. Liaison job may seem to be dead-end.

VII. *Liaison's career path.*

    A. User liaison should believe he or she has future with user.

        1. Helps establish and maintain loyalty.

        2. Assists in retaining personnel of sufficient competence.

    B. May become good candidate for CIO position if company expects to outsource long term.

VIII. *Personal characteristics for user liaison.*

    A. IS professional.

    B. Knowledgeable concerning user's applications.

    C. Willing to confront vendor.

    D. Attention to detail.

    E. Ability to see entire situation.

    F. Good communication skills.

        1. To management.

        2. To technical personnel.

    G. Willing to put things in writing.

    H. Loyal to user.

    I. Motivated to apprehend problems.

    J. Good sense of user's business objectives.

    K. Willing to work on widely ranging issues from technical details to strategic concerns.

    L. Persistent.

    M. Well organized.

    N. Some managerial skills.

    O. Promotable within user organization.

    P. Diplomatic.

    Q. Able to work with heads of user's departments.

IX. Important connections to other parts of the outsourcing relationship.

    A. Notice.

    B. Turnover.

    C. Turnback.

    D. Additional services.

    E. Existing employees.

CHAPTER 18

EXISTING EMPLOYEES

CONTRACT PROVISION FOR DISCUSSION:

EXISTING INFORMATION SYSTEMS EMPLOYEES. Exhibit ____ is a list of all of User's information systems employees (the "IS Employees"). Vendor expressly agrees to offer employment to certain IS Employees, in the same job categories as such IS Employees have with User, for a minimum of one year after the Effective Date of this Agreement and in accordance with this Section.

A. Vendor agrees that User intends to retain certain IS Employees in User's employ. Such IS Employees (the "Retained Employees") are specified by name or job title in Exhibit __.

B. Vendor also agrees to offer employment to such IS Employees listed or in job categories of people who are listed in Exhibit __ (the "Transferred Employees"). Any IS Employee not identified as a Retained Employee shall be deemed a Transferred Employee.

C. Vendor shall offer the Transferred Employees employment with Vendor at the salary and benefits specified by individual and/or job descriptions in Exhibit ___.

D. Vendor agrees for a period of three years not to solicit or to offer employment, as an employee or as an independent contractor, to any person or job title designated as a Retained Employee.

E. During the first year (the "Guaranteed Period"), Vendor may terminate a Transferred Employee only for cause.

F. After the Guaranteed Period, Vendor may terminate any Transferred Employee upon two weeks notice; provided, however, Vendor shall make reasonable efforts to assist a Transferred Employee in finding another job.

GENERAL DISCUSSION OF EXISTING EMPLOYEE PROVISIONS:

If you have an existing data processing department, then you will have existing IS employees. Existing employees create a number of issues for any user who wants to migrate to outsourcing. What are you going to do with them once you've outsourced? There's little point in outsourcing if you are going to keep most of the same people.

To some extent, moving to outsourcing is analogous to a large layoff or plant closing. Many of the considerations that you might have in such downsizing situations could become relevant in the transition to outsourcing.

YOU CAN FIELD ONLY SO MANY PLAYERS

The first big issue with your existing employees is deciding who stays, whom do you trade, and whom do you lay off on Christmas Eve. (There's never really a good day for layoffs, is there?) Keep in mind some general principles in trying to make such decisions. They are discussed here and, more extensively, as part of planning the transition in Chapter 9.

The answer to who goes and who stays is based on how much you plan to outsource, and resembles the decision of what and how much to outsource in the first place. If you're outsourcing only one application and that application exists, then consideration of what happens to employees should focus on that application. Consider also whether you plan to keep your existing applications, but let the vendor run them, or whether you plan to substitute any of the vendor's software for your own. The more vendor applications you are taking on, the less you will need, and the less the vendor will want your existing employees.

Do THEY DREAM OF ELECTRIC SHEEP?

In thinking about the disposition of an employee, consider how much that employee works with other employees versus how much he or she deals only with your computer system. This is a quick test for evaluating a person's retention potential. The more a person works with others, the more you may want to retain that person. The more that person talks to computers, the more you may want to find him or her another discussion group.

In general, keep your software applications people. They are too critical to your IS functions to lose. If you trade them to the vendor you will be completely at the vendor's mercy, unable to change even the heading on a report without incurring the vendor's fees. You will forever get software development and software maintenance services at retail prices instead of wholesale prices.

Also, the loyalty of personnel that you trade will always gravitate to the vendor's hardware and software configuration as a solution, rather than to the most cost-effective solution available. Even your former employees who don't dislike you for having sent them to the vendor will nevertheless think of software solutions that are most profitable to their employer then, and not of those software solutions that are the least expensive or most effective for you.

If you are moving to a new application, you can consider axing the applications personnel devoted to the old application once the conversion is complete. Even if the outsourcer supplies the applications, however, most of the same reasons for keeping the applications personnel in the first place would still apply.

Operations-dectomy

In general, trade the operations people to the outsourcer. The operations people are those people whose jobs involve working with the machines or computer systems more than they involve working with other people. This group includes computer operators, I/O control personnel, documentation control personnel, and systems programmers.

You will need all of these people up to and during the transition. But, once the transition is over, these people are better sent into the arms of the outsourcer. After all, without a computer system you won't need many operations people. Moreover, it is harder for operations personnel, who are not systems programmers, to get jobs than it is for software people. Trading them to the outsourcer will give them an opportunity to remain employed at least for some set period of time.

You should be safe in trading your systems programmers to the outsourcer, but don't expect them to behave in any predictable manner. Systems programmers tend to be among the most talented and unusual personalities in the IS department. They are just as likely to walk out the day that you inform them of the outsourcing agreement as they are to joyfully commence working for the outsourcer. If they stay, they may desert you before the transition is completed.

Give the outsourcer your headaches

A good reason to transfer employees to the outsourcer, even if you don't have any other reason, is to transfer your prospective personnel problems to the outsourcer. For instance, get the outsourcer to agree to offer employment to all of your operations personnel for a minimum of one year. After one year, the outsourcer will look like the bad guy if it throws all your former employees out into the cold. Your people may remember your company as the one that tried to get them a job in the face of certain economic realities and corporate restructuring decisions over which no one seems to have control.

Some employees should be neither retained nor transferred. You should boot right out the door the troublemakers:

whoever is going to undermine your efforts to make the transition to outsourcing while continuing to get your IS work done every day. Some of these people you may actually identify before your outsourcing announcement. Others may come to light once you have made the announcement. Remember that your goal is to retain those people that you need and will need during and after the transition to outsourcing, while securing offers of employment from the outsourcer for those employees you don't need. The people you discharge should be the few whom you cannot squeeze into either of the other two categories.

"THERE OUGHTA BE A LAW" AND THERE IS

In all of this employee shuffling, you must consider a number of legal issues as well. For instance, this is not a good time to discover that you don't have employment agreements with your key personnel. What you would prefer not to happen is to have those key people find employment with one of your competitors. Whatever trade secrets you may feel that you possess should not be subject to the vagaries of an agitated employee who fears for his or her job.

Again, this situation is analogous to a layoff or to a plant closing. Whether there are relevant state laws depends upon the state in which your operations are located. At least one state now requires a certain notification period for a plant closing, and some Federal laws may apply as well. A user would do well to seek legal advice to determine if it has any obligations under such a statute.

As part of the transfer of employees to the outsourcer, you will also need to address a transfer of those employees' benefits. There are ERISA and COBRA considerations to do such a transfer. It is worth your while to bargain hard with the outsourcer and attempt to have the outsourcer offer commensurate employment benefits to your workers. Don't forget that there may be also EEOC type issues in such an outsourcing transaction. For instance, often operations departments employ many members of protected groups, so you will need to be very careful that you do not run afoul of various employment laws concerning discrimination. Furthermore, if your shop is unionized, then you have a whole extra layer of concerns.

THE VENDOR'S EMPLOYMENT AGENCY

There are a number of reasons why during negotiations the vendor may resist hiring your people. The first is money. Although sometimes the vendor can take the same equipment and people and provide DP to the user at a lower cost, usually vendors' profits come from getting more work out of fewer people than their customers employed. Moreover, if your employees' functions duplicate the vendor's employees' functions, the vendor's staff could double. Your employees may not fit well with the vendor's staff either. Vendor and user management styles probably differ, if not conflict. Your personnel may be less skilled and less motivated for the vendor's purposes than those already on board. Whatever the reason, reconsider retaining these employees if you think you may want their services to remain available to you.

Any outsourcing vendor making a commitment to offer employment to a prospective customer's staff will want maximum discretion in how it does so. Nevertheless, it will work to your advantage to get certain minimum provisions for the employees who are going to the vendor. Almost all of these areas will be negotiable with the outsourcer. Moreover, if you want to retain your applications people, for example, secure an explicit promise from the vendor to refrain from raiding their ranks.

If you should fail to persuade the vendor to hire your employees, you must either take them home with you or discharge them. A layoff is never an easy task and it is particularly difficult for people who are the victims of the layoff. In addition, the term layoff is a misnomer. These people are not coming back so you should terminate their employment. Nevertheless, the moral issues of fair treatment remain relevant. At least treat people well while letting them go. Try your best to give them good severance packages, assistance in finding a new job, and so on. You'll like yourself better for having tried and you might avoid meeting the ghosts of Christmas past, present, and future on Christmas Eve.

EXISTING EMPLOYEES

CHECKLIST FOR CONTRACT PROVISIONS AND RELATED ISSUES

I. *The vendor may want some of the existing IS employees.*

    A. Assistance in the turnover.

    B. Operational assistance in the continuing relationship.

    C. Impact on user's morale.

    D. Easier to sell outsourcing to user.

II. *The vendor may not want existing employees.*

    A. Cost.

    B. Bad fit.

        1. Conflict between vendor's management style versus user's management style.

        2. Lower skill levels than vendor's personnel.

        3. Less motivated than vendor's personnel.

    C. Morale problems.

        1. Lingering resentment.

        2. Stress of losing one job and starting another.

III. *Post announcement morale problems.*

    A. Poor work performance.

    B. Job anxiety and related fear.

    C. Low self-esteem.

    D. Unhealthy competition fighting over the crumbs.

    E. Betrayal.

    F. Employees' exodus.

    1. May lose most talented employees first.

    2. Potential chaos.

    3. May retain least desirable employees.

IV. Failure to reduce staff vitiates outsourcing advantages.

  A. Disposition of superfluous personnel.

  B. Expense of retaining redundant personnel.

V. Making the cuts.

  A. In general, keep software applications personnel.

  B. In general, send all the operations personnel to the vendor.

  C. Get rid of troublemakers immediately.

VI. Implementing the cuts.

  A. Persuade those you want to retain.

  B. Persuade those you want to trade.

VII. Legal issues.

  A. Bad time to discover you lack employment agreements with key personnel.

  B. Check out layoff and plant closing laws.

  C. Employee benefits issues.

    1. Transfer.

    2. ERISA (Employee Retirement Income Security Act).

    3. COBRA (Consolidated Omnibus Budget Reconciliation Act of 1985).

  D. Discrimination issues.

    1. EEOC (Equal Employment Opportunity Commission).

      a. Race.

　　　　b. Gender.

　　　　c. Age.

　　2. ADA (Americans with Disabilities Act).

E. Union issues if unionized.

F. Tax issues, such as whether the severance pay is really severance pay or a settlement of claims.

G. Having legal disputes with departing employees draws resources from the turnover.

VIII. The moral issues.

A. You are responsible.

B. Instant conversions to free market economics are unkind.

C. Treating discharged IS professionals well is also an investment for when you will again need them or need their friends.

IX. Important connections to other parts of the outsourcing relationship.

A. Turnover issues.

B. Turnback issues.

C. Software development.

D. Software maintenance.

E. Secrecy.

F. Engaging consultants.

CHAPTER 19

EXISTING SOFTWARE LICENSES

CONTRACT PROVISION FOR DISCUSSION:

EXISTING SOFTWARE LICENSES. User acknowledges that obtaining consent for Vendor's use of the User Applications, specified in Exhibit ___, is User's responsibility. User shall employ reasonable efforts to obtain such consent.

A. If there are any fees associated with obtaining such consent, Vendor shall pay such fees up to a maximum of $_____ in the aggregate for all User Applications.

B. Vendor already has permission for User to use the software applications specified in Exhibit ____.

C. For any User Application for which User is unable to obtain consent, Vendor shall provide such application for User at Vendor's sole expense up to a maximum of $_____ in the aggregate for all such applications.

GENERAL DISCUSSION OF EXISTING SOFTWARE LICENSES PROVISIONS:

Unless you plan selective outsourcing using only the vendor's software, you need to use your existing software during your outsourcing relationship. Merely turning your existing software over to the outsourcing vendor is almost certainly illegal as it is a breach of your software license agreement. This chapter will try to keep you out of court.

There are many reasons why you might want to continue using your existing software. Changing to new software is expensive and time-consuming: you will have to pay new license fees, suffer through conversions, obtain training, etc. Certainly, your blood pressure will benefit from using the software you have.

Your company, if a typical user, negotiated the fees in its software licenses thoroughly, but the other license provisions not at all. You ought to read some of those license agreements; you would be surprised at their terms and conditions. Unfortunately, the license agreements are probably even more complicated than they appear as you read them.

THEY'VE GOT YOU CORNERED

In your software licenses, the two most common limitations you will discover are a non-disclosure provision and an internal use limitation. They mean that the agreement forbids you to disclose the software to anyone else and allows you to use the software only to process your own data.

Handing the software to an outsourcing vendor equals disclosing the software. So what? So, somewhere else in your software license there is probably a provision that gives the software licensor the right to spell relief i-n-j-u-n-c-t-i-o-n. The licensor can get a court order to prohibit your further use of the software. If you violate the order, you could go to jail until you cease violating the order. The licensor might be able to get some money damages out of your company as well. Perhaps worst of all, you end up without the use of the software on which your business depends.

Some users think they can get out of the non-disclosure restriction by making the outsourcing vendor the licensee. Occasionally this is possible, when the software license has no restriction on transfer. Unfortunately, though, the outsourcer cannot then disclose the software to you. What you need is for the software vendor to agree that you and the outsourcer can disclose the software to each other.

In addition, a license transfer, even when permitted, does not give the outsourcer the right to process your data when the license agreement also contains an internal use limitation. Under an internal use limitation, your data is not the outsourcing vendor's data. So a license that contains a prohibition on processing someone else's data also prohibits the outsourcer from processing your data without the software licensor's consent.

CHECK OUT THE CHECKLIST

These are but two common license restrictions that you must accommodate in running your software under an outsourcing relationship. There are many other restrictions that are listed in the checklist for this chapter. As unbelievable as it may seem, software licensors do not insert these license restrictions to torment users. The restrictions usually have the dual purpose of making money for the licensor and protecting the licensor's intellectual property. A software licensor that fails to restrict disclosure of its software risks losing its trade secrets. Nevertheless, every time an existing user must approach a software licensor for a concession to an existing software license, the licensor has another opportunity to charge the user a fee.

Outsourcing vendors tend to minimize the significance of dealing with licensors. A vendor may tell you it has never had difficulty with third-party software licenses. Of course, the speaker will be a marketing person. Or a vendor may think that in a "transaction your size," you won't mind another three million dollars or so. Doubtless your comptroller will have a different opinion.

Your current software license agreements raise issues for which there are no good substitutes for legal expertise. People without legal training usually are not in a good position to recognize license problems, or to address them. Even your paralegals may not be of much assistance. Much will depend on the training and experience that your paralegal possesses. Whoever reviews these agreements needs to be able to foresee provisions and phrases as being impediments to the proposed outsourcing relationship, as well as being able to read between the lines in some of the provisions.

FIRST, GET REAL

When you start addressing these problems, keep some practical considerations in mind. First off, determine how much software is involved. Every piece of software you obtained from outside your company will have an associated software license. Tabulating the license agreements will give you an idea of what you confront. If there are many license agreements—and there will be many license agreements if your company has a large IS department—start by making an inventory and making a copy of each agreement. Suggest that your attorney establish a system for reviewing and resolving the problems in each agreement.

Another practical consideration is your time frame constraints. How much time do you have to resolve everything? Coordinate the schedule of the outsourcing negotiations with the quantity of work relating to your software licenses. If there is not enough time to resolve the license issues before your outsourcing deal closes, your contract must accommodate this reality. Your outsourcing contract could state how you expect the unresolved license issues to be resolved, whether by you or by the vendor, and could provide for your fees to the vendor to be reduced by the amount of your unexpected payments to software licensors.

Another critical, threshold issue is financial. You already know the number of software packages and licenses you have, but what is the financial impact of the software involved? Efforts to straighten out your software licenses have associated costs, both to detect the problems in each license agreement and to solve those problems. A prime reason to suffer through this ordeal is to avoid paying a lot of additional fees to the software licensors. Your prospective savings in software-related costs should exceed the costs of resolving the license problems.

Likewise, the prospective savings in software expenses should exceed the cost of acquiring and converting to alternative software.

ALWAYS ASK IF THERE'S A GENERIC

Cost, though, is not the only issue. There are also some threshold technical questions that you need to answer. If there is a technically feasible alternative to the software you propose to use in the outsourcing relationship, you may be better off to acquire the alternative software. This will be especially true if the cost of resolving license problems on the existing software exceeds the cost of the other software. But the alternative software must be technically feasible for your use, and you cannot ignore potential conversion costs.

A closely-related question is whether the alternative software is more desirable from a technical standpoint. Your turnover to the outsourcer's operations may resemble a conversion from one software product to another, including conversion costs. If you could at the same time efficiently and economically replace software with more technically desirable software, your wisest choice could be to pay for the alternative product. For the new software, of course, you will negotiate the license provisions that you need to permit use of the software in your outsourcing relationship and to permit you to move that software to another outsourcer or in-house, someday. In other words, acquiring new software could allow you to do an "end-run" on the current and future licensing problems for your existing software.

DON'T WIND A CLOCK THAT CAN'T TICK

Another issue to examine, just in case, is the term of the existing software license. Not every license agreement is perpetual. Some of them are month-to-month, or annual, or for a term of years. Perhaps the license that you are evaluating is about to expire and you can renegotiate the outsourcing provisions as part of the overall renegotiation. Or perhaps you will soon lose the authority to use the software anyway and need to evaluate what alternatives exist.

You should also consider the type of third party software involved, such as systems software or applications software. Systems software tends to present fewer licensing problems for several reasons. Other than operating system and data base management systems, systems software tends to be generic software with several comparable alternatives. The licensor is more likely to cooperate with you rather than risking your business altogether.

Another reason is that, at least for operating systems, licensors tend to be flexible in arranging for outsourcing. There are issues, of course, but licensors of operating systems have a great deal of experience in outsourcing and are likely to have an established relationship with your prospective outsourcing vendor. This is good news because, unless you run in a UNIX or UNIX-clone environment, you're stuck with the operating system and its licensor. The story in licensing database management systems is improving, but still problematic. If your outsourcing vendor does not have an established relationship with the licensor of your DBMS, then probably someone must spring for a new or supplemental license fee.

Applications software licensors will be the most trouble. Many of these vendors have little—or bad—experience with outsourcing transactions and will approach your transaction very suspiciously.

When researching your applications software, the nature of the application may influence your chances of success in resolving the license problems. Some applications lend themselves to easy replacement. In those instances, if the vendor is not cooperative, you may have a number of economically and technically feasible alternatives. The other side of the coin is that some applications do not lend themselves to easy replacements, particularly if you customized extensively. Also, some applications are more critical to your business than others. If you have a critical application that does not lend itself to easy replacement and the vendor is uncooperative, you will have a real problem on your hands.

HAVE I GOT A MODULE FOR YOU

The outsourcing vendor's intentions with your software are also important. Does the outsourcing vendor intend to use your existing software for the benefit of only your company? Or, does the outsourcer intend to use your software to provide services to its other customers? The answers will substantially affect a software licensor's reaction when you ask to modify your license agreement. Some software vendors are happy to let you use their software with an outsourcer. Those companies view the outsourcer as an agent for you. Those same software vendors may go ballistic if they believe the outsourcer will use their software to service multiple end users. If the outsourcer plans this, the software vendor loses out on each end-user's license fees.

For any software, be it systems or applications, that could pose a problem for use in the outsourcing relationship, see if the outsourcer has a feasible alternative. The outsourcer is very likely to have systems software to bail you out. This is nowhere as likely for applications software, but it will not hurt to ask. Whatever of the vendor's software you can use in place of your current package will eliminate your burden to renegotiate the license for your current software.

SACK-CLOTH AND ASHES OR A DOZEN RED ROSES

You need a strategy for approaching your software licensors. Ideally you would begin this process before you make an irrevocable commitment to outsource. If you are discreet, you can approach software licensors before they know you have committed. However, you probably will have to negotiate with the licensors from a position of relative weakness because they will be fully aware of what is going on. As you negotiate with them, their calculators will be smoking while they estimate the additional fees. Nevertheless, circumstances may force you into the position of resolving license problems with licensors who know that you are outsourcing.

How you respond to the issues already discussed will influence your strategy. With a large number of licensors, the best strategy may be for your attorney to prepare a form to use to modify all of your software license agreements. Send the form with an appropriate cover letter, follow up, and be prepared to duck.

YOU MAY WISH YOU NEVER KNEW

The process of examining the existing license agreements and contacting the software licensors will sometimes stir up a hornets' nest, or at least raise issues that no one ever thought were there in the first place. This entire process may expose several embarrassing situations for you. For instance, your company may discover it has some pirated software on which it has come to depend.

Even more likely will be a revelation that your company is currently using some software in violation of your existing license agreements. A common license breach is using software on an unauthorized computer. Many software licenses restrict use to a central processing unit with a specific serial number. Over time, many companies substitute other CPUs without informing the software licensor or obtaining permission. Use on an unauthorized CPU would be a breach of that license agreement. Another commonly ignored license provision is a location restriction. Use of the software at an unauthorized location is also a breach of such a license agreement. You and your attorneys should endeavor to apprehend these problems before the vendor does.

Try to provide your legal advisors with accurate information, or at least access to people who might know the facts concerning your software. All too often, users continue to use software after the license agreements are no longer in effect, or have been terminated. Furthermore, don't waste your energy on existing licenses for software you've long since abandoned.

There are numerous specific issues and provisions for which your attorney should look in software license agreements. This section's checklist will assist you and your attorney.

EXISTING SOFTWARE LICENSES

CHECKLIST FOR CONTRACT PROVISIONS AND RELATED ISSUES

I. Threshold issues.

- A. Practical considerations.
- B. Financial considerations.
- C. Technical considerations.
- D. License term.
- E. Type of software involved.
- F. If application software, nature of application.
- G. Outsourcing vendor's intentions.
- H. Strategies in approaching the licensors.

II. Specific outsourcing, service bureau, or facilities management provisions in existing licenses.

III. Specific "transfer" provisions.

- A. Express prohibitions against transfers and/or assignments.
- B. Permitted transfers.
- C. Permitted assignments.
- D. Transfers or assignments permitted under certain conditions.

IV. Entity restrictions.

- A. Use is limited to a specific entity.
- B. Possession is limited to a specific entity.
- C. Use and possession are limited to a specific entity.
- D. Use is limited to a single, but not specific, entity.
- E. Access, but not possession, is limited.

V. Location restrictions.

    A. Limited to place of first installation.

    B. Limited to specific street address.

    C. Limited to general business premises.

    D. Limited to licensee's premises.

    E. Limited to one, but not specific, location at a time.

VI. Computer environment restrictions.

    A. Limited to specific, serial-numbered computer.

    B. Limited to a single computer.

    C. Limited to specific model of computer.

    D. Limited to computer owned by licensee.

    E. Limited to a maximum number of computers.

    F. Limited to a maximum number of copies.

VII. Data restrictions.

    A. Limited to processing only licensee's data.

    B. Limited to processing a specific type of data.

VIII. Disclosure restrictions.

    A. Claim or recitation of licensor's trade secrets.

    B. Limited disclosure to licensee's employees on need-to-know basis.

    C. Limited disclosure to licensee's employees.

    D. Limited disclosure to licensee's employees and agents.

    E. Limited disclosure to independent contractors pursuant to licensor's standard non-disclosure agreement.

IX. Software maintenance and support agreements.

A. Licensee's current maintenance and support status.

B. Future maintenance and/or support issues.

C. Outsourcing vendor's intentions concerning future maintenance and support from software vendor.

D. Outsourcing vendor's provision of its own maintenance and support for licensee.

X. Future post-outsourcing issues to consider in amending software license for outsourcing.

A. Reversion to licensee.

B. Ability to transfer to another outsourcing vendor.

C. Licensee's sale, merger, or acquisitions.

XI. Important connections to other parts of the outsourcing relationship.

A. Existing hardware-related agreements.

B. Turnover issues.

C. Turnback issues.

D. Licenses for vendor-provided software.

E. Self-defense issues.

F. Back-up and disaster recovery.

CHAPTER 20

EXISTING HARDWARE-RELATED AGREEMENTS

CONTRACT PROVISIONS FOR DISCUSSION:

ASSIGNMENT OF EXISTING HARDWARE-RELATED AGREEMENTS. Vendor and User hereby agree that the User shall assign to Vendor the leases identified in Exhibit __ for the hardware specified in Exhibit __. Such assignment shall occur upon the Effective Date or as soon thereafter as reasonably practicable. Vendor agrees that as of the Effective Date it shall assume all of the financial responsibility for such hardware leases, and that from the Effective Date on it shall pay such lease fees or negotiate with the appropriate lessors for termination of such leases.

EXISTING HARDWARE MAINTENANCE AGREEMENTS. User agrees to assign to Vendor or to terminate hardware maintenance for the hardware maintenance agreements specified in Exhibit __. As of the Effective Date, Vendor shall assume complete financial responsibility for such hardware maintenance agreements. If the assignments specified in this Section are not accomplished as of the Effective Date and User is obligated to make additional payments after the Effective Date, User may subtract such payments from all or any amounts due to Vendor.

GENERAL DISCUSSION OF EXISTING HARDWARE-RELATED AGREEMENTS PROVISIONS:

Typically, if a user has any existing hardware-related agreements, those agreements pertain to either leased hardware or hardware maintenance. Hardware leases generally have provisions that enable the lessee to terminate prematurely, usually with some type of cancellation penalty. Or the leasing companies readily permit assignment upon demonstrating the creditworthiness of the assignee. Likewise, rarely is there a problem with transferring hardware maintenance agreements to other entities. At a minimum, you or the vendor will have to notify the maintenance provider if you have relocated the hardware.

The practical and economic issues of existing hardware-related agreements usually outweigh legal considerations.

First, draft an inventory of all leased hardware and hardware maintenance agreements. Find someone persistent and detail-oriented. Lease agreements often designate the hardware by specific serial numbers, so that whoever constructs the inventory must find the location of each piece of serial numbered hardware—a task that is much more easily described than accomplished.

Don't be surprised, but the inventory may reveal some very ugly facts. For instance, some of the leased hardware quite likely has been replaced or sold, and no one has bothered to update the leases with the new serial numbers. For the typical lease, this situation would be an automatic breach of the lease's terms and conditions. While lessors want to receive their lease fees more than anything else, they also need to be able to identify their property and the location of their property. In fact, most lease agreements specify that the lessee must inform the lessor when the property is even moved to a new address. Imagine how your friendly car rental company would take to your substituting a different car for the one you rented.

Therefore, before you notify the lessors that you want to assign their leases, have a plan for reconciling the leases' "discrepancies." And get some tranquilizers for your attorneys because they will be very upset, and it wasn't even their hardware.

Once you have the inventory of leased hardware, determine who gets what. Are you transferring all leased hardware to the outsourcer or retaining some? (See Chapter 9 for more information.)

Existing Hardware-Related Agreements

Checklist for contract provisions and related issues

I. Inventory of existing hardware-related agreements including communications equipment.

   A. Purchase.

   B. Lease.

   C. Maintenance.

II. Compare list of agreements to list of existing hardware.

   A. Match agreements with related hardware.

   B. Identify discrepancies.

   C. Resolve discrepancies.

III. Leases.

   A. Review general creditor documents and determine if user has made any general pledges of assets to lenders.

   B. Review provisions for transferability.

   C. Match serial numbers in lease documents to actual hardware.

   D. Match authorized locations in lease documents to actual locations.

   E. Identify discrepancies.

      1. Serial numbers in agreement and on hardware do not match.

      2. Hardware missing.

      3. Hardware in location not authorized by lease.

    4. Payment status of lease payments.

F. Construct strategy to resolve discrepancies.

G. Implement strategy.

H. Determine what hardware user can purchase for nominal sum.

I. Determine which leased hardware user purchases from lessor.

    1. Purchases for a nominal amount.

    2. Purchases for fair market value.

J. Determine which leased hardware user transfers to vendor.

K. Determine which leased hardware user retains under lease.

L. Determine which leased hardware user turns over to lessor.

M. Establish procedure for tracking disposition of leased hardware.

    1. Resolving lease discrepancies.

    2. Updating or canceling lease agreements.

    3. Purchasing leased hardware from lessor.

    4. Transferring leased hardware to vendor.

IV. Maintenance agreements.

A. Review provisions for transferability.

B. Review provisions for termination.

C. Vendor not likely to want to retain the obligations of these agreements.

D. Vendor likely to have its own maintenance arrangements.

E. Allocate between vendor and user responsibility for paying hardware maintenance.

    F. Establish procedure for tracking disposition of user's hardware maintenance agreements.

V. Important connections to other parts of the outsourcing relationship.

    A. Turnover issues.

    B. Turnback issues.

CHAPTER 21

PERFORMANCE STANDARDS

CONTRACT PROVISIONS FOR DISCUSSION:

PERFORMANCE STANDARDS. "Performance Standards" means the measures specified in Exhibit ____.

A. Vendor agrees to provide the Vendor Services in accordance with the Performance Standards.

B. "Defective Performance" means Vendor's failure to perform in accordance with one or more of the Performance Standards.

REMEDIES FOR DEFECTIVE PERFORMANCE. In addition to such other remedies as are available to User, if there is a Defective Performance, User may avail itself of the remedies specified in this Section.

A. Types of Defective Performance are defined as follows:

(1) A "Defect" is any Defective Performance that occurs during a day.

(2) A "Level One Defect" is any Defect that lasts for more than two hours but less than 24 hours.

(3) A "Level Two Defect" is a Defect that lasts for more than 24 hours.

(4) A "Level Three Defect" is a Defect that occurs more than once during any seven-day period.

(5) A "Level Four Defect" is a Level Two Defect that occurs more than once during any thirty-day period.

B. For each Level One Defect, Vendor shall grant User a credit of $_____ against the Vendor fees.

C. For each Level Two Defect, Vendor shall grant User a credit of $_____ against the Vendor fees.

D. For each Level Three Defect, Vendor shall grant User a credit of $_____ against the Vendor fees.

E. For each Level Four Defect, Vendor shall grant User a credit of $_____ against the Vendor fees.

F. If a Level Four Defect occurs more than once in any ninety-day period, User may terminate this Agreement upon prior written notice to Vendor.

CORRECTION OF PROCESSING ERRORS. In addition to such other remedies as may be available to User, Vendor shall, at its own expense, promptly correct errors that occur in processing.

RIGHT TO AUDIT. Vendor agrees that User, at User's expense, may engage an independent accounting firm (the "Auditor") to audit Vendor's records and operations relevant to this Agreement to determine Vendor's compliance with this Agreement. Upon two business day's written notice, the Auditor may enter Vendor's premises and commence such audit. The Auditor shall use its reasonable best efforts to avoid disrupting Vendor's ordinary course of business. User shall pay Vendor for the Auditor's use of the Vendor Services in accordance with the Section entitled "VENDOR FEES."

General discussion of Performance Standards provisions:

At a minimum, your outsourcing agreement will require the vendor both to perform the services described in the description of services and related exhibits and to correct any errors. If that is the only description of the vendor's obligations, however, you will have difficulty complaining about poor performance.

Assume that your description of services states that the vendor will provide daily sales reports. The vendor sends the daily sales reports, but never before 4:45 P.M., and you needed them at 9:00 A.M. Or, of the reports for your ten sales regions, you receive only seven on a regular basis. Conceivably you can remedy the timing merely by alerting the vendor to the problem. Nevertheless, if the vendor balks, you can't say the vendor did not comply with the agreement unless the vendor fails to perform at all.

Perhaps your contract went a step further and stated that the vendor's performance had to be "timely," or "workmanlike," or words to that effect. Phrases such as "timely," "workmanlike," "professionally," "efficiently," or "customarily" are all useful to include in your outsourcing agreement, but their definition lacks precision and allows for subjective standards to apply.

If your company and the outsourcer always agree on what constitutes adequate performance, you will encounter few problems. Usually, though, a user and outsourcer will have very different concepts of satisfactory performance. Therefore, your contract needs performance standards that establish objective criteria by which you can evaluate and manage the outsourcing vendor. Without objective standards you will have many needless arguments—most of which you will lose.

Your standards need to make sense in light of your actual use of the outsourcer's services. For instance, if you have no online activities, a performance standard focused on response time is not very useful. You may find thinking of appropriate performance standards challenging, but do it. Such an inquiry is a vital part of the decision to outsource in the first place. You are forcing yourself to think through what you expect the outsourcer to deliver and what really matters to your company.

To THINE OWN STANDARDS BE TRUE

In addition to the discussion in this chapter, Chapter 7 and Chapter 10 discuss the importance of discovering, documenting, and enforcing your performance standards.

Examining your current IS operations is a good place to research performance standards. You probably already have some kind of internal, in-house performance standards. These performance standards may not be in writing; your department may never have documented them. Nevertheless, your operations people know the expected response time for online operations and the expected delivery time for output, etc.—their phones ring off-the-hook when performance is unacceptable.

Actually, your best source for appropriate performance standards is the prospective users of the outsourcing services, who are the existing users of your major applications. These users are likely to know what levels of outsourcing services will be deficient or excessive for their applications. A CIO usually has insufficient knowledge to develop performance standards for each user department without assistance. Knowing which level of service corresponds to the categories of necessary, desirable and overkill will greatly assist your drafting the performance standards.

The reason to know these necessary levels is straightforward. Any level of service below "necessary" is unsuitable for that user's operations. The "desirable" level of services is that measure of services at which the user department wishes to function. Maybe the current level of service such department receives from your IS department is the "desirable" level. "Overkill" means a service tier for which there is little purpose in the user's department or which fails a cost/benefit analysis. There is no point in having a performance standard requiring delivery of a report to a particular executive at 3 A.M. if that executive is not able to read those reports until 2 in the afternoon.

Occasionally, a vendor will seek to obtain what it calls a "baseline" of your current IS operations' performance. Often the vendor wants this prior to contract negotiations. Before agreeing to any such vendor research, determine if allowing the vendor to proceed will breach any confidentiality agreements to which your company is obligated, and think carefully why you want the vendor to know this information. You should know your IS performance statistics, but why should the vendor? Likely the information the vendor gathers will only be used against you when you want to negotiate higher standards than your old standards.

Fundamentally, your performance standards define your needs to potential vendors and then provide the measuring stick for vendor obedience school. Needs vary enough from company to company that you shouldn't just accept what a vendor volunteers. If you cannot develop performance standards with your internal resources, hire a consultant to do it. It's that important.

OVERVIEW OF SPECIFIC PERFORMANCE STANDARDS

Uptime/downtime

Uptime is the measure of the availability of the vendor's services. The easiest approach to uptime is to view it as encompassing all of the vendor services and not some fraction of those services. The converse of uptime is downtime — the period during which the vendor's services are unavailable. If you have online operations, you may want to divide uptime into uptime for online operations and uptime for other types of operations, such as batch.

Outsourcing agreements often calculate uptime and downtime as a percentage of time within a twenty-four hour period. This calculation can be very misleading because you may not require the uptime during certain times of the day. If you have an online system that runs automated teller machines (ATMs), those automated teller machines need to be available twenty-four hours a day, and your ATM uptime should be based on a twenty-four hour day.

On the other hand, there is little value in insisting that your online applications for human tellers be available twenty-four hours a day if your tellers work only from 9-5 Eastern Time. More importantly, you don't care whether those applications are up outside of the 9-5 window if you don't use them then. So, your calculation of uptime should not include uptime which you won't use. If you fail to exclude this unused uptime, the vendor can claim credit in the uptime calculations for having the system up during a period of time that is useless to you.

Output and delivery

Before online activity became so widespread, this was a relatively easy type of performance standard to construct. Almost every organization received daily printed reports and those reports had to be available—and accurate—for respective levels of management by a certain time each day in order for them to be useful.

As more and more reports have skipped the paper step, the delivery of such reports has become an electronic delivery and not a hard copy delivery. Nevertheless, the same type of standard that applied to paper reports and other types of physical output can apply to electronic reports and other types of electronic output. Say, for example, a sales manager needs the daily totals of sales for the Midwest region available to him or her at 9:15 every weekday morning. Even if the reports are in an electronic format, or are on a screen the manager calls up on a terminal, the performance standard for the delivery of such a report should be that such sales management report is due on or before 9:10 every morning, Monday through Friday.

You may want to include a definition of what delivery means. Does it mean, for instance, that the report must be correct? Must a report be produced, or is it sufficient for accurate information to be available for display?

Response time

In its simplest form, response time is the length of time between when someone at a terminal completes the entry of a transaction and the time when that user receives a response to the transaction initiated. However, once you go beyond that simple working definition, there are many options available in defining response time. For example, is the end of the response determined when the first part of the response comes back to the user, or when the complete response returns? That distinction in definition alone will have a significant impact on the actual measurement of response time. Commonly, when on-line applications perform update transactions, they give an initial response such as "please wait" or "update in progress, stand by," or a similar interim message. Under some definitions of a response, that interim message would count as a response. And the response time calculation would stop the clock at the reception of the interim message. However, at that point in time, the transaction remains incomplete. So, the definition of what constitutes a response for the purpose of response time measurement can make a difference.

Other complicating factors involve the communications lines themselves—those connections between the outsourcer's facilities and your user's terminal. Different communications' line speeds will affect response time. Moreover, if your outsourcer is not the same as the vendor providing the communications circuits, you will have additional response time measurement problems.

This technical reality begs the question of whether you should separate the response time measurement from line speed factors. If you have full-outsourcing, then the outsourcer is providing communications and a full panoply of data processing services. It is reasonable to consider the vendor's services as a closed loop beginning and ending at the user terminal. Therefore, you should not have to distinguish between a response time from the computer system to communications devices and a response time from the computer system to the user's terminal. The round trip in the closed loop is usually a reasonable way of measuring the response time.

Response time is a significant performance standard for a number of reasons. But of all those reasons, the most important one is that response time is the one factor that all users of a computer system experience. Both the CEO inquiring about back orders and someone on the shop floor checking parts in stock will notice how long the computer system takes to respond. Response time is an imperfect, but easy, measure of how well a computer system is performing. Even if your employees cannot define response time, they can all tell whether the computer system is "fast" or "slow" on a given day. People tend to get frustrated with "slow" computer systems. As a general rule non-technical personnel more easily use "fast" computer systems than "slow" ones.

Response time is also important in dealing with customers. At any point where your computer system must accommodate customers, such as taking orders or making computer inquiries on their behalf, customers likely will be even more sensitive to transaction delays than will your employees. It doesn't matter whether such behavior by customers is reasonable or not. People expect computers to operate quickly, and they do not like waiting in line or waiting on hold for a computer transaction to finish. Approach response time from several angles. You may want to have an overall response time for transactions and require that the average response time of all transactions be less than a specified number of seconds. Nevertheless, there are certain transactions, key transactions, for which you will want faster response time than the average response time. For instance, customer inquiry transactions should go extremely fast. In addition to average response time, then, you need maximum, permissible response times for specific transactions or types of transactions.

Frequently you will encounter vendors who wish those average performance standards to apply to less than all transactions. Your vendor might propose a performance standard such as, "No inquiry transaction shall take more than two seconds ninety-eight percent of the time." This type of qualification on a performance standard is not automatically unacceptable. But you must be very careful to understand the consequences of omitting two percent from the standard. Moreover, it would be wise to have another form of standard that has a limiting effect on the omitted two percent of transactions. One way is to provide a maximum amount of time for one hundred percent of the transactions. You might phrase such a standard like this: "All customer account transactions shall have a response time of two seconds or less ninety-eight percent of the time, and no response time for such transactions shall exceed thirty seconds."

Processing priorities

Most computer systems are able to establish a priority sequence for each application or "job." Very likely, your work at the outsourcing vendor will be running on a computer or computers with other customers of the vendor. Using the economies of scale in large expensive computer systems is one way outsourcers make money. Nevertheless, you want a performance standard that specifies what priority level your work will have relative to the vendor's other customers. If you are the vendor's biggest customer, or otherwise have significant negotiating leverage, you ought to request top priority. Conversely, you may not be in a position to obtain elevated priority. At a minimum, though, you want to ensure that your priority is no less than the priority of any other customer.

Resource availability

Your need for the outsourcer to keep certain resources available to you is another performance standard to consider. If you are on IBM mainframe systems, you may want to specify such items as the number of job initiators always dedicated to your company. You may also want to specify that a certain number of communications lines will always be available for data transmission. This could be an uptime performance standard for a communication circuit or the number of circuits that are always to be available for your use. Occasionally circuits that appear to be dedicated to a particular customer are switched to other customers in what are thought to be off-hours for the first customer. You may or may not find that practice acceptable.

Resource capacity

In addition, you may wish to specify that the vendor maintain the capacity of certain resources for your company. Perhaps once a month you need to employ some gigantic quantity of online storage because of the way your business operates. If so, you may want to specify that requirement explicitly in your performance standards.

COMPARE CONTRACT PROVISIONS

Finally, a way to look for holes in your performance standards is to contrast the performance standards with the description of services exhibit. You might want to think of the description of services exhibit as a list of what the outsourcer is supposed to do. Then the performance standards exhibit becomes a description of how well, or with what quality or level of service, the vendor is to perform those services specified in the description of services. As with your description of services provision and related exhibits, the details of actual performance standards are best left to an exhibit.

PERFORMANCE STANDARDS
___
CHECKLIST FOR CONTRACT PROVISIONS AND RELATED ISSUES

I. The need for performance standards.

  A. Subjective standards are useful, but not sufficient.
  B. Criteria to measure vendor's performance.
   1. Objective.
   2. Measurable.
   3. Specific.

II. Standards should measure the performance with which you are concerned.

  A. Minimum acceptable levels.
  B. Desired levels.

C. Overkill.

III. You may have difficulty selecting a single performance standard, so select many.

A. Useful to measure vendor's performance from many viewpoints.
B. Performance needs may change over time so the usefulness of specific performance measures may change over time.

IV. Performance reports.

A. Needed:
1. To compare vendor's performance against the standard.
2. To see if vendor is measuring up.
3. To provide an objective test of vendor's performance.
B. Frequent reporting advisable.
C. User may have existing reports.
D. Vendor may have existing reports.
E. Who should pay for the performance reports?

V. The vendor should suffer consequences if it fails to meet the performance standards.

VI. Investigate existing performance standards, if any.

A. Don't ignore informal standards.
B. Interview user departments.
1. Determine existing performance for department.
2. Determine desired performance for department.
C. Determine relevance to outsourcing environment.

D. Develop outsourcing standards from internal existing standards.

E. Engage consultants' assistance if necessary.

VII. *Possible system performance standards.*

A. Uptime/downtime.

　1. Definition.

　　a. Every system resource is available.

　　b. Certain system resources are available.

　2. How measured.

　　a. Twenty-four hour day.

　　b. Useful periods during day only.

　　c. By shift.

　　d. By software application.

　　e. By communications region.

　　f. Mean time between downtimes.

B. Delivery of output.

　1. Definition of delivery.

　　a. Output reaches destination.

　　b. Output reaches destination without errors.

　2. Hard copy delivery.

　　a. Physical receipt.

　　b. Issues related to intermediary.

　　c. Evidence of delivery.

　3. Electronic delivery.

　　a. Available for review.

　　b. Evidence of delivery.

　　c. EDI issues.

　　d. Network speed.

4. Each type of output may have its own delivery requirements:

    a. Reports.

    b. Negotiable instruments.

    c. Transactions such as wire transfers.

    d. Picking tickets.

    e. Delinquent tax notices.

    f. Parking citations.

C. Response time.

    1. Definition issues.

    2. Communications lines issues.

    3. Measurement issues.

    4. Maximum acceptable response time for a transaction.

    5. Maximum acceptable response time for certain transactions.

    6. Maximum acceptable response time for average of all transactions.

    7. Response time for percentage of all transactions.

D. Processing priority.

    1. Highest priority customer.

    2. Priority equal to or greater than all other customers.

E. Resource capacity.

    1. Direct access storage.

    2. MIPS.

    3. Job initiators.

    4. Servers and work-stations.

    5. Communications lines.

F. Adherence to production schedule.

VIII. Possible standards of personal services.

    A. Productivity.

        1. Lines of code per day.

        2. Adherence to development schedules.

    B. Service.

        1. Ratio of personnel to applications.

        2. Number of user department complaints.

IX. Contractual remedies for defective performance.

    A. Monetary.

        1. No fees due.

        2. Credit for fees paid.

        3. Liquidated damages.

    B. Job re-runs.

    C. Slightly inadequate performance.

    D. Repeated slightly inadequate performance.

    E. Serious non-performance.

    F. Termination of agreement.

X. Important connections to other parts of the outsourcing relationship.

    A. Fees.

    B. Payment of fees.

    C. Credit for inadequate performance.

    D. Escalating pressure on vendor when inadequate performance occurs.

    E. Breach of the agreement.

    F. Termination for breach.

    G. Force majeure.

    H. Dispute resolution.

CHAPTER 22

BACKUP AND DISASTER RECOVERY

CONTRACT PROVISIONS FOR DISCUSSION:

BACKUP. Vendor and User agree that Vendor shall, at a minimum, make copies of the data described in Exhibit __ as frequently as described in such exhibit. Vendor agrees, in addition, to make such backup as is reasonably required to protect User from loss of data, such that in the event that data is lost, User would have to repeat no more than one day's data entry.

DISASTER RECOVERY. Vendor agrees to provide disaster recovery in accordance with Exhibit ___. All of the cost of providing disaster recovery shall be borne by Vendor. Exhibit ___ describes in detail two annual tests no closer than three months to one another by which means User and Vendor can test the feasibility of such disaster recovery plans. Exhibit __ also contains the performance standards applicable to reestablishing the Vendor Services at the recovery site and the performance standards applicable to Vendor's performance at the recovery site.

GENERAL DISCUSSION OF BACKUP AND DISASTER RECOVERY PROVISIONS:

Unless your company is new to computer automation, it already has backup schedules and possibly a disaster recovery plan. If you are familiar with information systems backup needs and recovery issues, you may wish to skip to the next chapter. Just remember that your outsourcing agreement must specify which party is responsible for what. Don't assume the vendor will be responsible for your backups without stating that. Likewise, don't assume that you necessarily need to continue with your current disaster recovery plan. The vendor may already have arrangements at no extra cost to you.

BACKUP BASICS

For the computer portion of an IS function, such as payroll, to work, you need three ingredients: hardware (a computer), software (the programs), and data.

If a user loses any one of these three ingredients, the user will need another means of continuing that IS function. That "other means" is backup. The phrase "making a backup" means copying data or software so that if it becomes either unavailable or unusable (e.g., someone or some machine erases it) the copy can pinch hit for the original.

Loss of data and corruption of data (defects in the data that render it inaccessible or unusable) are occasional problems with computer systems. The cost of reproducing and re-entering the data into the computer system can be exorbitant in both out-of-pocket costs and in the cost of diverting resources from other important tasks. Thus, having a copy of your data on magnetic media so that you can quickly restore what you have lost is an obvious precaution.

The same considerations apply to the software that you use. The main difference between the backup needs of your software and your data is that software changes less frequently than data, and so you will need to backup software less often than you do data. Your data may change every second during a typical business day. On the other hand, your software probably changes once a week or even less frequently. So while you can probably backup your software every time it changes, some data backups will assume that you will have to reenter changes, manually or through a logging function, made since the most recent backup.

Some installations maintain a backup of certain hardware components of their computer systems, but such backup is unusual for a number of reasons. First, most large computer systems possess several of the devices that are most likely to fail, such as disk drives, tape drives, and printers. So the backup hardware is in a sense part of the existing configuration. In addition, most maintenance providers can solve hardware problems within a day. Moreover, the cost of having a backup for some hardware components, such as the CPU, might be prohibitive.

Try to commit your vendor to giving you use of DASD devices separate from any other user's data. Then the data to be backed up can be described more generically, by listing device names or specifying all devices whose names begin with your user code. This is less likely to change or be inaccurate than lists of data set names or other lengthy, detailed lists subject to frequent change. Having storage dedicated to your company may also allow additional security at the device level to further protect against the vendor's other customers accidentally accessing your data.

Disaster recovery dictates

What would you do if your computer were destroyed by a fire, flood, or a plague of locusts? However unlikely, as IS managers have discovered in Centralia, Illinois, South Florida and the World Trade Center—indeed, all over the U.S.—disasters happen. Moreover, there is no substitute for a plan to help cope with a disaster, that is, a disaster recovery plan. You can think of a disaster recovery plan as a backup or alternative for your entire IS function.

The typical disaster recovery plan has a simple framework:

1. Keep data and software backups at locations out of harm's way;

2. Have an alternative computer system, including communications, available; and

3. If a disaster occurs, combine parts 1 and 2.

A useful part of every disaster recovery plan is to have fire drills. That is, have a means of testing the feasibility of the plan without experiencing a real disaster.

The main purpose of backup and disaster recovery plans is to have an alternative means of continuing operations if something happens to disrupt your normal IS processing. Regardless of whether you outsource, you should have a disaster recovery plan. In outsourcing there is one additional basis or source of disruption for which you need to have backup and disaster recovery alternatives. That is, a disruption of the outsourcing relationship itself. You should coordinate your thoughts and solutions on backup and disaster recovery in general with the issues discussed in Chapter 23.

Obviously you need to coordinate your recovery and backup plans with the outsourcing vendor. This is true even when you outsource less than all of your IS function. In fact, the likelihood of confusion is even greater with selective outsourcing than with full-outsourcing, so you and the outsourcer must clearly delineate the responsibilities for backup and disaster recovery.

The outsourcing vendor may have a viable backup and disaster recovery plan. The outsourcer probably has many customers that have demanded such plans. So, it will not be uncommon to find vendors with experience in devising the plans and with established relationships with data storage facilities and hot site providers. Nevertheless, evaluate the vendor's plan carefully. Do not assume that because the vendor is otherwise knowledgeable in IS matters that the vendor has the right plan for your company.

All plans must meet two criteria: They must be able to get your IS department up and running as soon as reasonably required; and they must give your company a means to rapidly commence processing without using the outsourcer to do the work.

BACKUP AND DISASTER RECOVERY

CHECKLIST FOR CONTRACT PROVISIONS AND RELATED ISSUES

I. *Necessity for backup.*

   A. IS operations require:

      1. Hardware.

    2. Software.

    3. Data.

    4. Possibly communications.

B. Hardware.

    1. Malfunctions.

    2. Damage.

    3. Time-consuming repairs.

C. Software and data.

    1. Subject to accidental destruction.

        a. Erasure.

        b. Overlaid by existing software.

        c. Overlaid by new software.

        d. Hardware malfunction.

            (1) Erases or corrupts.

            (2) Inaccessible because of hardware malfunction (e.g., data on malfunctioning hard disk).

    2. Recording media subject to corruption.

        a. Partial erasures.

        b. Accidental alterations.

    3. Vulnerable to deliberate sabotage.

        a. Deliberate destruction.

        b. Deliberate alteration.

        c. By means of:

            (1) Employee's unauthorized use of computer system.

            (2) Outsider's unauthorized use of computer system.

            (3) Computer "virus," "worm," "logic bomb," "back door," "Trojan horse," "time bomb," etc.

(4) Connection to outside networks.

   d. Installation of new software.

4. Without a backup, re-entry of data or software is necessary.

   a. Expensive.

   b. Time-consuming.

II. *Means of backup.*

A. Hardware backup.

1. Hardware vendor's pre-positioning replacement parts in local area.

2. User's purchasing and maintaining inventory of spare parts.

3. User's purchasing extra units to provide backup.

4. Redundant hardware configurations.

   a. Disk shadowing/mirroring.

   b. Redundant processors.

5. Purchasing smaller model of large system.

6. Maintaining a backup system used for software development except when needed in backup.

B. Software backup.

1. Copies on magnetic media.

2. Printed copies of source code.

3. Copies on fast access, permanent media such as CD/ROM are becoming inexpensive.

C. Data backup.

1. Original documents recording data (source documents).

2. Copies on magnetic media.

3. Copies on fast access, permanent media such as CD/ROM.

    a. Source documents scanned in.

    b. Copies of files and data bases on magnetic media.

III. Need for disaster recovery.

A. Information systems facilities are vulnerable to partial and full-destruction.

    1. Fire.

    2. Flood.

    3. Earthquake.

    4. Hurricane.

    5. Tornado.

B. Alternate facilities needed when disaster occurs.

C. Disaster recovery is another way of considering a backup for everything.

    1. All hardware.

    2. All software.

    3. All data.

    4. All communications.

D. Requirement of alternate location for IS facilities.

    1. Disaster recovery requires more than merely making backups.

    2. If backups are at existing IS facility, backups will be subject to same disaster and useless.

    3. Alternate location should be protected against being victim of same disaster.

    4. Outsourcing vendor can usually provide alternative facilities.

    5. Alternate site often known as "hot-site."

E. Disaster recovery tactics.

1. Keep software and data backups at site remote from IS operations.
2. Consider the need for receiving communications services through an alternative local switching center.
   a. Connections to alternate central office.
   b. VSAT alternatives.
   c. Cellular alternatives.
3. Make a disaster recovery plan.
4. Test the plan frequently.
5. Train personnel in using the plan.
6. Seriously consider a secondary disaster recovery plan if primary disaster recovery plan is provided by outsourcing vendor.

IV. Important connections to other parts of the outsourcing relationship.

A. Self-defense provisions.
B. Performance standards.
C. Fees.

CHAPTER 23

SELF-DEFENSE

CONTRACT PROVISIONS FOR DISCUSSION:

OWNERSHIP OF DATA AND REMOVABLE MEDIA. Vendor expressly agrees that all data relating to User's business is the exclusive property of User. Vendor further agrees that all media provided to User or used pursuant to the Section entitled "BACKUP" is the exclusive property of User. Upon User's written request, Vendor shall, within twenty-four hours, provide User with a copy of all such data on the magnetic media of User's choosing. The fee that Vendor may charge for each such copy may not exceed $_____.

CONTINUITY DURING DISPUTE. In the event there is a dispute between User and Vendor, Vendor shall continue to perform the services described in the Section titled "VENDOR SERVICES." If such dispute relates to the payment of fees by User, Vendor may terminate this Agreement and cease to perform services only after six months notice to User.

GENERAL DISCUSSION OF SELF-DEFENSE PROVISIONS:

You ought to consider setting up a perimeter to provide for your company's self-defense. The reason you need some method of self-defense arises out of one of the disadvantages of outsourcing—your dependence on the vendor. In outsourcing, your company may relinquish control of its entire IS function to the outsourcer. Putting a substantial corporate asset under the possession and control of another leaves your company vulnerable. As discussed in Chapter 10, there are both practical and legal considerations in establishing a defense perimeter. The practical considerations will require the most thought and creativity on your part.

From a practical standpoint, you need to structure your relationship with the outsourcer in such a way that you can, if necessary, quickly retake and restart your own IS operations. The specific measures to employ will depend on what is possible, practical, and expedient in light of your relationship to the outsourcer. There is little point in establishing a process where your potential losses from a falling out are less than the costs you may incur through your self-help plan. Your goal should be to establish a means by which you can continue to process and to meet your IS needs even if you have a serious dispute with your vendor.

There are many similarities between a self-defense plan and a disaster recovery plan. In both you predicate your analysis on a scenario in which the outsourcer's facilities are unavailable. Your analysis of each will follow parallel paths. And in thinking through the issues, what solves a problem for one should also solve it for the other. Where self-defense and disaster recovery diverge is that the vendor should be more cooperative in disaster recovery. Should be is the key phrase here—but there are few ironclad guarantees in anything. If a disaster befalls your company and it alone, you'll have the vendor's cooperation. But if the disaster is widespread, like a blizzard, a hurricane, or old man river wanting to see the surrounding countryside, the outsourcer may have to face multiple disaster recoveries. If you don't happen to be the vendor's most important customer, you could find the vendor's recovery efforts for you to be a low priority.

Even if you cannot possibly imagine quitting your vendor except in a fond farewell embrace, your own self-defense plan as a disaster recovery "plan B" could come in handy. Think of the self-defense scenario as a disaster where the vendor's ability to help you continue processing is either non-existent or destroyed by the disaster.

SOME PRACTICAL STRATEGIES

Take sufficient daily, weekly, and monthly backups of software and data such that your company could supply those backups to another facility and commence processing quickly. If you cannot take your own backups, be sure your outsourcing agreement requires the vendor to do so, upon your request, so that you will have this ability to move your processing. For instance, if you have an online system where daily transactions update a customer information database, the database management software often creates a transaction log of each day's transactions. So, if you had to reconstruct a day's work, you could run today's transaction log against your backup of yesterday's database. If you get a copy of the daily tapes for each day of the week and you have a copy of last week's database, you could, in a pinch, recreate an entire week's work and make your database current. You'll need to backup both applications and systems software frequently as well to have a contemporary copy of all the data you'll need.

Whatever you establish as a disaster recovery facility, set it up so that you can transfer operations from the vendor's facility to the recovery facility quickly. If you didn't already know, that is why these facilities are often called hot-sites. Of course, this will do little good if the hot-site is another one of the outsourcer's facilities or otherwise available only through your vendor. So, if the outsourcer provides the primary hot-site, you should consider alternative secondary facilities that are not under the vendor's control. There is no need to be secretive about this. There will clearly be extra expense in having the relationship with the third party hot-site facility, but the money spent on this contingency could well serve to keep your outsourcer in line and provide a genuine secondary disaster recovery facility.

As with all contingency planning, threshold issues include deciding just how long you can survive without DP capabilities, or how long you can take to switch over; and how much work you are willing to redo, or how often you really need to make backups and logs. Reentering a couple of days of orders, for example, may be a cost-effective plan for a catastrophe that could occur but is unlikely.

THE LEGAL CONTEXT OF SELF-DEFENSE

While the practical structure of your self-defense strategy is the most important, you need to place the strategy in a legal context that reinforces the practical business approach. First of all, your agreement with the vendor must have contract provisions that establish your rights to implement your strategy. If you plan to obtain a daily transaction log tape, then you need a contract provision that delineates the outsourcer's duty to provide such tape.

Next, you must have the unequivocal right to your data and the media on which you have stored your data. Your contract should state explicitly that you own your data. Moreover, the contract should leave no doubt that at least one copy of the data's current version is on media that you own. As much as is humanly possible, articulate these rights without ambiguity and qualifications. Otherwise, some judges may not be clear about who owns what. They will then turn to the copyright law, which can create some additional confusion concerning ownership.

Consider for instance an arrangement where the people take your customers' orders work for the outsourcer. The outsourcer collects this data and runs it through an outsourcer-owned data entry application, which in turn feeds that data into another outsourcer application for shipping and receivables. Then imagine sometime in the future striving to clarify the situation for someone who doesn't know better, someone who is unfamiliar with data processing operations—that is, someone like a judge. The judge did not negotiate your agreement with the vendor. Even though you think there is no possible confusion, a judge might not conclude that because you pay the vendor, you own the data. Courts often review transactions where the parties have left significant points unresolved in their contracts. These contractual omissions are often the reason for the lawsuit in the first place.

If you have a dispute with the vendor, how will you convince a court that the data does belong to you? Easy you say, the data pertains to your business. Yet, doesn't the data also pertain to the outsourcer's business? You counter-argue, the customers are your customers and not the outsourcer's customers. True, but why does that mean that you own the data? The outsourcer collects the data, stores it, processes it. Does that make the data yours? If the data is somehow secret or confidential, maybe you have a claim. After several months of litigation you could convince a judge. Except for the fact that you are unemployed and your company is out of business, you won.

Your right to the data isn't enough. Maybe when you threaten to go to court, the outsourcer relents and offers you your one hundred gigabyte database, but in printed form. Even burning the midnight oil won't get the data onto magnetic media quickly enough, though it might set all that paper on fire.

Therefore, avoid situations where you must differentiate data and media. Your outsourcing agreement should specify that the media belongs to you too. Otherwise a court may also have difficulty in distinguishing between ownership of the data and ownership of the media where the data is recorded. You should not rely on a judge to figure out a distinction which as an IS professional is very clear to you. Some judges may be very confused about the idea of data and its being recorded on any media at all. In those situations, a judge could easily become baffled trying to sort out who should get possession when you claim that you own the data, but that you don't own the media.

Expect the vendor to grumble about the cost. Even if you are forced to pay for media, it will be worth the price. If your agreement is clear that you own not only the data but also the media, the outsourcer will be very hard pressed to assert a conflicting claim of ownership.

In establishing your claim of media ownership, however, focus on removable media. In general, you should not try to claim that the fixed media belongs to you, because in that case the outsourcer will have to convey entire DASD devices to you. That would be expensive. Even a reasonable outsourcer understandably would be quite reluctant.

Be careful to avoid undermining your ownership claims by allowing the outsourcer to get any kind of lien on the data and the media, such as a contract provision that allows a vendor security interest in the media. Also, avoid situations where your data is co-mingled with the vendor's other customers' data. You might want your agreement to have an express prohibition against co-mingling data.

Continuity during dispute

In the short term, the most practical out-of-court weapon you'll have against the vendor is to withhold a payment. If you and the vendor are in a dispute, you'll want to withhold some or all of your payments. However, you don't want the vendor to cease processing simply because you've withheld a payment. You should try to avoid contract provisions making the vendor's obligation to continue providing the services contingent upon your continuing to pay everything due. Of course, the vendor can't go without payment forever, nor should you be able to finance your fees by forcing the vendor to extend you credit for free, or by withholding a payment for anything other than a very serious problem. Vendors, as a general rule, do not allow users' pontifications upon the seriousness of a problem to determine whether they get paid.

Nevertheless, you need the ability to withhold payments while simultaneously compelling the outsourcer to continue performing for some period of time. One compromise is to allow the user to withhold payments, but, if it turns out that the withholding was unjustified, to tack some interest on to the payment. Another compromise would be requiring the user to pay some base fee, perhaps enough to cover vendor cost (if there is any way of determining vendor cost), but at the same time allow the user to withhold all other payments, or all payments above the base fee. Another way is structuring payment so the payments are not withheld upon poor performance, but rather that fees are earned only on an adequate performance as defined elsewhere in the agreement. Finally, you can establish an escrow account where the payment goes until the dispute settles.

Self-defense

Checklist for contract provisions and related issues

I. Necessary components for restarting operations if the vendor's facilities are unavailable.

    A. Software.

    B. Hardware.

    C. Communications.

    D. Data.

    E. Personnel.

    F. Duration.

II. Software.

    A. Application software.

        1. Critical applications.

        2. Non-critical applications.

    B. System software.

        1. Operating system release.

        2. Other system software.

            a. Data base management system.

            b. Language compilers.

            c. Other software tools.

        3. System software configuration for alternative hardware.

    C. Legal issues.

        1. Obtaining authority from software vendors.

        2. Insuring the outsourcing agreement permits this activity.

        3. Protective measures available in outsourcing agreement.

III. Hardware.

   A. Mainframe.

   B. Servers.

   C. Potential substitution of smaller but compatible system.

   D. Maintenance.

   E. In-house possibilities.

      1. Establish in-house on little notice.

      2. Keep a small in-house prototype system.

   F. Commercial hot sites.

   G. Hardware manufacturer hot-sites.

   H. Hardware manufacturer expedited delivery of systems.

   I. Usage of another company's facilities.

   J. Acquisition of enterprise with sufficient IS resources.

   K. Temporary use of another outsourcer's services.

IV. Communications.

   A. Circuits.

   B. Hardware.

   C. Software.

   D. Consider wireless/cellular alternatives.

   E. Satellites.

   F. VSAT substitution.

   G. FCC clearances.

   H. Duration.

V. Data.

   A. Identify critical data sets and data bases.

   B. Software and hardware requirements.

    C. Backup schedule.

    D. Backup location.

    E. Audit.

VI. Personnel.

    A. Operations personnel.

        1. Operators.

        2. Managers.

        3. Systems programmers.

    B. Application software.

        1. Maintenance programmers.

        2. Application specialists (systems analysts).

        3. User department personnel.

        4. Data entry personnel.

    C. Temporary personnel.

    D. Permanent hiring requirements.

VII. Alternative supplier of IS resources.

    A. Costs.

    B. Tests.

    C. Frequency of tests.

    D. Lead time.

    E. Bonding requirements.

    F. Standby system loaded with your software.

    G. On-going parallel operations with subset of processing already outsourced.

VIII. Duration.

    A. Temporary facility.

    B. Temporary operation.

    C. Permanent facilities and operations.

    D. Lead time necessary for establishing permanent facilities and operations.

    E. Alternative outsourcing provider.

        1. Lead time necessary to identify.

        2. Lead time necessary for transfer of operations.

    F. Multiple outsourcing providers.

IX. Important connections to other parts of the outsourcing relationship.

    A. Fees.

    B. Turnback.

    C. Backup and disaster recovery.

CHAPTER 24

DISPUTE RESOLUTION

CONTRACT PROVISIONS FOR DISCUSSION:

DISPUTE RESOLUTION AND ESCALATION PROCEDURES. Except for those disputes referred to in the section entitled "IMMEDIATE RELIEF," all disputes between Vendor and User shall adhere to the following procedures prior to the commencement of any arbitration [mediation] pursuant to the provisions entitled "BINDING ARBITRATION" ["NON-BINDING MEDIATION"] or any judicial proceedings.

A. The liaison shall notify the other party's liaison in writing of the occurrence of a dispute and shall establish a mutually convenient time and place to meet in order to discuss such dispute. In any event, such meeting shall occur within 48 hours of the time of the liaison's notice to the other liaison.

B. If the liaisons cannot resolve the dispute to the satisfaction of both parties within 24 hours of their first meeting, then either liaison may give written notice of the inability to resolve such dispute to the Mid-management Designee, designated below, of the other party. The Mid-management Designees of both parties shall meet within 48 hours of such written notice at a mutually convenient time and place.

C. If after 48 hours the Mid-management Designees cannot resolve such dispute to their satisfaction as agreed in writing, then either Mid-management Designee may give written notice of the inability to resolve such dispute to the Designated Executive, designated below, of the other party. Within 72 hours of receipt of such notice, the Designated Executives of both parties shall meet and in good faith attempt to resolve such dispute.

D. If after one week the designated executives have not resolved the dispute to their satisfaction as agreed in writing, then either party may proceed in accordance with its remedies stated elsewhere in this agreement.

E. The Mid-management Designees are

    (1) User Mid-management Designee: _____

    (2) Vendor Mid-management Designee: _____

F. The Designated Executives are

    (1) User Designated Executive: _____

    (2) Vendor Designated Executive: _____

NON-BINDING MEDIATION. If Vendor and User do not agree in writing that they have resolved a dispute, then after expiration of the periods referred to in the Section entitled "DISPUTE RESOLUTION AND ESCALATION PROCEDURES," either User or Vendor may by written notice to the other (a "Mediation Notice") invoke the provisions of this Section.

A. Upon receipt of a Mediation Notice, User and Vendor shall submit to non-binding mediation within ten days.

B. The mediator shall be mutually agreed upon in writing.

C. Each party shall bear its own costs and one-half of the mediator's fees, if any.

D. If Vendor and User cannot agree on a mediator, they shall use the mediator selected by the president of the User's state bar association.

BINDING ARBITRATION. If Vendor and User do not agree in writing that they have resolved a dispute, then after expiration of the periods referred to in the Section entitled "DISPUTE RESOLUTION AND ESCALATION PROCEDURES," either User or Vendor may by written notice to the other (an "Arbitration Notice") invoke the provisions of this Section.

A. All disputes which may arise between the User and Vendor will be finally settled by arbitration held according to the Commercial Arbitration Rules of the American Arbitration Association, to which User and Vendor hereby agree.

B. The arbitration panel shall consist of three arbitrators. Vendor shall select one arbitrator and User shall select one arbitrator. Such arbitrators shall select a third arbitrator.

C. The arbitration proceedings shall take place at User's location. User shall reimburse Vendor for coach class airfare for up to two Vendor representatives. Otherwise User and Vendor shall bear all of their own expenses.

D. The arbitration hearing shall be held within ninety days after receipt of the Arbitration Notice. The arbitrators shall give a written decision within 60 days after the last day of the arbitration hearing.

GENERAL DISCUSSION OF DISPUTE RESOLUTION PROVISIONS:

Every family fights. Likewise in every outsourcing relationship, there are bound to be disputes. Often the outsourcing customer has few choices as to how to handle such disputes.

Whine and whine some more, but unless you are willing to go to court, you may or may not get the vendor's attention that you think you deserve. You can threaten to go to court, but what will you do if the vendor calls your hand? You can actually go to court and see for yourself how slowly the legal system works and how much it really costs to litigate. You can play chicken with the vendor and withhold payment, but the vendor may decide to cease providing services or go to court itself.

TUXEDO ON A T-SHIRT

Therefore, it's a good idea to have some formally informal way of resolving disputes. You want to avoid the situation where you have a devil or deep blue sea kind of choice, where you have to either grin and bear the vendor's conduct or litigate.

Try to structure your agreement to head off disputes in the first place. A well-drafted and carefully negotiated agreement is the best place to start. Such an agreement means that both the vendor and user have evaluated the issues and tried to prepare for them.

The vendor's standard agreement is unlikely to take this approach. Many of the provisions that this book recommends, however, will aid in reaching such an agreement. Having liaisons and having them meet frequently helps to keep problems from festering and escalating. Having performance standards clarifies for both vendor and user the level of performance expected. Having practical and legal self-defense mechanisms are also useful means to avoid disputes.

LET THE PUNISHMENT FIT THE CRIME

A vendor's failure to meet performance standards illustrates the problems you may encounter in fielding disputes. Without an informal dispute resolution process, when the vendor fails to meet the performance standards, you can complain, shut up, or sue. You will not sue for one hour's downtime; only a fool would do so. You might sue if you were down for a day every week, but would you want to litigate if you were down only an hour a week? How about fifteen minutes every day? The continuum of vendor's performance failures ranges from an inconvenience to show-stoppers. You want a range of alternatives to accommodate the continuum of problems you may encounter.

When you and the vendor agree that the vendor has failed to meet a performance standard, your outsourcing agreement can specify a consequence for the vendor. For example, if the outsourcer promised that a CICS region was to be available from 8:00 A.M. to 6:00 P.M., but the region did not come up until noon, your contract could have a formula that gives you a credit. You can be creative in establishing such credits. The following is a list of some possibilities, but is by no means exhaustive:

- Establish a specific dollar amount as a credit.
- Employ a credit calculation that uses a flat percentage of your average daily fees.
- Estimate your lost profits as the amount to be credited.
- Obtain a credit equal to the cost of paying for data entry personnel's overtime to make up the lost time.

You should distinguish between an occasional failure and a repeated failure. Repeated failures should cause greater consequences to the outsourcer and at some point give you the opportunity to terminate your relationship.

FAILING TO DEFINE FAILURE

If you and the vendor disagree about whether it has failed to meet a performance standard, then to some extent your performance standards were inadequate in the first place.

Performance standards should be sufficiently objective that there is little "wiggle" room for the vendor. A failure to meet a performance standard should be easily determined. If you and your vendor disagree, ascertain if you have a genuine difference of opinion or if the vendor is being unreasonable. If you believe the situation is the latter, you might try talking to a higher level of management at the vendor. The contract can provide for such management escalation procedures. A genuine dispute may require more formal procedures.

You can draft performance standards of sufficient scope to anticipate most of the likely disputes you could have with the vendor and to receive a credit for vendor transgressions. Nevertheless, there will be circumstances that you did not anticipate or for which the "credit" approach is inadequate. For such situations, where performance standards and associated resolutions are inapplicable or ineffective, your agreement should have a dispute escalation procedure.

The procedure begins with the liaisons. When they disagree, one of the liaisons pushes the dispute to the next management level of both parties. If people at the next level cannot resolve the dispute, they pass the buck to both companies' top management. If top management cannot resolve the dispute, then more formal measures such as arbitration and litigation may be necessary. Nevertheless, the process of escalating the problem will increase the chances of capturing the vendor's attention and resolving the problem short of litigation. This escalation procedure will not always provide immediate relief. Nor will it work if the vendor plays you for the fool and is not committed to resolving your problem.

Generally, outsourcing agreements provide for arbitration or mediation, but not both. For more on arbitration and mediation see Chapter 10.

DISPUTE RESOLUTION

CHECKLIST FOR CONTRACT PROVISIONS AND RELATED ISSUES

I. Structure your outsourcing agreement to minimize disputes in the first place.

  A. Frequent liaison meetings.

  B. Objective performance standards.

  C. Self-defense mechanisms.

  D. An agreement that reflects what will actually occur.

  E. An agreement that reflects what both parties expect.

II. Structure your outsourcing agreement to provide litigation alternatives.

  A. Payments keyed to satisfactory performance.

  B. Credits for defective performance.

  C. Re-runs at no charge.

D. Informal dispute resolution procedures.

  1. Liaisons.

  2. Vendor and user management contact.

E. Formally informal dispute resolution procedures.

  1. Dispute escalation provisions in outsourcing agreement.

  2. Mediation by professional mediators (non-binding).

  3. Arbitration (binding).

III. Important connections to other parts of the outsourcing relationship.

A. Liaisons.

B. Performance standards.

C. Termination.

D. Fees.

CHAPTER 25

WARRANTIES AND LIMITATIONS OF LIABILITY

CONTRACT PROVISIONS FOR DISCUSSION:

VENDOR'S WARRANTIES. Vendor represents and warrants the following:

A. That Vendor is entitled to enter into this Agreement and that by entering into this Agreement it shall not violate any other Agreement to which Vendor is a party;

B. That Vendor is a corporation, duly organized, validly existing, and in good standing under the laws of the State of _____;

C. That Vendor has performed all necessary corporate action to have the appropriate authority to enter into this Agreement and comply with its provisions;

D. That Vendor's financial condition shall at all times comply with the Section entitled "FINANCIAL COVENANTS."

E. That Vendor shall perform in accordance with the Performance Standards; and

F. That Vendor's employees and agents shall perform their duties in a skillful and workmanlike manner.

USER'S WARRANTIES. User represents and warrants the following:

A. Subject to the Section entitled "THIRD PARTY SOFT-WARE" and the Section entitled "CONSENT OF SECURED CREDITORS," User represents and warrants that by entering into this Agreement, User will not be in default of any obligations pursuant to any other agreements to which User is a party;

B. That User is a corporation, duly organized, validly existing, and in good standing under the laws of the State of _____;

C. That User has performed all necessary corporate action to have the appropriate authority to enter into this Agreement and comply with its provisions.

LIMITATIONS OF LIABILITY. User and Vendor agree that this Agreement is subject to the following disclaimers and limitations of liability:

A. EXCEPT FOR THE EXPRESS WARRANTIES DESCRIBED IN THE SECTIONS ENTITLED "VENDOR WARRANTIES" AND "USER WARRANTIES," NEITHER VENDOR NOR USER MAKES ANY OTHER WARRANTIES, EXPRESS OR IMPLIED, INCLUDING WITHOUT LIMITATION THE IMPLIED WARRANTIES OF MER-CHANTABILITY AND FITNESS FOR A PARTICULAR PURPOSE.

B. In no event shall Vendor or User be liable for any incidental, special, indirect and/or consequential damages, even if Vendor or User was advised of the possibility of such damages.

C. In no event shall a cause of action be asserted by one party against the other party more than two years after such cause of action accrued.

GENERAL DISCUSSION OF WARRANTIES AND LIMITATIONS OF LIABILITY PROVISIONS:

While a technical and detailed explanation of warranties is beyond the scope of this chapter, think of warranties as the guaranties that an outsourcing vendor might give. These are guaranties rather than promises. When a vendor or a user breaches a warranty, the aggrieved party may gain additional remedies in litigation because a warranty rather than an ordinary promise, or covenant, was breached.

You can draft a warranty about anything, but typically warranties apply to the capacity to enter into an agreement; standards of care; and representations concerning performance under the agreement. There are two kinds of warranties, express and implied. Implied warranties are warranties that arise by law in a transaction, even though neither party has agreed to them. Neither party will have orally or in writing stated these implied warranties. An express warranty is an oral or written warranty. The law considers that one party intended to make the warranty. "Express" is the antonym of "implied," and that is why the law labels articulated warranties "express."

Express warranties do not have to be identified as such. A contract can contain them in almost any provision. They may or may not contain the word "warranty" or be in a paragraph identified as the warranty section. Frequently, though, agreements identify warranties in a section entitled "Warranties." In fact, most vendors will insist that a warranty section have a paragraph disclaiming any phrases outside that section that could appear to be warranties. So don't be surprised to see a phrase such as, "Except as specified in this section, this agreement contains no other warranties, express or implied."

The Role of Warranties in an Outsourcing Agreement

Contract warranties are useful and important, but, in the opinion of your author, over-rated in outsourcing agreements.

The attorneys of users and vendors will spend a lot of time arguing about warranties. Yet, most outsourcing vendors are relatively intransigent on the warranty issue. They will use warranty disclaimers and provisions known as "Limitation of Remedies" or "Limitation of Damages" to reduce their exposure, however meager it may be, in whatever warranties to which they agree. The user should try to avoid these provisions or minimize their impact.

Related to these is a limitation of liability, which limits the number of years within which to commence a lawsuit. You have undoubtedly heard of the "Statute of Limitations," at least as related to criminal matters. Actually, most states have several different statutes of limitations. These laws apply to a number of legal circumstances. Putting aside the criminal statutes of limitation, in civil matters two general principles apply: you cannot lengthen your state's statute of limitations, that is expand the time period within which you may file a lawsuit, but you can truncate it. The only question is how short a limitations period will your state permit.

In assembling an outsourcing agreement, the vendor usually fights very hard to disclaim warranties. The user is often left with warranties that, taken as a aggregate, do not provide a great deal of protection to the user and in any event will be useful only if the user and the vendor litigate their dispute. Thus, while neither user nor vendor should ignore warranties, those provisions concerning performance standards and the consequences of failure to meet those performance standards are likely to be of greater practical value than are whatever express warranties you extract from the vendor.

USER WARRANTIES

Vendors often will seek to have users make some warranties. But a user must be very careful in the warranties that it gives. As a general rule, a user should avoid giving any warranties concerning the transfer of existing software currently licensed to the user. The risks concerning the user's existing software licenses should be either entirely the vendor's risk, or clearly allocated between user and outsourcer for every software package. For more information, see Chapter 19.

WARRANTIES AND LIMITATIONS OF LIABILITY

CHECKLIST FOR CONTRACT PROVISIONS AND RELATED ISSUES

I. Vendor warranties to consider.

A. Capacity to enter the agreement.

B. That entering the agreement does not violate any other agreement of vendor.

C. That vendor will perform in accordance with the performance standards.

D. That the vendor will maintain certain promises related to its financial condition.

E. That before running software licensed to you, the vendor will obtain from the software's licensor the necessary authority to use such software.

F. That the vendor personnel will perform in a work-manlike manner and with due care.

G. That if the vendor provides software from third parties, the vendor has the authority to grant you the rights granted in the agreement.

H. That if the vendor licenses you its own software, the vendor has the authority to grant you the rights granted in the agreement.

II. Limitations of liability.

A. Warranty disclaimers.

B. Limitations on remedies or damages.

C. Limitations on litigation.

III. Warranty disclaimers.

A. Usually specific disclaimers.

1. Disclaiming express warranties not identified in the warranty provisions.

2. Disclaiming implied warranties of merchantability and fitness for a particular purpose.

B. Little negotiating room.

C. Consider a disclaimer applying to both vendor and user.

IV. Limitations on damages.

  A. Types of damages.

    1. Direct.

    2. Indirect.

    3. Incidental.

    4. Special.

    5. Consequential.

    6. Lost profits (a type of consequential damage).

  B. Limitations on types of damages.

    1. User should avoid limitations on direct damages.

    2. Very difficult to avoid limitation on other types of damages.

  C. Limitation on damage amounts.

    1. There does not need to be a ceiling on damages, but often there is.

    2. Fixed maximum amounts.

    3. Damages calculated as sum of recent fees paid to vendor (e.g., sum of most recent twelve months fees).

    4. Liquidated damages.

V. Limitations on litigation.

  A. Contract limitations period to replace statute of limitations.

    1. Cannot lengthen time within which to commence litigation.

    2. Can reduce time within which to commence litigation.

      a. Two year limitation common.

      b. Less than two years is of doubtful legality in some states.

          c. Some vendors want a longer period to sue for late payments than the user has to sue for anything else.

   B. Alternative dispute resolution procedures.

      1. Alternatives to litigation.

      2. Escalation of problems as prerequisite to filing lawsuit.

      3. Non-binding mediation.

      4. Binding arbitration.

VI. Important connections to other parts of the outsourcing relationship.

   A. Performance standards.

   B. Dispute resolution.

   C. Mediation.

   D. Arbitration.

   E. Self-defense provisions.

CHAPTER 26

TERMINATION AND EXPIRATION

CONTRACT PROVISIONS FOR DISCUSSION:

TERM. This Agreement shall become effective upon _____ , 19___ (the "Effective Date") and shall remain in effect for _____ years (the "Agreement Term").

EXPIRATION. Upon the end of the Agreement Term, the Vendor and User shall proceed in accordance with the section entitled "PROCEDURES UPON EXPIRATION OR TERMINATION."

RENEWAL. User may renew this Agreement for an additional term of _____ by giving Vendor _____ days notice prior to the end of the then current term.

TERMINATION FOR BREACH. If either party breaches this Agreement and fails to remedy such breach within 30 days after receiving written notice from the non-breaching party, the non-breaching party may terminate this Agreement upon ten days prior written notice. Upon such termination, the parties shall proceed in accordance with the section entitled "PROCEDURES UPON EXPIRATION OR TERMINATION."

TERMINATION FOR CONVENIENCE. User may terminate this Agreement for any reason whatsoever upon 180 days prior written notice and upon payment to Vendor of $_____ times the number of months remaining in the Agreement Term. Upon such termination, Vendor and User shall proceed in accordance with the section entitled "PROCEDURES UPON EXPIRATION OR TERMINATION."

TERMINATION UPON ACQUISITION. If an entity not a party to this agreement acquires a majority of the shares of User, User may terminate this Agreement upon _____ months notice. Upon such termination, Vendor and User shall proceed in accordance with the section entitled "PROCEDURES UPON EXPIRATION OR TERMINATION."

TERMINATION UPON DIVESTITURE. If User sells or exchanges ownership of a subsidiary or assets such that User's use of Vendor Services is reduced by more than _____ percent, User may terminate this Agreement upon _____ months notice. Upon such termination, Vendor and User shall proceed in accordance with the section entitled "PROCEDURES UPON EXPIRATION OR TERMINATION."

CHANGE IN CONTROL. If more than ___ percentage of ownership interest in Vendor changes during the term of this Agreement, then User may terminate this agreement upon __ days written notice to Vendor. Upon such termination, Vendor and User shall proceed in accordance with the section entitled "PROCEDURES UPON EXPIRATION OR TERMINATION."

PROCEDURES UPON EXPIRATION OR TERMINATION. If this Agreement expires or is terminated, then User and Vendor shall proceed in accordance with this section.

A. The date this Agreement expires is the "Expiration Date."

B. If this Agreement is terminated, the date on which termination is effective is the "Termination Date."

C. User either may immediately cease using the Vendor Services or, in the User's sole discretion, User may proceed in accordance with the provisions of the section of this Agreement entitled "TURNBACK."

D. User shall give Vendor express written notice of the election that User chooses in accordance with the following, as relevant:

(1) At least _____ days prior to the expiration of the Agreement Term;

(2) At least _____ days after giving Vendor notice that User may terminate for breach;

(3) Within _____ days after receiving Vendor's notice that Vendor may terminate for breach;

(4) At least _____ months prior to termination pursuant to the Section entitled "TERMINATION FOR CONVENIENCE."

(5) At least _____ months prior to termination pursuant to the Section entitled "TERMINATION UPON ACQUISITION."

(6) At least _____ months prior to termination pursuant to the Section entitled "TERMINATION UPON DIVESTITURE."

GENERAL DISCUSSION OF TERMINATION AND EXPIRATION PROVISIONS:

No outsourcing agreement lasts forever, but many vendors and users negotiate such agreements as though they will. As discussed in Chapter 11, there are many reasons your outsourcing relationship may end, but regardless of the details, it will end in either one of two ways, expiration or termination.

Expiration is the end of the outsourcing term. When the user and vendor initially signed their agreement, the agreement specified that it would remain in effect for some period of years, the agreement's term. Three years, five years, and ten years are common lengths in outsourcing agreements, although there is nothing unusual about other lengths. Non-attorneys need to distinguish the term of the agreement from the agreement's terms. The term is the length of the contract; the terms are the provisions of the contract.

Termination means any way in which your agreement may end other than by expiration of the term. Often termination occurs because one party has breached. Frequently outsourcing agreements will not distinguish between expiration and termination. Such failure is not critically wrong, but can confuse people unnecessarily.

The sample provisions cover several of the reasons you may want to opt-out of an otherwise acceptable agreement. Termination for special circumstances, such as deterioration in the vendor's financial condition, is another potential reason for termination. A vendor's failure to meet specific contractual financial covenants, a vendor's filing for bankruptcy, or some other re-structuring that substantially affects the vendor's financial circumstances all could be a good reason to terminate.

In considering expiration and termination provisions, all outsourcing agreements should also consider the issues of turnback, whether the transfer away from the outsourcing vendor is to the user or to another outsourcing vendor. See Chapter 27 for more detailed information.

Renewal is an issue that often arises in the structuring of an agreement's term. As a general rule, vendors want outsourcing agreements to renew, preferably automatically. The vendor's biggest profits come at the back-end of an outsourcing relationship. If the agreement renews with the same provisions in effect, the renewal will usually benefit the vendor. On the other hand, if the user can renegotiate, the user will gain some leverage.

The best situation for you, the user, is the option, but not the requirement, to renew. In that circumstance, you can keep an outsourcing deal with which you are satisfied, but attempt to renegotiate one with which you are dissatisfied. However, plan to avoid a situation where your only meaningful choice is to renew because you have failed to provide a transition period at the end of your agreement.

Termination and Expiration

Checklist for contract provisions and related issues

I. Expiration.

  A. All outsourcing agreements will end.

  B. You must have a plan for the day after expiration.

II. Termination.

  A. The agreement ends earlier than expected.

  B. Numerous possible reasons.

  1. Vendor or user breach.

  2. User convenience.

  a. Termination without an allegation of fault.

  b. Discretion of user.

  c. User must usually pay vendor an associated fee.

  d. Useful strategy for user.

  (1) Allows peaceable departure from bad relationship.

  (2) Allows peaceable departure when circumstances change.

  3. Acquisition.

  a. Should be an option for user to terminate, not a requirement.

  b. Acquired entity may have sufficient existing IS resources to accommodate user's processing requirements.

  c. Acquired entity may have existing outsourcing agreement.

  d. User may want to include new processing with user's existing processing.

4. Divestiture.

    a. Should be an option for user to terminate, not a requirement.

    b. User should have option for divested entity to remain under existing outsourcing agreement.

    c. Divested entity may have been significant factor in user's original decision to outsource.

    d. Entity acquiring divested entity may have existing outsourcing agreement.

5. Special circumstances.

    a. Substantial change in vendor's financial condition.

    b. Vendor's filing bankruptcy.

    c. Acquisition of vendor.

    d. Divestiture by vendor.

III. Other termination issues.

A. Notice.

1. Number of days in advance.

2. Possibly different number of days for different types of termination.

3. Opportunity to cure.

    a. If relevant.

    b. If possible.

    c. Does "cure" need definition?

4. Means of termination notice.

5. Prerequisite steps such as dispute escalation procedures.

B. Possible need for vendor services beyond termination.

1. Circumstances and conditions.
2. Fees.
   a. No change in fee structure.
   b. Contract mandated change in fee structure.
   c. "List price" fees.
   d. Fees negotiated at the time of termination (bad idea).

C. Necessity for turnback plan.

IV. Important connections to other parts of the outsourcing relationship.

A. Performance standards.
B. Self-defense.
C. Turnback.

CHAPTER 27

TURNBACK

CONTRACT PROVISIONS FOR DISCUSSION:

TURNBACK. If User elects to proceed in accordance with this Section and pursuant to the Section entitled "PROCEDURES UPON EXPIRATION OR TERMINATION," then Vendor, in accordance with this Section, shall continue to provide the Vendor Services and charge the Vendor Fees for up to _____ months after the Termination Date or Expiration Date, as relevant (the "Turnback Period").

A. Vendor may cease providing the Vendor Services after expiration of the Turnback Period.

B. During the Turnback Period, User may terminate the Vendor Services upon thirty days notice.

C. At no additional charge, Vendor shall provide User with the following services in addition to the Vendor Services (the "Turnback Services"):

(1) Vendor shall promptly answer User's inquiries concerning the Vendor Services.

(2) Vendor shall coordinate the orderly transfer of communications to User's facilities as designated in writing by the User.

D. At no additional charge, Vendor shall provide User with the following items (the "Turnback Deliverables"):

(1) A copy of User's data, User's software, User Licensed Software, and Vendor Software, as hereinafter defined:

    a. On magnetic media specified by User; or

    b. Electronically transmitted to User's facilities in accordance with User's written instructions.

(2) A copy of all runtime documentation that Vendor has for the User's software.

(3) A copy of all job control that Vendor has for User's software.

(4) A written description and graphic of the network topology for the client server network used to provide the Vendor Services.

(5) A written inventory of all of User's third-party software and documentation ("User Licensed Software").

(6) A written inventory of all of Vendor's third-party software and documentation used to provide the Vendor Services ("Vendor Licensed Software").

(7) A written inventory of all of Vendor's own software and documentation used to provide the Vendor Services ("Vendor Software").

E. Vendor shall provide the Turnback Deliverables within thirty days after a written request by User, but in any event prior to the expiration of the Turnback Period.

CONTINUING RIGHTS TO USE CERTAIN VENDOR SOFTWARE. Vendor and User hereby agree that upon expiration or termination of this Agreement, User has the option to use the software specified in this Section in accordance with the provisions of this Section.

A. User's option is exercisable upon written notice to the Vendor prior to the Termination Date or Expiration Date.

B. Upon exercising the option, User may use the Vendor Software, and all associated documentation, specified in Exhibit _____.

C. User shall use the Vendor Software in accordance with the license agreement contained in Exhibit _____(the "Vendor License Agreement").

D. Upon receipt of the notice and license fees due Vendor, if any, Vendor shall provide User with a copy of the Vendor Software in source and object code format on magnetic media specified in writing by User.

GENERAL DISCUSSION OF TURNBACK PROVISIONS:

The purpose of a turnback provision is to accommodate the period between the expiration date or termination date of your outsourcing agreement and the time when you have re-started your operations in-house or with another outsourcer.

Chapter 9 and its checklist explore the transition away from outsourcing in detail. The above provision for licensing software supplied by the vendor as part of the turnback from the vendor, however, is a legal matter that merits additional discussion.

The prime motivation for entering into some outsourcing relationships is access to unique software. In such instances, a critical decision for the user is defining its access to that software at the contract's end. Should the user acquire a license for the software that the outsourcing vendor has used to provide the services? Or, should the user be content with taking its application requirements to some other software vendor or some other outsourcer with a competing product? If the latter, the user will be wise not to rely on software that it must abandon once outsourcing is over.

Processing when the outsourcing relationship ends is an obvious issue in selective outsourcing, where you have selected only certain applications for the vendor to provide. Yet it can be a significant factor, even in full-outsourcing, when the time for turnback arrives. You can become just as dependent on a vendor application in a full-outsourcing relationship as you will in selective outsourcing. Perhaps you enter the outsourcing relationship wanting to use only a little software provided by the vendor. Nevertheless, before using any software, you need to evaluate what you will do without it. If you intend to use only vendor utilities that you can easily replace on the open market, you shouldn't have problems. But if those "utilities" are a data base management system or software that grows into a significant application, you may become addicted to using them, and withdrawal will be painful.

There is nothing wrong with dependence on particular software as long as you have permission to use it. If you want to continue using the vendor's software after your outsourcing relationship is over, you will need that permission. Permission to use software is a software license. To avoid negotiating from a position with no leverage, establish the terms and conditions, including license fees, up front. Trying to negotiate a license for the software when the outsourcing relationship is terminating will be too late to get any kind of reasonable deal. The vendor will want you to continue outsourcing and will not want to facilitate your exit.

Don't assume that you must commit upfront to a license with a lump-sum fee. Consider structuring your prospective software license as an option to obtain the license for a fixed fee, rather than obligating yourself to definitely become a licensee. You protect yourself with the option, without being required to pay whatever license fees are then due, or any fee at all if you opt out. Obviously, if the vendor believes that it will get additional money at the back end of its relationship with you, you may be able to negotiate a different price at the front end. If you are relatively certain that you will want to retain the vendor software, but you don't want a lump sum balloon payment lurking, try structuring an installment plan that pays for the software over the length of the outsourcing relationship.

Important also among the rights you need in order to continue using the vendor's software, are the rights to use the vendor's software as a customer of another outsourcing vendor.

This is a sensitive area. An outsourcing vendor whose main product is its specialized software will, of course, be extremely reluctant to grant such rights. In some cases though, and for enough money, it may be willing.

In full-outsourcing relationships, the ability to use vendor software is not the central reason that a user enters into the agreement in the first place. Rather, vendor software is an additional inducement that vendors use to get your outsourcing business. The vendor-supplied software will probably reduce the vendor's and thus a user's costs, since both can avoid some license fees. The outsourcer's experience with its own software often reduces the user's transition trauma in outsourcing for that application. Finally, the software itself may have attractive features and functions that enhance the appeal of the outsourcing vendor's proposal. Whatever reason motivates you to take advantage of the vendor's software, negotiate at the beginning of the relationship for the rights you want when the relationship is over.

Don't limit your concept of vendor software only to software the vendor owns. Include software for which the vendor is an authorized distributor or an outsourcing licensee. The vendor may be an authorized distributor for the exact database management software you require. A wise user will consider obtaining an option to license this software for terms and conditions and fees negotiated before becoming dependent. Negotiation for this third party software probably will require negotiation with the third party.

The negotiation and drafting of a software license is a complicated and involved subject. This chapter's checklist will give you a taste of all the issues involved, but what you really need is an attorney familiar with software licenses.

TURNBACK

CHECKLIST FOR CONTRACT PROVISIONS AND RELATED ISSUES

I. Threshold issues.

    A. Bring outsourced items in-house.

B. Transfer to another outsourcer.

C. Plan for the reasonably likely scenarios.

D. See Chapter 11 checklist.

II. *Turnback triggering events.*

A. Termination for breach.
1. "Major."
2. "Minor."
3. Material breach.
4. Chronic minors.
5. Performance standards violations evolving into breaches.

B. Expiration of agreement.
1. Outsourcing agreements are supposed to end someday.
2. Many of the original players will be long gone.

C. Economic failure of either party.

D. Technological weaning.
1. Can you reduce the amount of the outsourcer's services you need by changing the technology that you require, e.g., moving from a centralized mainframe environment to a distributed environment?
2. Does your outsourcing agreement permit this possibility?

E. Change in control.
1. User.
2. Vendor.

F. Merger/acquisition/divestiture.
1. User.
2. Vendor.

III. Establish legal procedures.

    A. Establish your right to the following:

        1. Your data on magnetic media and the descriptions of the data's layout.

        2. Your software.

        3. The vendor's cooperation.

        4. The vendor's assistance.

        5. The vendor's disclosure of technical information necessary and useful for the transition back.

        6. Licenses for software owned by the outsourcing vendor for which you will have a continuing need.

    B. Breaches.

        1. Minor breaches.

        2. Repeated breaches.

        3. Serious, or material, breaches.

    C. Notice.

        1. Of termination, if applicable.

        2. Of your intent to continue to use the vendor's services.

        3. Of any other relevant provision for which your agreement requires notice.

    D. Opportunity to cure.

    E. Injunctive relief.

    F. Change in control.

    G. Associated fees for the vendor's services.

    H. The repurchase of the things sold to the vendor, such as hardware.

    I. The retransfer of things transferred to the vendor, such as software licenses and software maintenance agreements assigned to the outsourcer.

J. Reduced usage of vendor's services.

IV. Third party agreements—particularly software licenses.

A. Plan ahead.

B. When establishing the relationship with the outsourcer try to provide for turnback.

C. Establish your right to a license for software from a third party, but supplied by the outsourcing vendor, for which you will have a continuing need.

D. See Chapter 19.

V. Need for vendor supplied software after outsourcing relationship ends.

A. Vendor supplied software.

    1. Software owned and provided by vendor.

    2. Third-party software provided by vendor.

B. Dependency developed during the relationship.

C. Transition from selective outsourcing customer to end user of software.

VI. Negotiate for the software before entering into the outsourcing relationship.

A. You have the most leverage before you are obligated to the outsourcing relationship.

B. You will have almost no leverage as the contract ends.

VII. Terms and conditions possibly applicable for software license.

A. Specifications.

B. Deliverables.

    1. Executable code.

  2. Source code.
    a. Delivered.
    b. In escrow.
    c. Released by vendor on specific conditions.
  3. Documentation.
    a. User documentation.
    b. Technical documentation.
C. Granting of license.
  1. Exclusive or non-exclusive.
  2. Transferable or non-transferable.
  3. License term.
    a. Fixed number of years.
    b. Month-to-month.
    c. Perpetual.
  4. Possible usage rights.
    a. Use.
    b. Possess.
    c. Modify.
    d. Copy.
    e. Prepare derivative works.
    f. Incorporate into other software.
  5. Possible usage limitations.
    a. Designated CPU by serial number.
    b. Designated model CPU.
    c. Number of CPUs.
    d. Transfer to another CPU.
        (1) Location.
        (2) CPU model.
        (3) CPU vendor.
        (4) Backup.

  e. Network limitations.

  f. Number of user limitations.

  g. Data limitations.

   (1) User's own data.

   (2) No limitation.

   (3) Outsourcing permitted or prohibited.

   (4) User's subsidiaries' data.

   (5) User's affiliates' data.

  h. Location limitations.

   (1) Specific location where first installed.

   (2) Backup CPU.

   (3) Transfer to new location upon written consent.

D. Software maintenance.

 1. Party responsible for software maintenance.

  a. Outsourcing vendor.

  b. User.

  c. Third party.

 2. Requires access to source code.

 3. Definition of software maintenance.

  a. Telephone support and general hand holding.

  b. Support via modem.

  c. Access to bulletin boards.

  d. Error correction.

  e. Updates.

   (1) Batched error corrections.

   (2) Modifications to accommodate changes to hardware and software environment.

   (3) Small improvements in functions.

f. Enhancements.

    (1) Significant modifications to software to enhance functionality.

    (2) Often not included in software maintenance definition.

    (3) Enhancement may be equivalent of "new release."

g. New products.

    (1) Somehow distinguished from enhancements.

    (2) Usually vendor's discretion.

    (3) Sometimes is a new release of software.

    (4) Often unrelated to functions of existing software but has interface to existing software.

h. Duration of maintenance.

E. Fees.

  1. Categories.

    a. License fees.

    b. Installation fees.

    c. Conversion fees.

    d. Maintenance fees.

    e. Time and materials fees.

    f. CPU transfer fees.

    g. Fees to increase number of users.

  2. Payment of fees.

    a. Usually one-time fees.

      (1) License fees.

      (2) Installation.

      (3) Conversion.

          (4) CPU transfer fees.

          (5) Fees to increase number of users.

      b. Payment according to a payment schedule.

      c. Payment according to milestones achieved.

      d. Payment tied to software acceptance.

      e. Recurring fees.

          (1) Maintenance.

          (2) Occasionally license fees.

      f. Payment upon invoicing.

          (1) Time and materials.

          (2) Installation fees occasionally.

          (3) Conversion fees occasionally.

F. Schedule of events.

    1. Notice of outsourcing relationship's end.

    2. Notice that user is exercising option for software license.

    3. User's acquisition of software and hardware environment to run software.

    4. Installation of software in user's environment.

    5. Conversion.

    6. Testing.

    7. Interim acceptance.

    8. Final acceptance.

    9. Warranty period commences.

    10. Warranty period ends.

    11. Maintenance period commences.

G. Acceptance testing.

    1. Vendor-defined test.

    2. Demonstration to user.

3. User-defined test.

4. Jointly-defined test.

5. Performance in substantial accordance with-specifications.

6. Ad hoc user testing within defined period.

7. Indication of acceptance.

8. Indication of rejection.

9. Procedures for vendor to correct errors and resubmit to user for evaluation.

10. Period within which vendor must cause software to become acceptable.

11. Period within which user must decide to accept with faults or reject altogether.

H. Training.

1. Is training necessary?

2. Operations training.

3. User department training.

4. Fees.

5. Additional training.

6. Training new employees.

7. Location.

8. Methods.

9. Training a user trainer.

I. Software ownership.

1. Title to software.

a. Vendor.

b. User.

c. Third party.

2. Title to modifications.

a. Vendor provided.

(1) Pursuant to maintenance.

    (2) Paid for by user.

  b. User developed.

  c. Intellectual property rights.

    (1) Patent.

    (2) Copyright.

    (3) Trade secrets.

    (4) Marks.

      (a) Trade.

      (b) Service.

      (c) Usage of marks.

 3. Ownership of media upon which software is recorded.

J. Non-disclosure.

 1. Is non-disclosure provision required?

 2. Limitation concerning to whom you may disclose.

  a. Employees.

  b. Consultants.

  c. Customers.

  d. Other third parties.

  e. Need to know basis.

 3. Reproduction of notices.

 4. Restrictions on number and locations of copies.

K. Representations and warranties.

 1. Ownership of software.

 2. Authority to grant the rights granted to user.

 3. Performance of software.

  a. Substantially in accordance with specifications.

  b. Other standards.

(1) Results.

(2) Capacity.

4. Commencement of warranty.

5. Length of warranty.

6. Remedy for breach of warranty.

    a. Repair.

    b. Replace.

    c. Procedures.

        (1) Notice of errors.

        (2) Correction.

7. Are exclusive remedies acceptable?

8. Warranty exclusions.

L. Indemnification for infringement.

1. Scope of basis.

2. Scope of indemnities.

3. Scope of losses.

4. Notification of vendor.

5. Control of defense.

6. Control of settlement.

7. Vendor option to remedy.

    a. Acquire rights from complainant.

    b. Repair.

    c. Replacement.

    d. Pro-rated refund.

VIII. Important connections to other parts of the outsourcing relationship.

A. Existing software licenses.

B. Termination and expiration.

C. Self-defense.

D. Existing hardware-related agreements.

E. Turnover.

F. Fees.

G. Schedules.

H. Growth provisions.

I. Technological developments.

J. Employee considerations.

CHAPTER 28

CHANGE OF CHARACTER AND SUBSTITUTION

CONTRACT PROVISIONS FOR DISCUSSION:

CHANGE OF CHARACTER. No change in character or change in function of the software used by User shall cause User to be charged for any additional fees unless such change substantially affects User's usage of vendor resources in accordance with the section entitled "Fees."

SOFTWARE SUBSTITUTION. Without the prior express written consent of the User, Vendor may not substitute or replace any software used by User, including, without limitation, software provided by User, software provided by Vendor, and software provided by Vendor from third parties.

GENERAL DISCUSSION OF CHANGE OF CHARACTER AND SUBSTITUTION PROVISIONS:

Some vendors will seek to increase the fees payable by a user if the user changes the character of the software that it is using. This is especially true in fixed fee arrangements. In such instances, the vendor generally argues that its cost structure has changed. This argument has some validity even in situations where the fees are based on a usage charge. If the vendor has agreed to provide software maintenance for this software and the user switches the software, then the vendor may incur charges in retraining its maintenance personnel or in actually performing the maintenance.

The problem with this vendor argument is that it is not necessarily the case. The replacement software may actually be less expensive to maintain, particularly after the vendor's maintenance personnel have experienced the requisite training. In agreements that are not fixed fee, and where the vendor does not have to maintain the software, the vendor has no excuse at all for wanting to change the fees.

To some extent, a vendor has the same incentive to change the software that it provides a user, as the user might have to substitute software. That is to reduce costs. You may have problems if you do not want to change your software. Rarely is software identical in function. Any change in software is likely to cause you at least minor problems, if not compel a significant conversion effort as well as retraining your personnel. Even if the substitute software were identical in function, you may be more comfortable with one particular application as opposed to another. You may be more confident in the present software licensor's ability to produce a top quality product and not want to risk a new licensor. Or perhaps the existing software has functions you will use in the future, but that the replacement software lacks.

Software substitution is an issue for the vendor from the additional standpoint of maintaining the computer hardware and software environment within which it runs the User's software. Over time, it is possible that the vendor will encounter good reasons to upgrade its hardware and software. There is nothing unusual about this, of course. However, some of those upgrades may require you to modify your software. This too may be inevitable. On one hand, you can try to prohibit the vendor upgrade, but such prohibition is unreasonable if the vendor is running other outsourcing customers in that same hardware and software environment.

The second issue when the vendor upgrades is who pays for any modifications your software requires because of changes to the operating environment. A reasonable position would seem to be that the vendor cannot make the changes without your prior consent or the vendor pays for all the changes.

The issues of change of character, change in function, and substitution of software are issues that should be addressed in the description of services, particularly in the provisions providing for change and growth in those services.

CHANGE OF CHARACTER AND SUBSTITUTION

CHECKLIST FOR CONTRACT PROVISIONS AND RELATED ISSUES.

I. Change of character.

  A. Can apply to changes in goods or services that the vendor must provide.

  B. Changing the specific software application (e.g., changing payroll application from ABC, Inc. to payroll application from XYZ).

  C. Changing the software application in general (e.g., changing a payroll application to an application that includes employee benefits administration).

  D. Changing the quantity of items subject to the agreement (e.g., adding to the number of sales offices that require daily transmissions).

II. Change of character and related fee structures.

  A. The more the fees are fixed, the stronger the argument that a change should lead to adjusted fees.

  B. A change in character should not necessarily increase fees.

  C. A change in character may lower vendor costs.

  D. The more the fees vary with usage, the weaker the vendor argument for adjusted fees.

III. Software substitution.

  A. Vendor's equivalent to a user's "change in character."

  B. Vendor's motivation usually to lower its costs.

C. User may find substitution objectionable.

    1. Substitute software may perform differently.

    2. Licensor of substitute software may lack reputation for quality.

    3. User may have planned on access to features only in prior software.

D. Vendor substitution is closely related to change in hardware and software operating environment.

    1. Vendor may need to make change for business reasons.

    2. Change may require conversion by user or modifications to user software.

    3. Primary issue is who pays for conversion and modifications required.

    4. If vendor initiates change, it is reasonable for vendor to pay.

    5. Additional issue is whether change causes user to increase its usage of vendor resources.

    6. Additional issue of whether change will necessitate change in usage fee structure.

IV. Important connections to other parts of the outsourcing relationship.

A. Description of services.

B. Additional Services.

C. Fees.

D. Turnback.

CHAPTER 29

ASSET TRANSFERS AND EQUITY INFUSIONS

CONTRACT PROVISIONS FOR DISCUSSION:

VENDOR'S PURCHASE OF CERTAIN ASSETS OF USER. Vendor hereby agrees to purchase from User, and User hereby agrees to sell to Vendor, the assets listed in this Section. Such purchases shall occur subject to the purchase agreements attached hereto as exhibits and described in this Section.

A. The assets that Vendor shall purchase from User are as follows:

1. The land and improvements thereon that consist of User's computer center, identified in Exhibit __;
2. The mainframe computer systems identified in Exhibit __, located in San Francisco, Chicago and Boston.

B. Vendor shall acquire such assets pursuant to the agreements in the following exhibits.

1. The Real Estate Purchase Agreement in Exhibit ___; and
2. The Computer Purchase Agreement in Exhibit __.

EQUITY PURCHASE BY VENDOR. Vendor agrees that within 90 days after the Effective Date, Vendor shall purchase 100,000 shares of Class B Common Stock of User at a price of $12.50 per share pursuant to Exhibit ___: Stock Purchase Agreement.

GENERAL DISCUSSION OF ASSET TRANSFERS AND EQUITY INFUSIONS PROVISIONS:

Many outsourcing transactions involve the transfer of significant assets of the user, such as real estate, buildings, expensive computer equipment, and other similar assets. The agreement between the vendor and user must account for such transfers. Since the transfers can run the continuum from real estate to high tech, this chapter does not attempt to accommodate all the possible transactions that might occur.

Nevertheless, when a particular type of property is the subject matter of a transfer from the user to the vendor, the user should engage someone with expertise in that type of transaction to contribute to the overall drafting and negotiation of the outsourcing agreement. If you intend for the vendor to purchase any real estate, for example, then engage the services of competent real estate counsel. A number of issues in the real estate transaction would need to be evaluated and factored into the outsourcing agreement.

While the range of possible equity infusions is narrower than the range of possible asset transfers, no two equity infusions are likely to be identical. Most often the user will receive cash in return for shares of stock or some similar indicia of ownership or contingent ownership. The specifics such as number of shares, shareholders' rights, and price per share will always vary.

From a negotiating standpoint and for an efficient division of work, the most logical way to deal with these asset transfers and equity infusions is to include the appropriate provisions as exhibits to the overall outsourcing agreement.

ASSET TRANSFERS AND EQUITY INFUSIONS

CHECKLIST FOR CONTRACT PROVISIONS AND RELATED ISSUES

I. Changing the balance sheet.

    A. Asset transfers.

    B. Raising equity.

II. Asset transfers.

A. Assets not yielding income.

B. Transferred for cash.

C. Transferred for relief from payment obligations.

    1. Mortgages.

    2. Real estate leases.

    3. Hardware leases.

D. Real estate.

    1. Buildings owned by user.

    2. Buildings leased by user.

E. Computer equipment.

    1. Mainframes.

    2. Supporting peripherals.

    3. Often purchased for more than fair market value.

III. Raising equity.

A. Cash for stock.

B. Loan.

C. Stock swap.

D. Securities law considerations.

IV. Selected issues in computer equipment purchase.

A. Inventory of all hardware.

B. Identification of hardware to be purchased.

C. Price.

D. Payment.

    1. Cash.

    2. Credit against future fees.

E. Title.

F. Confusion of hardware owned by user and hardware leased by user.

G. Exercise of lease's purchase option.

H. Risk of loss and when the risk passes to the buyer.

I. Encumbrances.

    1. Subject to

        a. Lease.

        b. Purchase money security interest.

        c. Any pledge of user assets.

    2. Release of liens and encumbrances.

J. Outsourcing vendor's assumption of notes payable.

K. Site.

    1. Removal and relocation.

    2. Payment for restoring former site.

L. Warranties.

    1. Title.

    2. Free from liens and encumbrances.

    3. Pass through of any remaining manufacturers' warranties.

M. Warranty disclaimers.

N. Existing hardware maintenance agreements.

O. Schedule to effectuate transfer.

P. Option to repurchase.

Q. Disposition of operating system and other system software licenses.

V. Important connections to other parts of the outsourcing relationship.

A. The decision to outsource.

B. Existing software licenses.

C. Turnover.

D. Turnback.

Chapter 30

Definitions

Contract provisions for discussion:

AGREEMENT DEFINITIONS. The following terms shall have the meaning specified below:

"Effective Date" means _____, 19_____.

"Vendor Services" means the services described in Exhibit __.

TECHNICAL DEFINITIONS. The following terms shall have the meaning specified below unless the context provides otherwise:

"Application" means computer software that performs a specific business function, such as payroll, accounts receivable, word processing, or inventory control.

"Application software" means one or more applications.

"System Software" means a type of software required by all computers and that performs such computer functions as control of printers and terminals, management of a computer's memory, scheduling program execution, and data storage and retrieval.

GENERAL DISCUSSION OF DEFINITIONS PROVISIONS:

Most agreements need a definitions section or exhibit. Even if the agreement defines its terms somewhere else in the agreement's provisions, having a definitions section or exhibit provides a convenient reference. In outsourcing agreements, the parties may find it useful to define technical terms in the definitions section along with other terms. Or, you could draft two definitions sections: one section for technical definitions and one for definitions particular to the specific agreement.

A technical definitions section can be valuable when one party has substantially less computer expertise than does the other. Also, you can include technical definitions just to make sure that both parties are singing from the same hymnal. For instance, the word "system" has several different meanings in computer technology. "System" can mean hardware, it can mean software, it can mean a combination of hardware and software, and it can mean the logical organization of software. If your turnover provisions state, "Vendor shall convert user's existing systems to the vendor's systems," the quotation probably refers to a software conversion, but why not clarify it? Otherwise, you may discover that you and the vendor have different interpretations.

CHAPTER 31

ASSIGNMENT

CONTRACT PROVISION FOR DISCUSSION:

ASSIGNMENT. Vendor may not assign this agreement without User's prior express, written consent. Vendor may not subcontract any of its obligations without User's prior express, written consent.

GENERAL DISCUSSION OF ASSIGNMENT PROVISIONS:

As a general proposition in contract law, contracts are freely assignable, i.e., the rights and obligations of one party may be transferred to another party unless there is a specific restriction against assignment. Also as a general proposition, a user should have no restriction on assignment. This is true because over the course of an outsourcing agreement the user company may be sold, or change its corporate structure. The outsourcing agreement should not serve as an impediment to whatever changes the company needs to make in its corporate structure. Say, for example, the company is a Delaware corporation and it wants to become a Nevada corporation by means of a merger into a Nevada corporation. Each corporation is a separate legal entity. If there is a prohibition on the Delaware corporation's assigning the agreement to the Nevada corporation, then the outsourcer might have some say over the user's corporate reorganization—generally not an area in which the outsourcer should have any say whatsoever.

On the other hand, the user as a general rule, should prohibit the outsourcer from assigning the agreement, or at least from assigning the agreement without the user's consent. An outsourcing agreement is at its heart a service-based agreement. Presumably there are some organizations that provide services, even some that provide outsourcing services, with which the user may not want to do business. Why should a user be forced to do business with any vendor other than the one with which the user signed up? This is true even for a subset of the user's work. The prohibition on assignment should contain an express prohibition against subcontracting any of the user's work without the user's prior express, written consent.

Of course, the vendor is going to make the same arguments about its need for corporate organizational flexibility as does the user. However, the situations are not analogous. The vendor's main concern is whether or not it gets paid. As long as the assignment does not operate to prevent its getting paid, then the vendor should have no complaint. On the other hand, the user is the recipient of the services. All of the qualitative as well as quantitative issues involved in the providing of services are relevant to the user's having selected this particular vendor. The user didn't select vendors A, B, C and D; it selected the one with which it entered into an agreement, and it should be able to keep that vendor or terminate the agreement.

Nevertheless, a prohibition on the vendor's assignment of the agreement will not prevent a new company from taking over the vendor, for example, through the acquisition of a controlling interest in the vendor's stock. If the user does not want to run this risk of having to deal with an unknown purchaser of the outsourcing vendor, then the user will need an additional provision. That is a provision that allows it to terminate upon a change in control. See Chapter 26.

CHAPTER 32

MISCELLANEOUS PROVISIONS

For every agreement, outsourcing or otherwise, you need to consider the provisions contained in this chapter.

GOVERNING LAW.
CONTRACT PROVISION FOR DISCUSSION:

GOVERNING LAW. User and Vendor agree that this Agreement shall be governed by the laws of the state of _____ without regard to the state of _____'s choice of law rules.

GENERAL DISCUSSION OF GOVERNING LAW PROVISION:

As everyone learned in elementary school, the United States consists of fifty states and the District of Columbia. While the following fact may seem crazy to someone who would design a logical and sensible legal system, the fact of the matter is that in the United States there are a minimum of fifty-two separate legal jurisdictions, each with its own laws: the fifty states, Washington, D.C., and the federal government.

Most commercial laws tend to be the same throughout the United States, fortunately for interstate commerce, but there are some significant differences nonetheless. For some areas of the law, there could be fifty-two different answers to the same legal question. In most instances where there is a conflict between federal and state law, the federal law prevails. State and federal laws usually apply to different subjects and so they are generally not in conflict. However, when businesses or people from different states make an agreement, there is always the question of which state's law applies.

If the parties to an agreement fail to specify which state's laws apply and then there is a dispute, determining the appropriate state's law becomes another issue in a lawsuit. The answer is rarely straightforward. You could spend significant time and money trying to convince a judge to see things your way, i.e. to apply whichever state's law is most favorable to you. Determining at the outset which state's law governs a transaction not only can be useful, but could determine the outcome of certain disputes.

Therefore, in an outsourcing agreement, as in any significant agreement, it is in both the user's and the vendor's best interests to select a particular state's law to apply. The main limitation on such selection is that the state must have some connection to the transaction. Either the vendor's state or the user's state is the most likely state's law to apply.

As a general rule, a user is better off selecting the law of the state in which it resides for several reasons. First of all, that is the law with which your top management will be familiar, if they are familiar with any commercial law. Secondly, that is also the law with which your attorneys are most likely to be familiar. Conversely, there may be some legal advantage to the user's selecting the vendor's state as the governing law, if that state has statutes that would apply more favorably to the user.

The vendor has a good argument for choosing its own state's law. Its argument will be that the vendor has to do business in many different places and doing business under several different legal regimes adds to its cost. If the vendor can have all of its agreements covered by its home state's law, then it does not have to confront multiple sets of laws. This vendor argument is more persuasive when the vendor does no business with governmental entities, because the latter almost always insist on the law of their own states.

While the parties may agree on which state's law governs, they must also determine whether or not the governing state's law will apply to issues that lawyers call conflicts of law or choice of law. For instance, if you specify that Kansas law governs the transaction, the Kansas choice of law rules which you have invoked might actually choose the law of a state other than Kansas to govern the actual dispute. This is not a very desirable situation where your goal is to know in advance which state's law applies. Therefore, parties to a contract will often agree to apply a certain state's law, but specify that the state's conflicts of law or choice of law rules will not apply.

CONFIDENTIAL INFORMATION
CONTRACT PROVISION FOR DISCUSSION:

CONFIDENTIAL INFORMATION. Vendor and User expressly agree that all information communicated to Vendor with respect to this agreement and with respect to the services provided by Vendor pursuant to this agreement, including, without limitation, any confidential information obtained by Vendor by reason of its association with User, is confidential. Vendor further agrees that all information, conclusions, reports, designs, plans, project evaluations, data, advice, business plans, customer lists and/or other documents available to Vendor pursuant to this agreement are the confidential and proprietary property of User. Except as otherwise provided by law, Vendor and User agree that all proprietary and confidential information disclosed by the other during performance of this agreement and identified in writing as proprietary or confidential shall be held in confidence and used only in performance of this Agreement. If such information is publicly available, already in the disclosing party's possession or knowledge, or is thereafter rightfully obtained by the disclosing party from sources other than the other party, then there shall be no restriction in its disclosure.

GENERAL DISCUSSION OF CONFIDENTIAL INFORMATION PROVISIONS:

The vendor should keep your secrets. Every company has information that it does not want to disclose to the world or to competitors. Unless your information is what the law recognizes as a "trade secret," an outsourcing vendor has no obligation to keep your secrets unless you put such an obligation in your outsourcing agreement.

The legal definition of a trade secret varies from one state to another. Broadly speaking, a trade secret is information that is not generally known in your trade or business and that gives you an advantage over competitors. Software is often protected as a trade secret. You do not want to gamble with any of your trade secrets or other confidential information. So, make sure the vendor is obligated to keep confidential information confidential.

The main issues to resolve in any confidentiality provision are as follows:

1. How does a party identify its confidential information? Is all information disclosed deemed confidential, or must the party disclosing the information identify the information as confidential? If so, how must the discloser make the identification—in writing, orally, or both?

2. For how long does the non-disclosure obligation last—a set number of years or forever?

3. Are there any circumstances where, even if a party identifies information as confidential, the other party can still disclose it?

4. What if a court or a government agency demands disclosure of the other party's confidential information? Is disclosing the information in compliance with a lawful subpoena a breach of your agreement?

FORCE MAJEURE (IRRESISTIBLE FORCE)
CONTRACT PROVISION FOR DISCUSSION:

FORCE MAJEURE. Neither the Vendor nor the User shall be in default by reason of any failure to perform under this agreement if such failure results, whether directly or indirectly, from fire, explosion, flood, acts of God or of the public enemy, war, civil disturbance, act of any government, dejure or de facto, or agency or official thereof, quarantine, restriction, epidemic or catastrophe (separately and collectively a "Force Majeure Event"). If there is a Force Majeure Event that prevents Vendor from performing a substantial part of its obligations under this agreement and such Force Majeure Event lasts more than 24 hours, then User may terminate this Agreement upon 48 hours prior express, written notice.

GENERAL DISCUSSION OF FORCE MAJEURE PROVISIONS:

Many events outside the control of the vendor or the user may prevent one or both of them from performing their parts of the agreement. The range of events that could prevent performance varies from bankruptcy all the way to hellfire, damnation, and plagues of locusts. Typically these types of events are in the fire, flood, riot, war and other "acts of God" category. In many agreements, whether the agreement has to do with outsourcing or not, there is a Force Majeure provision.

In an outsourcing agreement, a user must scrutinize the Force Majeure provision very carefully. The user's focus should not be to insert a provision to force the vendor to provide services when the vendor has been burned out, but rather to provide for continued receipt of services by the user, even if there is a Force Majeure event that prevents the vendor from performing. The user needs to decide what events are acceptable as a Force Majeure excuse for the vendor's failure to perform and, even if those events are acceptable excuses, how long the user will tolerate the vendor's inability to perform before the user seeks other sources of outsourcing services.

Along with this analysis, a user should consider how the disaster recovery and backup procedures connect to the occurrence of a Force Majeure event. Certain Force Majeure events ought to trigger disaster recovery procedures immediately. Other events of Force Majeure ought to start disaster recovery procedures if they last too long. Moreover, even if disaster recovery processing commences successfully, a user does not want to remain processing at disaster recovery facilities indefinitely. In other words, if the vendor cannot perform, even though it is through no fault of the vendor, and even if there is a disaster recovery facility that can perform for some period of time, how long must the user wait before it seeks other outsourcing providers?

NOTICE
CONTRACT PROVISION FOR DISCUSSION:

NOTICE. All notices and demands required to be given pursuant to this Agreement shall be given to the parties in writing and by certified mail, return receipt requested, at the addresses specified in this Section or to such other addresses as the parties may hereinafter substitute by written notice given in the manner prescribed by this Section.

A. Notice to User.

_____
_____
_____
_____

B. Notice to Vendor.

_____
_____
_____
_____

GENERAL DISCUSSION OF NOTICE PROVISIONS:

While the notice provision of any agreement is fairly standard, you should consider the following issues nevertheless:

1. To whom to give the notice.
2. To whom to give a copy of the notice.
3. When the notice becomes effective, whether upon sending the notice, or upon the receipt of the notice, or upon some fixed time after sending the notice.

4. What forms of transmitting the notice will be acceptable: letter, facsimile, telex, Federal Express, certified mail with return receipt requested, e-mail, in person, or via a courier service.

5. When notice is accomplished through facsimile or telex or in person, whether a confirming letter or telephone call is required to serve as evidence that the first notice was sent.

VENUE
CONTRACT PROVISION FOR DISCUSSION:

VENUE. Vendor and User expressly agree that this Agreement is entered into and performable in _____ County and that all, if any, suits arising under this Agreement shall be brought in courts located in that county or, if in federal court, in the _____ district of _____.

GENERAL DISCUSSION OF VENUE PROVISIONS:

If there is a lawsuit between the vendor and user, the governing law provision will have selected which state's law applies, but such a provision will not select where the lawsuit will occur. Venue is the answer to the question of where the lawsuit will occur. Without the selection of a venue, certain rules will apply. If the vendor and the user are in the same state, then the venue rules of that state will apply and they are beyond the scope of this chapter. On the other hand, if the vendor and user are located in different states and the amount in controversy exceeds $50,000.00, then both the vendor and user may have the right to go to federal court to sue the other.

The venue provision contained in the outsourcing agreement represents the parties' attempts to pick the venue in advance. Venue is a complicated and somewhat uncertain legal issue. Nevertheless, it is worth at least trying to establish the venue if the parties are amenable.

As a general rule, it is cheaper to go to a venue that is in your home town than it is to go all the way across the country to a venue in the vendor's hometown. So, if you have a choice, choose a venue of your hometown. However, you cannot deprive the other party of its right to go to federal court. Those courts may not be located in your hometown or home county, depending upon where you live.

If the vendor and user cannot agree on a venue, then it is better left out of the agreement. In that instance, the general rule is that whoever goes to court first will get to pick the venue.

Other miscellaneous contract provisions:

INTEGRATION OF AGREEMENT. Vendor and User agree that this Agreement and the Exhibits attached hereto embody the entire agreement of Vendor and User in relation to the subject matter herein and that there are no other oral or written agreements or understandings between Vendor and User at the time of the execution of this Agreement.

MODIFICATION OF AGREEMENT. Vendor and User expressly agree that this Agreement cannot be modified except by a writing executed by both Vendor and User.

LEGAL CONSTRUCTION. If one or more of the provisions of this Agreement are for any reason held to be invalid, illegal, or unenforceable in any respect, such invalidity, illegality, or unenforceability shall not affect any other provision of this Agreement; and this Agreement shall be construed as if such invalid, illegal, or unenforceable provisions had never been contained in this Agreement.

WAIVER. Any waiver by Vendor or User of any provision of this Agreement shall not imply a subsequent waiver of that or any other provision. And, further, any waiver must be signed in writing by the party against whom such waiver is to be construed.

BINDING EFFECT. This Agreement shall inure to the benefit of and bind the parties hereto, their successors, and permitted assigns.

AUTHORITY. Vendor and User hereby warrant and represent that their respective signatures set forth below have been, and are on the Effective Date, duly authorized by all necessary and appropriate statutory and/or corporate action to execute this Agreement.

CAPTIONS. All captions contained in this Agreement are for convenience or reference only and are not intended to define or limit the scope of any provision of this Agreement.

EXPENSES FOR ENFORCEMENT. In the event that either party is required to employ an attorney to enforce the provisions of this Agreement or is required to commence legal proceedings to enforce the provisions of this Agreement, then the prevailing party shall be responsible for the payment of the other party's attorneys' fees, including costs, collection agency fees, costs of investigation or any other costs arising out of the litigation of this Agreement.

TAXES. User shall pay sales or use taxes imposed upon the services provided by Vendor pursuant to this Agreement; provided, however, in no event shall User be responsible for any other taxes, including, without limitation, taxes based on Vendor's net income and franchise taxes of Vendor.

MISSPELLINGS. Misspelling of one or more words in this agreement shall not vitiate this Agreement. Such misspelled words shall be read so as to have the meaning apparently intended by the parties.

NO JOINT VENTURE. Vendor and User agree that each are independent contractors under this Agreement. In no event shall this Agreement be construed as creating any partnership, joint venture, agency or other relationship between Vendor and User.

COMPLIANCE WITH LAWS. Vendor expressly agrees that during the term of this Agreement it shall observe and comply with all relevant laws, including, without limitation, federal, state, and local laws, ordinances, orders, decrees, and regulations.

HIRING OF OTHER PARTY'S EMPLOYEES. Except as permitted in the Section entitled "TRANSFER OF EMPLOYEES," neither party may hire the employee of the other party while this Agreement is in effect without the express, written consent of the other party.

PART IV

APPENDICES

WARNING: The sample outsourcing agreement is intended for illustrative purposes only. It is not intended to be used as a form. You should obtain competent legal advice to draft and negotiate any outsourcing contract.

OUTSOURCING AGREEMENT

This agreement (the "Agreement") is made on the 15th day of September, 2003 (the "Effective Date") by and between STICKY WICKET, a Texas corporation, with its principal place of business at 1500 Limitless Boulevard, Dallas, Texas (the "User"), and OUTSOURCERS-R-US, a Delaware corporation, with its principal place of business at 1000 Larchwood Avenue, Cambridge, Massachusetts (the "Vendor").

RECITALS

A. User is in the business of sorghum distillation and owns and operates a data center facility in Tarboro, North Carolina, which has communications links to its headquarters in Dallas, Texas and communications links to its manufacturing facilities in Linden, Tennessee (collectively "User's Current Operations").

B. Vendor is in the computer outsourcing business.

C. User and Vendor intend that User shall transfer all of User's Current Operations to Vendor and that Vendor shall provide to User all of the services provided by User's Current Operations.

NOW THEREFORE, the parties mutually agree as follows:

ARTICLE ONE - SERVICES

1.1 DESCRIPTION OF VENDOR SERVICES. With the exception of the Excluded Services, as hereinafter defined, Vendor agrees to perform the following services (the "Vendor Services"):

A. All the services provided by User's IS department prior to the Effective Date (the "Prior Services") and more specifically defined in Exhibit __, except the services specified in Exhibit __ (the "Excluded Services");

B. All the services specified in Exhibit __ (the "New Services");

C. All services for converting the Prior Services to the Vendor Services and more specifically described in Exhibit __ (the "Turnover Services"); and

D. The services specified in Exhibit __ for converting the Vendor Services to the User's or another vendor's operation (the "Turnback Services").

1.2 OMISSION IN VENDOR SERVICES. If an item of Prior Services is omitted from both the Vendor Services and the Excluded Services, then such omitted item of Prior Services shall be deemed to be included within the scope of Vendor Services.

1.3 GROWTH IN SERVICES. At no additional charge, Vendor shall acquire the necessary hardware and software to perform the Vendor Services irrespective of the volume of User's use of the Vendor Services. Any services that User requires from Vendor because of increases in User's volume that are not specified as Vendor Services shall be performed pursuant to the Section entitled "ADDITIONAL SERVICES."

1.4 ADDITIONAL SERVICES. Vendor shall perform all services requested by User that are not Vendor Services (the "Additional Services") on a time and materials basis at the rates specified in Exhibit ___.

A. User shall not pay Vendor for Additional Services except in accordance with the following:

(1) User requests Additional Services in writing; and

(2) Vendor gives User a written estimate of the total cost of performing the Additional Services (the "Task Estimate"); and

(3) User gives Vendor written authorization to perform the Additional Services.

B. User shall have no liability to pay any fees that exceed the Task Estimate by more than ten percent.

C. Vendor shall maintain time records for all time expended on the Additional Services and provide User with a copy of such records relating to each invoice.

ARTICLE TWO—FEES

2.1 FIXED FEE. For the Vendor Services, User shall pay Vendor a fixed fee of $_____ per month in advance ("Vendor Fees").

2.2 FIXED FEE ADJUSTMENT. User and Vendor agree that the Vendor Fees shall increase if User's transaction count exceeds 100,000 transactions in a given month. In such event, the fixed fee shall increase by $_____ for each transaction more than 100,000 transactions in a month.

ARTICLE THREE—TURNOVER

3.1 TURNOVER TO VENDOR OPERATIONS. User and Vendor agree that User's transition to the use of all the Vendor Services shall proceed in accordance with Exhibit __ (the "Turnover Plan"). The Turnover Plan describes the User's and Vendor's respective obligations as well as the schedule for accomplishing the Turnover Plan. Until the completion of the transition period, Vendor expressly agrees that User shall have no obligation to pay for the Vendor Services consumed by User except in accordance with the section of the Turnover Plan entitled "Phase-in of Fees."

3.2 SCHEDULE OF EVENTS. Vendor and User agree to perform their respective obligations in accordance with Exhibit __ (the "Schedule of Events"). The Schedule of Events can be modified only with the written consent of both parties.

3.3 LIAISONS. Vendor and User hereby agree that the following individuals shall serve as their respective liaisons. The liaisons shall serve as a point of contact by which the parties may communicate on a frequent basis. Either party may change its liaison upon written notice to the other party. User acknowledges that the User Liaison may accept goods and services provided under this agreement and thereby bind User. Vendor expressly agrees that Vendor Liaison may obligate the Vendor in all matters pertaining to this agreement.

A. "Vendor Liaison" means _____.

B. "User Liaison" means _____.

3.4 EXISTING INFORMATION SYSTEMS EMPLOYEES. Exhibit ____ is a list of all of User's information systems employees (the "IS Employees"). Vendor expressly agrees to offer employment to certain IS Employees, in the same job categories as such IS Employees have with User, for a minimum of one year after the Effective Date of this agreement and in accordance with this Section.

A. Vendor agrees that User intends to retain certain IS Employees in User's employ. Such IS Employees (the "Retained Employees") are specified by name or job title in Exhibit __.

B. Vendor also agrees to offer employment to such IS Employees listed or in job categories of people who are listed in Exhibit __ (the "Transferred Employees"). Any IS Employee not identified as a Retained Employee shall be deemed a Transferred Employee.

C. Vendor shall offer the Transferred Employees employment with Vendor at the salary and benefits specified by individual and/or job descriptions in Exhibit ___.

D. Vendor agrees for a period of three years not to solicit or to offer employment as an employee or as an independent contractor to any person or job title designated as a Retained Employee.

E. During the first year (the "Guaranteed Period"), Vendor may terminate a Transferred Employee only for cause.

F. After the Guaranteed Period, Vendor may terminate any Transferred Employee upon two weeks notice; provided, however, Vendor shall make reasonable efforts to assist a Transferred Employee in finding another job.

3.5 EXISTING SOFTWARE LICENSES. User acknowledges that obtaining consent for Vendor's use of the User Applications as such are defined in Exhibit ___, is User's responsibility. User shall employ reasonable efforts to obtain such consent.

A. If there are any fees associated with obtaining such consent, Vendor shall pay such fees up to a maximum of $_____ in the aggregate for all User Applications.

B. Vendor already has permission for User to use the software applications specified in Exhibit ____.

C. For any User Application for which User is unable to obtain consent, Vendor shall provide such application for User at Vendor's sole expense up to a maximum of $_____ in the aggregate for all such applications.

3.6 ASSIGNMENT OF EXISTING HARDWARE-RELATED AGREE-MENTS. Vendor and User hereby agree that the User shall assign to Vendor the leases identified in Exhibit __ for the hardware specified in Exhibit __. Such assignment shall occur upon the Effective Date or as soon thereafter as reasonably practicable. Vendor agrees that as of the Effective Date it shall assume all of the financial responsibility for such hardware leases and that from the Effective Date on it shall pay such lease fees or negotiate with the appropriate lessors for termination of such leases.

3.7 EXISTING HARDWARE MAINTENANCE AGREEMENTS. User agrees to assign to Vendor or terminate hardware maintenance for the hardware maintenance agreements specified in Exhibit __. As of the Effective Date, Vendor shall assume complete financial responsibility for such hardware maintenance agreements. If the assignments specified in this Section are not accomplished as of the Effective Date and User is obligated to make additional payments after the Effective Date, User may subtract such payments from all or any amounts due to Vendor.

3.8 VENDOR'S PURCHASE OF CERTAIN ASSETS OF USER. Vendor hereby agrees to purchase from User, and User hereby agrees to sell to Vendor the assets listed in this Section. Such purchases shall occur subject to the purchase agreements attached hereto as exhibits and described in this Section.

A. The assets that Vendor shall purchase from User are as follows:

1. The land and improvements thereon that consist of User's data center in Tarboro, North Carolina;

2. The mainframe computer systems located in Dallas, Texas and Tarboro, North Carolina.

B. Vendor shall acquire such assets pursuant to the agreements in the following exhibits.

1. Real Estate Purchase Agreement in Exhibit ___; and

2. Computer Purchase Agreement in Exhibit ____.

ARTICLE FOUR - PERFORMANCE STANDARDS

4.1 PERFORMANCE STANDARDS. "Performance Standards" means the measures specified in Exhibit ____.

A. Vendor agrees to provide the Vendor Services in accordance with the Performance Standards.

B. "Defective Performance" means Vendor's failure to perform in accordance with one or more of the Performance Standards.

4.2 REMEDIES FOR DEFECTIVE PERFORMANCE. In addition to such other remedies as are available to User, if there is a

Defective Performance, User may avail itself of the remedies specified in this Section.

  A. Types of Defective Performance are defined as follows:

  (1) A "Defect" is any Defective Performance that occurs during a day.

  (2) A "Level One Defect" is any Defect that lasts for more than two hours but less than 24 hours.

  (3) A "Level Two Defect" is a Defect that lasts for more than 24 hours.

  (4) A "Level Three Defect" is a Defect that occurs more than once during any seven-day period.

  (5) A "Level Four Defect" is a Level Two Defect that occurs more than once during any thirty-day period.

B. For each Level One Defect, Vendor shall grant User a credit of $_____ against the Vendor Fees.

C. For each Level Two Defect, Vendor shall grant User a credit of $_____ against the Vendor Fees.

D. For each Level Three Defect, Vendor shall grant User a credit of $_____ against the Vendor Fees.

E. For each Level Four Defect, Vendor shall grant User a credit of $_____ against the Vendor Fees.

F. If a Level Four Defect occurs more than once in any ninety-day period, User may terminate this Agreement upon prior written notice to Vendor.

4.3 PRODUCTION SCHEDULE. Vendor shall perform User's daily, weekly, and monthly production processing in accordance with Exhibit __ (the "Production Schedule"). User may modify the Production Schedule upon thirty days written notice.

4.4 RESOURCE SCHEDULE. Vendor agrees to provide the resources and facilities described in Exhibit ___ (the "Resource

Schedule") at the times specified in the Resource Schedule. The Resource Schedule can be modified only with the written consent of both parties.

4.5 OWNERSHIP OF DATA AND REMOVABLE MEDIA. Vendor expressly agrees that all data relating to User's business is the exclusive property of User. Vendor further agrees that all media provided to User or used for backup pursuant to the Section entitled "DESCRIPTION OF VENDOR SERVICES" is the exclusive property of User. Upon User's written request, Vendor shall, within twenty four hours, provide User with a copy of all such data on the magnetic media of User's choosing. The fee that Vendor may charge for each such copy may not exceed $_____.

4.6 CONTINUITY DURING DISPUTE. In the event there is a dispute between User and Vendor, Vendor shall continue to perform the services described in the Section titled "DESCRIPTION OF VENDOR SERVICES." If such dispute relates to the payment of fees by User, Vendor may terminate this Agreement and cease to perform services only after six months notice to User.

4.7 CORRECTION OF PROCESSING ERRORS. In addition to such other remedies as may be available to User, Vendor shall, at its own expense, promptly correct errors that occur in processing.

4.8 RIGHT TO AUDIT. Vendor agrees that User, at User's expense, may engage an independent accounting firm (the "Auditor") to audit Vendor's records and operations relevant to this Agreement to determine Vendor's compliance with this Agreement. Upon three day's written notice, the Auditor may enter Vendor's premises and commence such audit. The Auditor shall use its reasonable best efforts to avoid disrupting Vendor's ordinary course of business. User shall pay Vendor for the Auditor's use of the Vendor Services in accordance with the Section entitled "ADDITIONAL SERVICES."

ARTICLE FIVE–DISPUTES

5.1 DISPUTE RESOLUTION AND ESCALATION PROCEDURES. All disputes between Vendor and User shall adhere to the following procedures prior to the commencement of any mediation pursuant to the provision entitled "NON-BINDING MEDIATION" or any judicial proceedings.

A. The Liaison shall notify the other party's Liaison in writing of the occurrence of a dispute and shall establish a mutually convenient time and place to meet in order to discuss such dispute. In any event, such meeting shall occur within 48 hours of the time of the Liaison's notice to the other Liaison.

B. If the Liaisons cannot resolve the dispute to the satisfaction of both parties within 24 hours of their first meeting, then either Liaison may give written notice of the inability to resolve such dispute to the Mid-management Designee, designated below, of the other party. The Mid-management Designees of both parties shall meet within 48 hours of such written notice at a mutually convenient time and place.

C. If after 48 hours the Mid-management Designees cannot resolve such dispute to their satisfaction as agreed in writing, then either Mid-management Designee may give written notice of the inability to resolve such dispute to the Designated Executive, as designated below, of the other party. Within 72 hours of receipt of such notice, the Designated Executives of both parties shall meet and in good faith attempt to resolve such dispute.

D. If after one week the Designated Executives have not resolved the dispute to their satisfaction as agreed in writing, then either party may proceed in accordance with its remedies stated elsewhere in this agreement.

E. The Mid-management Designees are

(1) User Mid-management Designee:_____

(2) Vendor Mid-management Designee: _____

F. The Designated Executives are

    (1) User Designated Executive: _____

    (2) Vendor Designated Executive:_____

5.2 NON-BINDING MEDIATION. If Vendor and User do not agree in writing that they have resolved a dispute, then after expiration of the periods referred to in the Section entitled "DISPUTE RESOLUTION AND ESCALATION PROCEDURES," either User or Vendor may by written notice to the other (a "Mediation Notice") invoke the provisions of this Section.

> A. Upon receipt of a Mediation Notice, User and Vendor shall submit to non-binding mediation within ten days.
>
> B. The mediator shall be mutually agreed upon in writing.
>
> C. Each party shall bear its own costs and one-half of the mediator's fees, if any.
>
> D. If Vendor and User cannot agree on a mediator, they shall use the mediator selected by the president of the User's state bar association.

ARTICLE SIX–WARRANTIES AND LIMITATIONS OF LIABILITY

6.1 VENDOR'S WARRANTIES. Vendor represents and warrants the following:

> A. That Vendor is entitled to enter into this Agreement and that by entering into this agreement it shall not violate any other Agreement to which Vendor is a party;
>
> B. That Vendor is a corporation, duly organized, validly existing, and in good standing under the laws of the State of Delaware;
>
> C. That Vendor has performed all necessary corporate action to have the appropriate authority to enter into this Agreement and comply with its provisions;

D.That Vendor shall perform in accordance with the Performance Standards; and

E. That Vendor's employees and agents shall perform their duties in a skillful and workmanlike manner.

6.2 USER'S WARRANTIES. User represents and warrants the following:

A. That by entering into this Agreement, User will not be in default of any obligations pursuant to any other agreements to which User is a party;

B. That User is a corporation, duly organized, validly existing, and in good standing under the laws of the State of Texas;

C. That User has performed all necessary corporate action to have the appropriate authority to enter into this Agreement and comply with its provisions.

6.3 LIMITATION OF LIABILITY. User and Vendor agree that this Agreement is subject to the following disclaimers and limitations of liability.

A. Except for the express warranties described in the sections entitled "VENDOR'S WARRANTIES" and "USER'S WARRANTIES," neither Vendor nor User makes any other warranties, express or implied, including without limitation the implied warranties of merchantability and fitness for a particular purpose.

B. In no event shall Vendor or User be liable for any incidental, special, indirect and/or consequential damages, even if Vendor or User was advised of the possibility of such damages.

C. In no event shall a cause of action be asserted by one party against the other party more than two years after such cause of action accrued.

ARTICLE SEVEN–TERM AND TERMINATION

7.1 TERM. This Agreement is effective upon the Effective Date and shall remain in effect for 100 years (the "Agreement Term").

7.2 EXPIRATION. Upon the end of the Agreement Term, the Vendor and User shall proceed in accordance with the section entitled "PROCEDURES UPON EXPIRATION OR TERMINA-TION."

7.3 RENEWAL. User may renew this Agreement for an additional term of 10 YEARS by giving Vendor 180 days notice prior to the end of the then current term.

7.4 TERMINATION FOR BREACH. If either party breaches this Agreement and fails to remedy such breach within 30 days after receiving written notice from the non-breaching party, the non-breaching party may terminate this Agreement upon ten days prior written notice. Upon such termination, the parties shall proceed in accordance with the section entitled "PROCE-DURES UPON EXPIRATION OR TERMINATION."

7.5 TERMINATION FOR CONVENIENCE. User may terminate this agreement for any reason whatsoever upon 180 days prior written notice and upon payment to Vendor of $_____$ times the number of months remaining in the Agreement Term. Upon such termination, Vendor and User shall proceed in accordance with the section entitled "PROCEDURES UPON EXPIRATION OR TERMINATION."

7.6 TERMINATION UPON ACQUISITION. If an entity not a party to this Agreement acquires a majority of the shares of User, User may terminate this Agreement upon six months notice. Upon such termination, Vendor and User shall proceed in accordance with the section entitled "PROCEDURES UPON EXPIRATION OR TERMINATION."

7.7 TERMINATION UPON DIVESTITURE. If User sells or exchanges ownership of a subsidiary or assets such that User's use of Vendor Services is reduced by more than twenty percent, User may terminate this Agreement upon three months notice. Upon such termination, Vendor and User shall proceed in accordance with the section entitled "PROCEDURES UPON EXPIRATION OR TERMINATION."

7.8 CHANGE IN CONTROL. If more than thirty percent of the ownership interest in Vendor changes during the term of this Agreement, then User may terminate this agreement upon thirty days written notice to Vendor. Upon such termination, Vendor and User shall proceed in accordance with the section entitled "PROCEDURES UPON EXPIRATION OR TERMINA-TION."

7.9 PROCEDURES UPON EXPIRATION OR TERMINATION. If this Agreement expires or is terminated, then User and Vendor shall proceed in accordance with this Section.

A. The date this Agreement expires is the "Expiration Date."

B. If this Agreement is terminated, the date on which termination is effective is the "Termination Date."

C. User either may immediately cease using the Vendor Services or, in the User's sole discretion, User may proceed in accordance with the provisions of the section of this Agreement entitled "TURNBACK."

D. User shall give Vendor express written notice of the election that user chooses in accordance with the following, as relevant:

(1) At least ___ days prior to the expiration of the Agreement Term;

(2) At least _____ days after giving Vendor notice that User may terminate for breach;

(3) Within ___ days after receiving Vendor's notice that Vendor may terminate for breach;

(4) At least ___ months prior to termination pursuant to the Section entitled "TERMINATION FOR CONVENIENCE."

(5) At least ___ months prior to termination pursuant to the Section entitled "TERMINATION UPON ACQUISITION."

(6) At least ___ months prior to termination pursuant to the Section entitled "TERMINATION UPON DIVESTITURE."

7.10 TURNBACK. If User elects to proceed in accordance with this Section and pursuant to the section entitled "PROCEDURES UPON EXPIRATION OR TERMINATION," then Vendor, in accordance with this Section, shall continue to provide the Vendor Services and charge the Vendor Fees for up to _____ months after the Termination Date or Expiration Date, as relevant (the "Turnback Period").

A. Vendor may cease providing the Vendor Services after expiration of the Turnback Period.

B. During the Turnback Period, User may terminate the Vendor Services upon thirty days notice.

C. At no additional charge, Vendor shall provide User with the following services in addition to the Vendor Services (the "Turnback Services"):

(1) Vendor shall promptly answer User's inquiries concerning the Vendor Services.

(2) Vendor shall coordinate the orderly transfer of communications to User's facilities as designated in writing by the User.

D. At no additional charge, Vendor shall provide User with the following items (the "Turnback Deliverables"):

(1) A copy of User's data and User's software:

a. On magnetic media specified by User; or

b. Electronically transmitted to User's facilities in accordance with User's written instructions.

(2) A copy of all runtime documentation that Vendor has for the User's software.

(3) A copy of all job control that Vendor has for User's software.

(4) A written description and graphic of the network topology for the client server network used to provide the Vendor Services.

(5) A written inventory and copies of all of User's third-party software and documentation ("User Licensed Software").

(6) A written inventory of all of Vendor's third-party software and documentation used to provide the Vendor Services ("Vendor Licensed Software").

(7) A written inventory of all of Vendor's own software and documentation used to provide the Vendor Services ("Vendor Software").

E. Vendor shall provide the Turnback Deliverables within thirty days after a written request by User, but in any event prior to the expiration of the Turnback Period.

7.11 CONTINUING RIGHTS TO USE CERTAIN VENDOR SOFTWARE. Vendor and User hereby agree that upon expiration or termination of this Agreement, User has the option to use the software specified in this Section in accordance with the provisions of this Section.

A. User's option is exercisable upon written notice to the Vendor prior to the Termination Date or Expiration Date.

B. Upon exercising the option, User may use the Vendor Software, and all associated documentation, specified in Exhibit _____.

C. User shall use the Vendor Software in accordance with the license agreement contained in Exhibit _____ (the "Vendor License Agreement").

D. Upon receipt of the notice and license fees due Vendor, if any, Vendor shall provide User with a copy of the Vendor Software in source and object code format on the magnetic media specified in writing by User.

ARTICLE EIGHT–MISCELLANEOUS

8.1 ASSIGNMENT. Vendor may not assign this Agreement without User's prior express written consent. Vendor may not subcontract any of its obligations without User's prior express written consent.

8.2 GOVERNING LAW. User and Vendor agree that this Agreement shall be governed by the laws of the state of Texas without regard to the state of Texas's choice of law rules.

8.3 CONFIDENTIAL INFORMATION. Vendor and User expressly agree that all information communicated to Vendor with respect to this Agreement and with respect to the services provided by Vendor pursuant to this Agreement, including, without limitation, any confidential information obtained by Vendor by reason of its association with User, is confidential. Vendor further agrees that all information, conclusions, reports, designs, plans, project evaluations, data, advice, business plans, customer lists and/or other documents available to Vendor pursuant to this Agreement are confidential and proprietary property of User. Except as otherwise provided by law, Vendor and User agree that all proprietary and confidential information disclosed by the other during performance of this Agreement and identified in writing as proprietary or confidential shall be held in confidence and used only in performance of this Agreement. If such information is publicly available, already in the disclosing party's possession or knowledge, or is thereafter rightfully obtained by the disclosing party from sources other than the other party, then there shall be no restriction in its disclosure.

8.4 FORCE MAJEURE. Neither the Vendor nor the User shall be in default by reason of any failure to perform under this Agreement if such failure results, whether directly or indirectly, from fire, explosion, flood, acts of God, or of the public enemy, war, civil disturbance, act of any government, dejure or de facto, or agency or official thereof, quarantine, restriction, epidemic or catastrophe (separately and collectively a "Force Majeure Event"). If there is a Force Majeure Event that prevents Vendor from performing a substantial part of its obligations under this Agreement and such Force Majeure Event lasts more than 24 hours, then User may terminate this Agreement upon 48 hours prior express, written notice.

8.5 NOTICE. All notices and demands required to be given pursuant to this Agreement shall be given to the parties in writing and by certified mail, return receipt requested, at the addresses specified in this Section or to such other addresses as the parties may hereinafter substitute by written notice given in the manner prescribed by this section.

A. Notice to User.

_____

_____

_____

_____

B. Notice to Vendor.

_____

_____

_____

_____

8.6 VENUE. Vendor and User expressly agree that this Agreement is entered into and performable in Dallas County, Texas and that all, if any, suits arising under this Agreement shall be brought in courts located in that county or, if in federal court, in the Northern District of Texas.

8.7 INTEGRATION OF AGREEMENT. Vendor and User agree that this Agreement and the Exhibits hereto embody the entire agreement of Vendor and User in relation to the subject matter herein and that there are no other oral or written agreements or understandings between Vendor and User at the time of the execution of this Agreement.

8.8 MODIFICATION OF AGREEMENT. Vendor and User expressly agree that this Agreement cannot be modified except by a writing executed by both Vendor and User.

8.9 LEGAL CONSTRUCTION. If one or more of the provisions of this Agreement are for any reason held to be invalid, illegal, or unenforceable in any respect, such invalidity, illegality, or unenforceability shall not affect any other provision of this Agreement; and this Agreement shall be construed as if such invalid, illegal, or unenforceable provisions had never been contained in this Agreement.

8.10 WAIVER. Any waiver by Vendor or User of any provision of this Agreement shall not imply a subsequent waiver of that or any other provision. And, further, any waiver must be signed in writing by the party against whom such waiver is to be construed.

8.11 BINDING EFFECT. This Agreement shall inure to the benefit of and bind the parties hereto, their successors, and permitted assigns.

8.12 AUTHORITY. Vendor and User hereby warrant and represent that their respective signatures set forth below have been, and are on the Effective Date, duly authorized by all necessary and appropriate statutory and/or corporate action to execute this Agreement.

8.13 CAPTIONS. All captions contained in this Agreement are for convenience or reference only and are not intended to define or limit the scope of any provision of this Agreement.

8.14 EXPENSES FOR ENFORCEMENT. In the event that either party is required to employ an attorney to enforce the provisions of this Agreement or is required to commence legal proceedings to enforce the provisions of this Agreement, then the prevailing party shall be responsible for the payment of the other party's attorneys fees, including costs, collection agency fees, costs of investigation or any other costs arising out of the litigation of this Agreement.

8.15 TAXES. User shall pay sales or use taxes imposed upon the services provided by Vendor pursuant to this Agreement; provided, however, in no event shall User be responsible for any other taxes, including, without limitation, taxes based on Vendor's net income and franchise taxes of Vendor.

8.16 MISSPELLINGS. Misspelling of one or more words in this Agreement shall not vitiate this Agreement. Such misspelled words shall be read so as to have the meaning apparently intended by the parties.

8.17 NO JOINT VENTURE. Vendor and User agree that each are independent contractors under this Agreement. In no event shall this Agreement be construed as creating any partnership, joint venture, agency or other relationship between Vendor and User.

8.18 COMPLIANCE WITH LAWS. Vendor expressly agrees that during the term of this Agreement it shall observe and comply with all relevant laws, including, without limitation, federal, state, and local laws, ordinances, orders, decrees, and regulations.

8.19 HIRING OF OTHER PARTY'S EMPLOYEES. Except as permitted in the section entitled "EXISTING INFORMATION SYSTEM EMPLOYEES," neither party may hire the employee of the other party while this Agreement is in effect without the express written consent of the other party.

IN WITNESS WHEREOF, Vendor and User through their duly authorized representatives make this Agreement effective upon the Effective Date.

User: _____   Vendor:_____

By: _____   By: _____

_____   _____

Title   Title

GLOSSARY

ADR means Alternative Dispute Resolution.

Alternative Dispute Resolution is a means other than litigation to resolve legal disputes and includes mediation and arbitration.

Application has two meanings: the first is a computer program; the second is the business problem which certain computer software is intended to solve.

Application Software or **Applications Software** is software that is intended to solve business problems such as payroll, general ledger, health claims management, and word processing and is to be distinguished from systems software and operating system software.

Arbitration is a form of alternative dispute resolution, and generally the outcome of arbitration is binding upon the parties.

Arbitrator is the person in arbitration who serves as a quasi-judge.

Asynchronous Telecommunications Method is a type of communications transmission suitable for voice, video, and data.

ATM has two meanings: one meaning is automated teller machine, and the other meaning is asynchronous telecommunications method.

Autocoder was an early programming language.

Automated Teller Machine is a type of computer terminal that serves to receive bank deposits, dispense cash, and answer account inquiries. The main purpose of an automated teller machine is to replace a bank teller or to provide teller services outside of banking hours.

Back-up is a process by which one copies software and data to have alternative sources for software and data if the originals are destroyed or damaged.

BASIC is a computer language that is predominately used on personal computers.

Bit is the smallest form of representing and storing data and information in a computer system. A bit is always a 0 or a 1.

Bridge is a communications device that connects one network to another.

Byte is a collection of bits, usually eight bits.

C++ is a computer programming language used mainly on personal computers.

Cache is a type of computer memory used to speed up operations—usually CPU operations.

CEO is Chief Executive Officer.

CFO is Chief Financial Officer.

CICS means Customer Information Control System. It is an IBM software product used for data communications.

CIO is Chief Information Officer.

Circuit has several meanings, but the meaning in this book is a communications connection.

COBOL is a computer programming language used predominantly on large computer systems.

Communications is the means by which computer terminals communicate to computer systems and computer systems communicate to one another. Communications most often refers to connections via telephone circuits.

Confidential is not a term with a clear legal definition and generally must be defined as part of a definition of confidential information in an agreement.

Conversion is the process of changing software that runs on one computer to run on another, or changing from the use of one application software product to another application software product.

Copyright is the right granted by the Federal Government in certain works or materials that are authored. Copyright gives certain exclusive rights to the copyright holder such as the right to copy and the right to produce derivative works. You can have copyrights in software and in documentation.

CPU means the Central Processing Unit of a computer system.

DASD is Direct Access Storage Device.

Data means information for the purposes of this book.

Data Base is a set of related computer files.

Data Base Management System means software that manages data bases.

Data Processing means the use of computers to perform various business functions.

DBMS is Data Base Management System.

Defendant is the person or company that is the object of a lawsuit.

Development usually means the writing of computer software.

Direct Access Storage is a type of computer storage that is relatively fast and usually refers to some type of disk drive.

Disaster Recovery is the process by which one restarts data processing or IS operations after the main operations facilities are damaged or destroyed.

Documentation is the written information that instructs a user how to use software and/or informs a programmer how software is designed.

DP means Data Processing.

Gigabyte means approximately one billion bytes of information.

Hardware Independent means software that can function on a variety of computer hardware, unlike most computer software.

Hardware Maintenance is the process by which computer hardware is kept in good operating condition.

Hardware Vendor is a manufacturer or distributor of computer hardware.

Hexadecimal is a base sixteen numbering system.

Hot-site is a computer facility generally available on short notice to provide alternative computer facilities when a company has experienced a disaster at its main facilities.

Hub is a type of interconnection between various components of a network.

Information Systems is another name for Data Processing or Computer Systems.

Infringement means misappropriating the rights of an owner of a patent or copyright.

Injunction is an order issued by a court to do something or to refrain from doing something.

Intellectual Property is a general reference to a patent, copyright, trade secret, or trademark.

Interface is a connection between software and software, hardware and software, or hardware and hardware.

IS means Information Systems.

IT Provider is an Information Technology Provider, or outsourcer.

Lawsuit is the formal legal proceeding that begins when one party sues another. ADR is an alternative to lawsuits.

Lessee is the person or entity who leases equipment from a lessor.

Lessor is the person or entity who provides equipment to a lessee.

License is a limited right to use and/or possess computer software.

Licensee is the person or entity who possesses or uses computer software pursuant to a license.

Licensor is the person or entity who licenses computer software to licensees. The licensor is usually, but not always, the owner of the computer software.

Line is a communications circuit.

Litigation is the general name for the process of pursuing a lawsuit.

Maintenance is the means by which hardware and/or software are kept in good working order.

Management Information Systems is another name for application software.

Mediation is a form of alternative dispute resolution where the outcome does not bind the participants.

Mediator is the person who facilitates dispute resolution in mediation.

Megabyte means approximately one million bytes of information.

MIPS means Million Instructions per Second and is a measure of CPU speed.

MIS means Management Information Systems.

Misappropriation is the wrongful taking of the property of another, usually in reference to disclosing or using the trade secrets of another.

Module means a computer program or a subroutine of a computer program.

Multiplexer (multiplexor) is a device that allows multiple computer terminals to share a single communications circuit.

Network is the interconnection of several computers usually through communications circuits.

Object Code is the translated version of computer software in source code format.

Open Systems, used in its imprecise sense, means software applications that are hardware independent—usually meaning applications that run on one or more variants of the operating system software known as UNIX.

Operating System Software means software that manages the operations and interaction of computer hardware in a computer system and may provide resource scheduling, basic input/output functions, and computer memory management.

Operations are the people and department that actually run a computer on a daily basis.

Outsourcer is a company that provides one or more outsourcing services and is also known as an outsourcing vendor or IT Provider.

Out-sorcerer is an outsourcer who is a magician.

Outsourcing Vendor means outsourcer.

Outsourcing is not a word (see Chapter 2) and therefore there is no need to define it.

Patent is an intellectual property right granted by the Federal Government which allows the patent holder the exclusive rights to make, use, or sell the patented invention.

Performance Standards are criteria to use in evaluating an outsourcer's performance.

Permanent Injunction is a type of injunction that lasts forever unless terminated by a court.

Plaintiff is the party that initiates a lawsuit.

Processing, in this book, is another word for data processing or IS.

Program is a discrete unit of computer software.

Random Access Storage is a type of computer storage, e.g., DASD.

Repair Time is a phrase used to mean the interval between when a repair organization is summoned and when the repair is completed.

Response Time can have several different meanings; the most common meaning is the time between the pressing of the enter key on a computer terminal's keyboard and the first meaningful response on the computer terminal.

Router is one of the network devices that can connect one network to another network.

Run-time means the length of time that it takes for a particular application to complete its processing.

Services has no special meaning, but in the outsourcing context is meant to be a description of what the outsourcer will provide and what the outsourcer will not provide.

Shrink-wrap License is a type of software license that does not require the licensee to sign it. The purchaser, in theory, becomes the licensee by opening the package containing the software.

Software is another name for computer programs and can mean one or more computer programs.

Software License is the license that allows the licensee to possess and/or use certain computer software.

Software Maintenance consists of procedures to keep software in good working order.

Software Vendor is the licensor of software and/or the owner of software.

Source Code is software in its human (meaning programmer) readable form. Compiling source code produces object code.

Specifications are the detailed requirements to perform various data processing functions, including development and conversion.

SQL is Structured Query Language.

Structured Query Language is a language initially specified by IBM but now used by many vendors as a language to access data bases.

System has many meanings. Sometimes system refers to a group of application programs; sometimes it refers to a combination of hardware and software; and sometimes system refers to a set of procedures.

System Software or **Systems Software** is software that is dedicated to management of various computer resources and includes the operating system and utilities.

Temporary Restraining Order is a type of court order, similar to a temporary injunction, of extremely limited duration.

Temporary Injunction is a type of injunction of limited duration.

Tetrabyte means approximately one trillion bytes of information.

Third-Party Software in the outsourcing context means software that does not belong to the outsourcer or to the user, but is licensed from some other licensor.

Trade Secret is a type of intellectual property that has different meanings in different states, but generally means any information that is a relative secret and gives the possessor of that information a competitive advantage over others who do not know or use the trade secret.

TRO means Temporary Restraining Order.

Tsunami means tidal wave in Japanese.

Turnback is the process of moving data processing operations from one outsourcer back to in-house operations or to another outsourcer.

Turnover is the process of cutting over, transferring, converting, or moving data processing operations to an outsourcer.

UNIX is a registered trademark licensed exclusively by X/Open Company Ltd., but often refers to operating system software that is similar to Unix and is hardware independent.

Vendor has at least two meanings in the outsourcing context. One means software vendor and the other means outsourcing vendor. This book uses the word "vendor" interchangeably with the phrase "outsourcing vendor" and refers to a software vendor as a licensor.

INDEX

A

Accounts receivable billing/collection, 32
Additional services
    checklist for, 202-3
    contract provision, 201-3
    Rochester Quake, 14
Alternative dispute resolution (ADR),
    159-60
    See Dispute resolution, 381
Applications development personnel, 123
    See Personnel
Applications maintenance personnel,
    123-25
    See Personnel
Asset transfers/equity infusion
    See also Capital
    checklist for, 332-34, 355-56
    contract provision, 331-34
    equity infusion methods, 333
    equity purchase by vendor, 331
    types of asset transfers, 332-33
    vendor purchase of user assets, 331
Assignment, contract provision, 337-38,
    365-66
Audit, client's right to, 358
Authority, contract provision, 347, 368

B

Backup/disaster recovery, 4
    backup basics, 270-71, 273-75
    checklist for, 272-76
    contract provision, 269-76
Balance sheet, changes and outsourcing,
    23
Bank processing, 14, 17-18
Bankruptcy, of vendor, 170-71
Binding effect, contract provision, 346,
    368

Bonuses, for meeting performance stan-
    dards, 112, 149-50
Business reply mail processing, 19

C

Capital
    asset transfers/equity infusion, con-
        tract provision, 331-34
    cash infusion methods, 92
    and outsourcing, 23
Captions, contract provision, 347, 368
Change of character/software substitu-
    tion
    checklist for, 329-30
    contract provision, 327-30
Checklists
    additional vendor services, 202-3
    asset transfers/equity infusion, 332-34
    backup/disaster recovery, 272-76
    change of character/software
        substitution, 329-30
    cost/performance measures for
        assessment of IS department, 103-5
    description of vendor services, 196-99
    dispositions for hardware/tangible
        property, 139-41
    dispute resolution, 292-93
    evaluation of need for outsourcing,
        63-68
    existing employees, 233-35
    fees, 209-10
    hardware, 251-53
    liaisons, 221-26
    performance standards, 264-68
    schedules, 216-17
    self-defense, 283-86
    software, 245-47
    termination, 307-9
    for termination of vendors, 182-86
    turnback, 315-26

Checklists, *continued*
warranties/limitations of liability, 298-301
Competition, maintaining competitiveness, 43-44
Compliance with law, contract provision, 347, 369
Computer expertise
and evaluation of need for outsourcing, 66
and outsourcing, 25-26, 30-31, 46-47
Computer operations
changes in computer industry/technology, 27-30, 47-49
selling to outsourcing vendor, 23
Computer system. *See* Information systems
Computers, decline in cost of, 23-24
Confidentiality
contract provision, 341-42, 366
and outsourcing, 38-42
about outsourcing plans, 60-62, 127-28
Consultants, 69-85
advantages of, 70-71, 75
disadvantages of, 71-72
do's and don'ts in dealing with, 83-84
locating consultants, 75-77
multiple consultants, use of, 78
myths related to, 72-75
and non-disclosure agreement, 79
qualities/skills needed, 78-79, 82-83
questionnaire for evaluation of, 80-82
and tasks of outsourcing transaction, 77-78
and use of request for proposal (RFP), 101-2
Continental Bank, 16
Contract provisions, 4-5
additional services, 201-3
asset transfers/equity infusion, 331-34, 355-56
assignment, 337-38, 365-66
authority, 347, 368
backup/disaster recovery, 269-76
binding effect, 346, 368
captions, 347, 368
change of character/software substitution, 327-30
compliance with law, 347, 369
confidentiality, 341-42, 366
definitions, 335-36

description of vendor services, 189-99, 351-52
dispute resolution, 287-93, 358-60
exclusivity provisions, 163
existing employees, 227-35, 354, 369
expenses for enforcement, 347, 368
fees, 205-10, 353
force majeure, 342-44, 366
governing law, 339-41, 366
hardware-related provisions, 249-53, 355
integration of agreement, 346, 367
legal construction, 346, 368
liaisons, 219-26, 353-54
misspellings, 347, 369
modification of agreement, 346, 367
no joint venture, 347, 369
notice, 344-45, 367
performance standards, 255-68, 356-58
remedies by vendor provision, 180
schedules, 215-17, 353, 357
self-defense, 277-86
software licenses, 237-47, 354-55
taxes, 347, 368-69
termination/expiration, 168-71, 303-9, 361-65
turnback, 173-75, 311-26, 364-65
turnover, 211-14, 353-56
venue, 345-46, 367
waiver, 346, 368
warranties/limitations of liability, 295-301, 361
Contracts
breach of, 168
evaluation of, 84-85
expiration of, 168
performance standards in, 148
provisions of. *See* Contract provisions in request for proposal (RFP), 100-101
statute of limitations, 179
and vendor risk, 37
Control, and in-house data processing, 54-55
Corporate restructuring, and termination of outsourcing relationship, 161-62, 170, 304
Cost control
methods of, 93
and outsourcing, 3, 24-25
Cost of outsourcing, 25
and changes in services, 44
vendor tactics, 107-9

D

Data processing. *See* Information systems
Definitions, contract provision, 335-36
Delivery, 266-67
    meaning of, 145, 260
Dependency relationship, and outsourcing, 36
Description of services
    checklist for, 196-99
    contract provision, 189-99, 351-52
    for full outsourcing, 194-95, 196-98
    growth in services, 190, 192-93
    omission in services, 189, 191-92
    for selective outsourcing, 195-96, 198
    services at no additional charge, 193-94
    in terms of value to client, 194-95
Disaster recovery. *See* Backup/disaster recovery
Dispute resolution, 157-62
    alternative dispute resolution (ADR), 159-60
    checklist for, 292-93
    contract provision, 287-93, 358-60
    and failure to meet performance standards, 290-91
    and preservation of rights, 160-61
    about substandard performance, 112, 150-52
    and top management, 158-59
Downsizing, and outsourcing, 16-17, 29

E

Eastman Kodak, 15
Electronic Data Systems (EDS), 13
Electronic mail, 38
Employees. *See* Personnel
Employment laws, and termination of employees, 66-67, 127, 231-32
Enron Corp., 16
Evaluation of outsourcing needs, 55-68
    alternatives to outsourcing, 92-93
    checklist for, 63-68
    clarification of needs, 90-91
    consultants for, 69-85
    decision-making test, 94-98
    and future of company, 55-57
    impact on company functions, 62-63
    and learning about IS functions, 87-90

    and personnel, 59
    sources of assistance for, 68
Exclusivity, conditions for, 4
Expenses for enforcement, contract provision, 347, 368
Expiration. *See* Termination of outsourcing arrangement
Express warranties, 297

F

Facilities, sale to outsourcer, 62
Facilities management, 10, 14, 17
    nature of, 14
Fees
    adjustments to, 209-10
    bottom line approaches, 208-9
    checklist for, 209-10
    contract provision, 205-10, 353
    fixed fees, 205, 207
    from shared revenue, 206, 208
    from shared savings, 206, 208
    usage fees, 205-6, 207-8
Financial function, impact of outsourcing on, 62, 65
First Boston Corp., ix, 16
First City Bank Corp., 16
Fixed fees, 205, 207
Flexibility
    and outsourcing, 31-32
    technical, methods of, 93
Force majeure, contract provision, 342-44, 366-67
Full outsourcing, 10, 118, 194-95, 196-98
    and transition to outsourcing, 212
    See also Description of services
Future of company, and outsourcing decision, 55-57

G

Gates, Bill, 13
General Dynamics, 16
Governing law, contract provision, 339-41, 366

H

Hardware
    checklist for, 251-53
    contract provisions for, 249-53, 355

Hardware, *continued*
  leases, 250, 251-52
  maintenance agreements, 249,
    252-53
  transferring to vendor, 121, 139-40
Health claims processing, 14, 19, 32
Hot-sites, 279

I

Implied warranties, 297
Information systems (IS)
  checklist of measures for assessment
    of, 103-5
  communication costs, 104
  communications functions, 88
  costs related to, 89-90
  evaluation of department, 87-88,
    91-92
  increased access to technical
    resources, 93
  miscellaneous costs, 105
  miscellaneous services, 89
  operational costs, 103
  operational functions of, 88
  software development/maintenance
    costs, 104-5
  software development/maintenance
    functions, 88
Information Technology (IT) provider,
  See Vendor
Inland Revenue, 16
Insurance claims processing, 14, 31, 32
Integrated Systems Solutions Corporation
  (ISSC), 15
Integration of agreement, contract provision, 346, 367
IS department. *See* Information systems (IS)

L

Leases, hardware, 250, 251
Legal construction, contract provision,
  346, 368
Legal issues
  related to outsourcing, 63, 66-67
  See also Contract provisions
Liability
  limitation of, contract provisions,
    296, 298, 299-301
  risks related to outsourcing, 49-51

Liaisons
  alternate liaison, 220
  assistants to, 155, 222
  characteristics of, 154, 225
  checklist for, 221-26
  communication methods, 223
  contract provision, 219-26, 353-54
  issues related to, 155-56, 224
  loyalty of, 156, 224
  meetings with, 223
  office for, 154-55, 224
  procedure in use of, 153-57
Licenses, software, and outsourcing, 5,
  49-50, 237-47
Litigation with vendors, 178-81
  notice of, 180
  and paper trail, 178-79
  self defense strategy, 280-82
  time frame for, 179
  views of, 180
  See also Dispute resolution

M

Maintenance agreements, for hardware,
  249, 252-53
Maintenance programmers, 123-25
Management, focus of, 26-27
Medicare/Medicaid claims processing, 14,
  32
Misspellings, contract provision, 347,
  369
Modification of agreement, contract pro-
  vision, 346, 367
Monitoring, of vendor performance, 147-
  48

N

National Car Rental, 16
Negotiations with vendor, 112-13
  (*See* Chapter 8)
  pressure from vendor, 112
Network communications, and transition
  to outsourcing, 141
Network services, 32
No joint venture, contract provision,
  347, 369
Non-disclosure agreement, and consul-
  tants, 79
Notice, contract provision, 344-45, 367

O

Optical scanning services, 19
Output, 260, 266-67
Outsourcing
    advantages of, 2, 21-33, 90
    alternatives to, 92-93
    basic rules of, 1-6
    categories of, 10-11, 118
    disadvantages of, 2-3, 17-18, 35-51,
        91-92
    evaluation for use of, 54-68
    facilities management, 10, 17
    fees.
    See Fees
    See Cost of outsourcing
    history of, 12-18
    need for. *See* Evaluation of outsourc-
        ing needs
    service bureaus, 10
    time-sharing, 10, 11
    transition to, 117-41
    trends related to, 19
    types of activities for, 19, 32
    types of transactions for, 12
    use of term, 9-10
    See also Vendors
Outsourcing agreement, example of, 351-69

P

Parallel operation, 134-35
Parking ticket management, 19
Payroll processing, 13, 32
Penalties, for substandard performance,
    112, 151-52
Performance standards, 6, 109, 112, 145,
    278
    baseline measure, 259
    checklist for, 264-68
    contract provision, 148, 255-68, 356-58
    defective performance, definition of,
        255-56
    desirable level, 258
    dispute resolution about, 290-91
    incentives for vendor, 149-50
    measures of, 145
    and monitoring of performance, 147-
        48
    output and delivery, 260
    overkill, 258
    processing priorities, 263, 267

    remedies for defective performance,
        112, 150-52, 167, 255-56, 268
    repeated problems with performance,
        153
    resource availability, 263
    resource capacity, 264, 267
    response time, 260-63, 267
    sources of information on, 258-59
    uptime, 259-60
Perot, Ross, 12-13
Personnel
    application development personnel,
        123
    application maintenance workers,
        123-25
    applications personnel, 123
    contract provision for existing
        employees, 227-35, 354, 369
    disclosure about outsourcing, 128
    and downsizing, 16-17, 29
    emotional issues and outsourcing,
        127-28, 233-34
    enthusiasm about vendor, 130
    evaluation for retention, 229
    job titles, 126-27
    legal employee termination issues, 66-
        67, 127, 231-32, 234-35
    loss of jobs, 128-29
    operations personnel, 230
    problems related to outsourcing, 131-
        32
    quitting of, 129, 131
    resentment to outsourcing, 59
    sabotage of outsourcing plan, 130, 131
    systems programmers, 122
    transfer to outsourcer, 47, 59, 123,
        129, 230-33
    and transition to outsourcing, 122-25,
        126-32
Pricing
    alternative structures, 3
    cost control, 3
Processing priorities, 263, 267
Production schedule, 215, 217
Property, transfers in transition to out-
    sourcing, 139-40
Property tax collection, 19, 32

Q

Quality, improvement with outsourcing,
    26

R

Redoubt, 175-77
Renewal of outsourcing agreement, 306
Request for proposal (RFP), 98-102
  contents of, 99-100
  contract in, 100-101
  and use of consultant, 101-2
  usefulness of, 98-99, 100-101
Resource availability, 263
Resource capacity, 264, 267
Resource schedule, 215, 217
Response time, 260-63, 267
  and customer dealings, 262
  meaning of, 145
  as performance standard, 261-62

S

Schedules
  checklist for, 216-17
  contract provision, 215-17, 353, 357
  production schedule, 215, 217
  resource schedule, 215, 217
  schedule of events, 215, 216-17
Security risk, and outsourcing, 42-43
Selective outsourcing, 10, 118, 195-96, 198
  See description of services
  and transition to outsourcing, 137-38,
    213
Self-defense
  checklist for, 283-86
  contract provision, 277-86
  compared to disaster recovery, 278
  legal context of, 280-82
  withholding payments, 282
Service bureaus, 10
  history of, 13
Shared revenue, fees from, 206-8
Shared savings, fees from, 206, 208
Software
  checklist for, 245-47
  contract provision for licenses, 237-
    47, 354-55
  contract provision for software substi-
    tution, 327-30
  conversion to new software, 50
  development, phases of, 146
  evaluation of third party software,
    125-26, 242
  licensing and outsourcing, 5, 49-50,
    237-47
  non-disclosure restriction, 238
  protection of in-house software, 5
  right to use and turnback, 312-13,
    318-25
  strategic software, 38-39
  transferring to vendor, 121-22, 140-41
  updating by maintenance personnel,
    124
  user manual, draft of, 146-47
Strategic issues, related to outsourcing,
  63-65
Systems programmers, 122

T

Taxes, contract provision, 347, 368-69
Termination of outsourcing arrangement, 161-86
  checklist for, 182-86, 307-9
  contract provision, 303-9, 361-65
  and corporate restructuring, 161-62,
    170, 304
  expiration of contract, 168
  and litigation, 178-81
  planning for, 165-68, 172, 173-74
  redoubt, 175-77
  and substandard performance, 167
  and technical changes, 177
  termination for breach of contract,
    168, 184, 303
  termination for convenience, 168-70,
    303-4
  termination for special circumstances,
    170-71
  turnback, 172-75, 183-84
Third Party Software
  See Licenses
  See Software
Throughput, meaning of, 145
Time-sharing, 10, 11
Trade secrets, and outsourcing, 39-42
Transition to outsourcing, 117-41
  application conversion procedures,
    135-36
  checklist of dispositions for
  hardware/tangible property, 139-41
  contract provision for turnover, 211-
    14, 353-56
  flip-the-switch approach, 118-19, 123,
    132
  and full outsourcing, 212
  with no existing application, 136-37

Transition to outsourcing, *continued*
  and parallel operation, 134-35
  and personnel, 122-25, 126-32
  phases of, 132-33
  plan for, 117-18, 119-20, 138
  procedures for, 133-34
  resources in, 119-22
  and selective outsourcing, 137-38, 213
  vendor assistance in, 138
Turnback, 172-75, 183-84
  checklist for, 315-26
  contract provision, 173-75, 311-26, 364-65
  legal procedures in, 317-18
  period of time for, 175
  procedures in, 172-73
  requirements for, 174
  and right to use vendor software, 312-13, 314-15, 318-25
  triggering events for, 316
Turnover
  checklist for, 212-14
  contract provision, 211-14, 353-56
  See also Transition to outsourcing

U

Uptime, 259-60, 266
  meaning of, 145
Usage fees, 205-6, 207-8
User warranties, 298

V

Vendors
  approach to technical contra-indications to outsourcing, 109-10
  approach to top management, 110

bankruptcy of, 170-71
bonuses to, 112
consequences of substandard performance, 112
dispute resolution, 157-62
inheriting of outsourcing relationship, 181
liaison with, 153-57
litigation with, 178-81
negotiations with, 112-13
performance claims of, 110-12
performance standards, 109, 112, 145
pricing tactics, 107-9
renegotiation with, 161
termination of relationship, 161-86
vendor/client relationship, 36-37, 45-46, 153-56
Venue, contract provision, 345-46, 367
Video transmission services, 19

W

Waiver, contract provision, 346, 368
Warranties
  checklist for, 298-301
  contract provision, 295-301, 360-61
  disclaimers, 299
  express warranties, 297
  implied warranties, 297
  nature of, 296-97
  role in outsourcing agreement, 297-98
  user warranties, 296, 298
  vendor warranties, 295, 299
Worker compensation claims processing, 19

X

Xerox Corporation, 15, 16